PLAY TO YOUR STRENGTHS

PLAY TO YOUR STRENGTHS

Managing Your Internal Labor Markets for Lasting Competitive Advantage

HAIG R. NALBANTIAN
RICHARD A. GUZZO
DAVE KIEFFER
AND JAY DOHERTY

McGraw-Hill

New York   San Francisco   Washington, D.C.   Auckland   Bogotá
Caracas   Lisbon   London   Madrid   Mexico City   Milan
Montreal   New Delhi   San Juan   Singapore
Sidney   Tokyo   Toronto

1 2 3 4 5 6 7 8 9 0 DOC/DOC 0 9 8 7 6 5 4 3

ISBN 0-07-142253-6

McGraw-Hill books are available at special discounts to use as premiums and sales promotions, or for use in corporate training programs. For more information, please write to the Director of Special Sales, Professional Publishing, McGraw-Hill, Two Penn Plaza, New York, NY 10121-2298. Or contact your local bookstore.

This book is printed on recycled, acid-free paper containing a minimum of 50% recycled de-inked paper.

Library of Congress Cataloging-in-Publication Data

Play to your strengths : managing your internal labor markets for
lasting competitive advantage / by Haig R. Nalbantian ... [et al.].
    p. cm.
  ISBN 0-07-142253-6 (alk. paper)
  1. Human capital. 2. Labor productivity. 3. Organizational
effectiveness. 4. Competition. I. Nalbantian, Haig R.
  HD4904.7.P56 2003
  658.3'01—dc21
                    2003014194

Contents

Preface

THERE ARE TOO MANY myths and too much conjecture about the management of people.

Considering the sophistication of the tools and metrics commonly used in major companies—inventory tracking, logistics, customer experience management, and financial measures—most tactics and measurements for workforce management seem almost primitive. Thus few, if any, companies know the return on investment (ROI) on their various investments in people practices. The same thing is true for the people tactics that most often drive overall business results.

Ten years ago, we set out to bridge that measurement gap, starting as a research and development group and gradually evolving into a consulting practice. Since that time we have worked with over a hundred global and national firms—some the best in the world, some average, some struggling. More to the point, we have had complete access to company data—covering more than 2 million employees—that enabled us to measure and define actual people management practices, how those practices affect the workforce, and what their impact is on business performance.

Along the way we have learned a lot about the process of discovering organizational realities and turning that knowledge into strategies for business success:

- Some of the most profound learning in business comes from understanding your own organization.
- The opportunity exists to capitalize on what others cannot possibly know about your business.
- New methods for measuring and optimizing your workforce practices are now available.

In place of platitudes or meaningless generalities, this book explains the new science for making fact-based, firm-specific decisions. Unlike most business books, it does not urge you to adopt practices used successfully at other companies or in other industries. There's no reason to believe that those practices will work for you. Instead, this book gives you a framework for thinking strategically about the people side of your business and introduces you to new tools for measuring and managing your most valuable asset.

Whether you're a CEO approving a $175 million initiative, a CFO trying to judge the return on investments in people, or a human resources chief who needs to make a compelling case for change, this book will show you new ways to resolve those issues—and to make smarter decisions. For the first time, you will see how to understand and measure the contributions of human capital to business success. Not only will you see things differently (and better), you will think and talk about your business differently.

*   *   *

Dozens of clients and colleagues have made this work possible. Clients that supported this work—particularly early on when its power was only emerging—include Karl Fischer, Kurt Fischer, LuAnn Jarnagin, Sarah Meyerrose, Steve Michel, Pat Nazemetz, Shelley Seifort, and Anne Szostak. We wish to acknowledge scholars who variously stimulated and encouraged our thinking, including organizational psychologist Cheri Ostroff (Columbia) and economists Bengt Holmstrom (MIT), Ed Lazear (Stanford), and Lalith Munasinghe (Barnard). Consultant and former ITT executive Bob Braverman spent months with us, challenging our assumptions and the practical applications of the work.

Internally, the work was kept alive solely by the vision and support of CEO Peter Coster. More recently, EVP Mac Regan has begun to advance these capabilities globally. Numerous colleagues at Mercer have invested their time and reputations in introducing this work to their clients and have contributed insights and expertise to enhance what we deliver. We thank them all.

And, of course, we also thank our team—especially those with us in the early years who helped us build the foundation: Douglas Dwyer, Luis Fernando Parra, Mike Spratt, Bruce Wang, and Wei Zheng. Our crackerjack analysts in those early years were Steve Blader, Gigi Foster, Sonya Kim, Katie Noonan, Michael Wolosin, and later Sara Hertog. Since then, Stefan Gaertner, Wendy Hirsch, Brian Levine and Matt Sato have developed new extensions of our work. Mark Chandler, David Lee, and Matt Stevenson have invented software for managing the huge databases we use. They have been joined by other talented professionals who offer fresh perspectives and enhance our core capabilities. These include: Ilse de Veer, Damien DeLuca, Pete Folcy, Helen Friedman, Gail Greenfield, Rosemary Hyson, Julie Kim, Lingzi Liang, Susan Merino, Kanishka Ray, Bill Sipe, and Roy Wellman. Thanks too to our desktop publisher Deneen Jones and our assistants Tammy Miller and Melissa Wilkison.

Finally, we appreciate the efforts of John Campbell, Debra Joseph, Graham Leigh, and Pat Pollino in moving this book project forward. We particularly thank Richard Luecke of Salem, Massachusetts, for helping us frame and write the book. We appreciate his fine editorial judgment and his willingness to accommodate the schedules and idiosyncrasies of four strong-willed authors with different writing styles. We also thank Ryan Risk for his exceptional efforts under great time pressures to bring all the edits and figures together and move the book into production. And, needless to say, we acknowledge our editor at McGraw, Mary Glenn, who has steered this project to completion.

Introduction:
The Last Asset

The CEO knew it was a bold play, but he was determined to get it past the board.

"Ladies and gentlemen," he said, "I propose to invest 36 percent of next year's sales—roughly $5 billion—in a venture I'm confident will produce great gains for the company."

He knew he had to take the high ground before they started asking questions.

"Let me say at the outset that I can't estimate a specific return on investment, but we will be able to benchmark our spending against other companies, so I am confident we can manage this venture effectively."

There was silence.

He was relieved.

They were stunned.

STRANGE AS IT may seem, an unspoken version of that dialogue takes place *every* year in *every* company from Germany to the United States to Japan. This is what it would sound like if CEOs had to ask their boards for permission to fund all the investments associated with their workforce—equivalent to an average of 36 percent of an American company's revenue each year.[1] The question for companies goes like this: Is the return you're getting on your various human capital investments exceptional, marginal, or negative? Unfortunately, that question seldom is asked and virtually never is answered. That's why for many companies human capital is the biggest investment about which they know the least.

The reason executives know so little about their human assets isn't a lack of interest or concern. Indeed, CEOs and senior managers spend most of their time dealing with people problems. The problem has been their inability to measure, assess, and predict the outcomes of workforce tactics in the same way they do with other parts of the business. The tools simply have not been available. They didn't miss the boat. There wasn't any boat.

The only good news in this is that there has been parity among companies in their inability to measure and manage human capital factors. The bad news is that this situation is changing dramatically. Measurement and management tools are now available. Companies that adopt them and learn to use them well will gain substantial advantages over organizations that are slow to catch on.

The Last Major Source of Competitive Advantage

Every company has tangible assets (financial and physical) and intangible assets (brands, customer relationships, and people). In the past, tangible assets were prime sources of competitive advantage, but their power to differentiate or confer special power has faded. For example, it was not long ago that executives struggled to obtain the capital they desired to run their companies. Nowadays capital flows relatively easily even during significant economic downturns. In early 2003, in a distinctly down economy, companies continued to get the money they wanted, ranging from the $900 million Volkswagen was putting into new manufacturing facilities in China,[2] to $21 million in private financing for Chicken Out, a fledgling restaurant chain in Maryland.[3] Access to financial capital doesn't differentiate enterprises or give a business a competitive advantage over its rivals anymore.

Nor does technology set most companies apart for very long. Until recently first movers with new technologies could establish competitive advantages they could ride for years, as FedEx did with its logistics/tracking system. Today advantages rooted in new technology are short-lived. What one company has often can be acquired or replicated easily by others, making technology no longer special, just required.

At the same time the competitive landscape is tumultuous. Almost unthinkable things are happening: smaller companies taking on bigger ones, less developed countries going toe to toe with larger ones. The Royal Bank of Scotland, like a latter-day Robert the Bruce, charged into England to buy Nat West, and it's now expanding overseas. Chile is crating off its counterseasonal produce to northern markets and hooking those markets on its year-round fishery. Lowe's is chiseling away at Home Depot's seemingly uncontested market dominance. Big pharmaceutical houses find the performance of upstarts like Forest Labs depressing. China continues its Mao-defying revolution into a new economic dynasty. Nothing can be taken for granted anymore.

Thus, earlier sources of value creation and advantage—access to capital, technology, and economies of scope and scale—have become much less critical. What's left—the last unexploited source of advantage—is the largest part of most companies' intangible assets: human capital and the *system* each company uses to manage it. Nobody has ever denied that people are important. Companies routinely profess that "people are our most important asset" although many behave otherwise. However, in a world where knowledge and connections to customers matter more and more, human capital—a company's stock of knowledge, technical skills, creativity, and experience—is becoming increasingly important.

A great workforce alone is not, however, the source of advantage. If it were, today's best-endowed companies would simply outpay all others, staff themselves with the best people, and enjoy a permanent advantage. Obviously, this doesn't happen. The reason is that the real and competitive advantage comes not merely from the people, but more importantly from the way firms *manage* them. We call that set of management tactics, policies, and practices an organization's *human capital strategy*. That strategy—that *system*—is the last asset with which companies can gain enduring advantages.

Human capital strategy is the sum of all actions—in both line and staff functions—used to manage people throughout an organization. It is the people analogue to a firm's business model or strategy.

Six Essential Factors

Human capital strategy consists of six factors that most affect business results (Figure P-1). For details on the empirical basis for these factors, see Appendix A, "The Research Roots of the Six -Factor Framework."

I. People

From the executive suite to the mail room, the nature and quality of individuals in the workforce obviously influence the performance of an organization. Specifically, this factor represents the human capital itself, the collective mix of attributes individuals bring into the company and then develop over time.

2. Work Processes

Dominant work processes have both direct and indirect effects on organizational performance. Two companies in the same industry may organize their work quite differently; for example, General Electric builds jet engines on an assembly line, and Allison builds them in small work groups. Those differences often require different kinds of talent.

Figure P-1

"Six-Factor Framework"

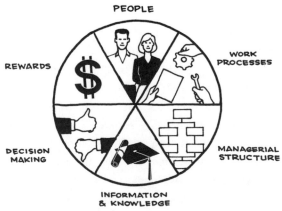

© 2003, Mercer Human Resource Consulting LLC

3. Managerial Structure

This factor characterizes how organizations direct the work of employees across dimensions of managerial direction (high control) versus individual discretion (low control).

4. Information and Knowledge

The flow of information and knowledge in an organization also drives productivity. This factor includes both internal dynamics (up, down, across) and external dynamics (to and from customers, suppliers, regulators, etc.).

5. Decision Making

This factor focuses on important business decisions (not on day-to-day job-level decisions) that affect major areas of strategy, operations, finance, marketing, and sales.

6. Rewards

The motivational component of human capital strategy is reflected in an organization's reward structure: both the financial and the non-financial motivators that influence employees to work hard, innovate, and develop.

All organizations have a human capital strategy made up of these six elements, whether intended or not. The factors come together in unique combinations to fit the individual companies; thus different patterns work best for different enterprises (Figure P-2).

Some drivers are critical for success, but all of them always are in play. At its best, a company's unique human capital strategy is a major barrier to competitors.

Context Is Everything

We emphasize that these six factors operate as a system in which they interact with, balance, and complement one another and their various parts. Of course, this human capital strategy system exists within the context of larger systems, just as one's family "system" resides in a social system, an ecosystem, and a political system. In the case of organizations the human capital system must fit and complement other sys-

Figure P-2

Symbolic Best Fit Patterns

© 2003, Mercer Human Resource Consulting LLC

tems—the company's marketplace, its business model, and its strategy for financial and physical asset management (including technology). Effective decision making must take into account those points of context.

We will talk more about this system's reality in Chapter 1 because ad hoc or silo-based decisions are *always* suboptimized, and usually dysfunctional, when they are made without regard to the overall system.

Together with the market and the business model context, the human capital system inherently shapes the unique character of a company. That creates two potent competitive advantages. First, the sum of a company's human capital practices is relatively stable and persistent, typically more enduring than the effects of technology and financial capital. Second, because it is unique to its context and goals, a successful company's system for managing human capital is very difficult to copy. Indeed, what works well for Company A is unlikely to work for Company B. A copycat may try to adopt two or three "best practices" from a top company, but that approach will not produce great competitive advantages. Why? Because the best practices of the highly successful company are part of its system of interrelated practices and values. It is the sum of a company's whole system that makes a company great. Thus, copying one or two discrete practices produces one of two outcomes: The first result is that the transplanted tactic works but generates no competitive advantage because, since it's easily adopted, it quickly becomes a new standard used by most companies. The second, more likely outcome is that it fails—sometimes quietly, sometimes stunningly—because the "borrowing" company can't copy all the other factors that support and interact with the adopted tactic at the great company. In other words, it doesn't fit into that company's unique context.

Our work shows that these two competitive advantages—longevity and inimitability—hold true even for close competitors in the same industry. Think about trying to copy a successful rival's entire system. Consider what would happen if BMW decided that the only way for it to be ultimately successful would be to transform itself into another Toyota and then beat Toyota at its own game. Or if Oracle aspired, as impossible as that might be, to copy Microsoft. Or Komatsu chose to model itself after Caterpillar.

Each would struggle for years to emulate its competitor. It would have to change long-standing values, practices, and policies. It would have to match its workforce to the new strategy. It would have to train people for new ways of doing things. Key people would leave in disgust or have to be replaced because they weren't "wired" to lead or perform in the new system. There would be major turmoil before there were results. It would take years—if it were even possible. (Paradoxically, companies can change their business models more easily than they can change their human capital strategies.)

Thus a company that gets its system of people management "right" has an extraordinary competitive advantage over its rivals. It will obtain better performance from what is often its largest asset and won't have to worry about its rivals copying the key to its success. In doing this, a company is playing to its strengths.

Three Critical Questions

These realities—the sheer size of the human capital asset, its enduring character, and its competitive advantages—are pushing people both inside and outside organizations to try to better measure the value and drivers of workforce performance. From the inside, organizations have long measured productivity in either broad financial terms (revenue per employee, etc.) or on an individual or operational basis (units produced per hour, etc.). Such measures are easily made, but they don't provide much insight into what tactics produce the outcomes. The real question is: What does it take for an organization to create more value, more effectively and more predictably with human capital? To respond to that issue, companies must answer a whole set of questions that typically aren't asked in most organizations:

- What are we actually spending on human capital (cost), and what is it buying us (value)?
- Are we sure our human capital strategy is aligned with our business design?
- What can we change in the way we manage people to generate greater returns by cutting, reallocating, or increasing investments?

The answer to those questions in virtually all companies is that no one really knows, but that fact gets clouded by historical storytelling, anecdotes, speculation, or questionable "correlations."

Look inside any company and the worst, least reliable performance metrics are those used for people tactics, practices, and policies. It is difficult to know what's working and what isn't because there is no science to it. This is not the case in most critical areas of business. Financial economists in universities and on Wall Street over the years have provided CFOs with solid techniques for optimizing the use of financial capital and managing risk. On the operating side, the disciplines of statistical quality control and process engineering have improved product quality and cut cycle times. Thanks to advances like these, the physical and financial assets of today's organizations are in general much better measured and managed. Thus, most managers can answer these questions when they are focused on financial or physical assets. They know what to measure and have the tools and systems to measure it. They have developed disciplines for tracking and evaluating their activities. The same thing cannot be said for human capital, and this makes comparably good decision making on major outlays practically impossible.

Because basic questions on the human capital side seldom are asked, let alone answered, companies end up tolerating more variance in the performance of their human capital investments than in the performance of any other asset they manage.

In light of the history of business and protocols of most companies, the chances are great that these questions will remain unasked until perhaps CEOs or board members—maybe even institutional shareholders—start demanding answers. This is the case because there are strong biases against and even structural barriers to such inquiries.

Barriers to Change

There are four fundamental barriers to change. First, although companies may say somewhere in the first couple of pages of the employee handbook that people are their greatest asset, few really live by those words. The heart of the problem, which virtually never is acknowledged, is the pervasive sense that employees are merely an operating cost, not a source of value creation that can be changed and leveraged. Thus, expenditures on human capital almost always are considered as costs to be minimized rather than investments to be optimized. And while from an accounting standpoint the workforce is deemed a fixed expense, in down cycles it is treated as anything but fixed.

A second, more complex phenomenon is that no one really "owns" the human capital issue. Organizations are not structured to create accountability for human capital. Think about it. In your company, someone is directly responsible for R&D, production, sales, customer service, finance, facilities, computers, trucks, and so on. Who is in charge of human capital? The human resources HR department? Not really—not in the same way someone is in charge of accounts receivable or buildings. HR has important administrative duties. It helps with recruiting. It usually takes the lead in training and development. It has major responsibilities in advising senior management on rewards and other policies. The best HR managers act as consultants to business units, but they aren't responsible in an ultimate sense for the people throughout the enterprise. If anything, at least on their bad days, they tend to blame line managers for mishandling people and people issues.

So what about the line side? Obviously these managers look after people on a day-to-day basis, but their responsibility for people is more limited than most might think. They typically don't make many people policies or prescribe people practices; they seldom are allowed to "experiment" with people tactics; they are in no position to see or influence strategic decisions about human capital. Most line managers would say, therefore, that they don't own the people issues. On their bad days they tend to blame HR for their people difficulties.

Of course, no one will ever be fully in charge of people, but that begs the question. Who is going to think strategically about human capital? Who is going to assure that the company's human capital strategy is aligned properly with its business model? Who is going to measure the impact of people on the firm's performance? Managing the purse strings is not sufficient. Swings of several percentage points in returns on labor costs are in play. For most large companies, even a 1 percent greater return on the labor bill would represent tens of millions of dollars falling straight to the bottom line.

The subject needs top-of-the-house attention and leadership, which we'll take up in detail in Chapter 12. In many companies that will require CEOs to wade into this untidy mess with some of the tough questions we have just mentioned. Those who do will launch a new era of creative and effective human capital management.

The third problem is that most practices and policies are made one at a time and are not connected to the others. Therefore, companies sometimes make decisions about leadership selection exclusive of the business model, decisions about benefits independent of pay decisions, decisions about pay in isolation from performance drivers, decisions about spans of control decisions decoupled from staffing models, and so on. Finally, all those individual decisions are exclusive of the larger organizational context. As we've said, organizations are systems, but most are managed like a set of discrete and unrelated events.

The fourth and most challenging factor that confounds the management of people is the long-standing lack of good internal measures. To fill the void companies resort to all kinds of inputs. Decisions are based on instincts, anecdotes, and management myths—legends that have, in the absence of better science, taken on the mantle of "truth."

In the absence of sophisticated measures, the most commonly used assessment is benchmarking. It is a "natural" process. It's baked into all people to want to know how they, not to mention their houses, dogs, and cars, compare with others. One can't get away from it, and it certainly has utility in business. But it also has limitations. Most benchmarking leads to the identification and use of best practices, which can make for terribly wrong decisions. Why, for example, would we expect the benchmarks or best practices at a GE appliance factory to be uniquely meaningful to SAP?

These barriers can be hurdled by measuring what up to now has been largely immeasurable: finding those things in your organization

---

Myth Busting

Here are some management myths we'll blow up in this book.

- There is one best way.
- Strong cultures are winning cultures.
- The past doesn't matter.
- It's always good to "pay for performance."
- Employee turnover hurts the bottom line.
- Major people decisions are best informed by employee surveys.
- Acquisitions should be integrated as fast as possible.

---

that uniquely contribute to your firm's performance (or erode it) and managing them aggressively. The requirement for doing that effectively is establishing *causal* evidence with which to make powerful business decisions. All that amounts to a new science for managing people, and that is what this book is all about.

The New Science of Human Capital Management

Unlike in the past, new, sophisticated means are available to get over those long-standing barriers. Thanks to many years of research in microeconomics, organizational psychology, and related fields and to new developments in statistical methods and information systems, a fact-based "science" of human capital management has taken form. This science has its own theory, discipline, and metrics, not unlike the evolution of "modern" finance. Beginning in the late 1950s and running through the 1970s, there was a flurry of research (some of it Nobel Prize–winning) by economists and financial experts in academia that revolutionized thinking about financial markets and instruments. The practical significance of that research was seized by some far-sighted financial institutions, such as Wells Fargo, Merrill Lynch, and Goldman Sachs. By the early 1980s the core concepts and methods were being embraced and transformed into new products and even whole new markets. In the end, those concepts reshaped financial markets in fundamental ways that remain in place today.

We believe that we are on the edge of a similar revolution in the way human capital is seen and managed. This new science measures human capital drivers of business performance. More important, it gives decision makers the power to *predict* the impact of their choices involving human capital on future results with reasonable confidence.

This is quite revolutionary. Executives will have to change the way they think about these issues:

TODAY'S THINKING . . .	THE NEW ERA . . .
What does the employee survey *say* we should do?	What do our employees' behaviors—that is, what they actually *do*—say we should do?
What works at GE and Microsoft?	What works here?
What does our function or group want?	How does this fit into the overall system?
What do the experts think?	What do the patterns over time in our company tell us?
How much does it cost?	What is the ROI?
What data do we have?	What data do we need?

This new path to better business performance and distinct competitive advantages relies on the discipline to enact three core principles. The first is to "insist on *systems* thinking." Business models and human capital strategies must match. Decisions about each one are intertwined and are certain to fail if they are addressed independently. Furthermore, they must be in accord with the marketplace: the customer and the competitive and regulatory spheres in which your company lives.

The second is to "get the *right* facts." Go beyond external sources and internal perceptions and tap into the running record of your company—its performance trends and human capital patterns—to get firm-specific insights.

The third is to "focus on value." There's a floor to cost reduction but no ceiling to value creation. Find the points of leverage.

We're going to take up each of those three principles in Part I. Then, in Part II, we'll explain the core tools and statistical methods, with an emphasis on the concept of internal labor markets and how to measure their dimensions and implications. This is where the real science of our work shows up. It's not beach reading, but if you get your hands around this material, you'll be positioned to transform the way you think about and manage your greatest asset.

In Part III we'll shift to common business challenges and applications ranging from implementing strategy shifts to managing risk. The last section, Part IV, looks to the future: what investors, CEOs, staff executives, and employees need to do to maximize the opportunities of this new science of human capital strategy.

Key Points

- For most organizations, human capital is their most important asset.
- Human capital strategy is the last asset with which companies can create a sustained competitive advantage since financial and physical assets, including technology, are typically no longer major points of differentiation.
- Companies tolerate more variance in the performance of human capital than in any other asset because measures and analytics comparable to those used in other parts of the business have not been available.
- Most decisions about people, even in the best companies, are driven by hunches and what the competition is doing.
- One of the greatest risks on the people side of the business is missed opportunity—not knowing how to maximize the return on human capital.
- A new science for human capital management now makes it possible for executives to identify and understand the real human capital drivers of business performance.

Principles

Insist on Systems Thinking

THE CHIEF EXECUTIVE officer (CEO) of a global manufacturing company we'll call ProductCo faced painful, widely known problems. First, new product introductions were running behind schedule, throwing a monkey wrench into the company's marketing plans and delaying the receipt of hundreds of millions of dollars in new revenues. Second, many products were experiencing quality problems, draining away cash for warranty settlements. Third, and equally alarming, customer satisfaction had taken a dip. There was no denying these problems, each of which was tangible and measurable.

To the casual observer ProductCo should not have been having these troubles. It had strong senior management, its product development teams had years of experience, and it had implemented several state-of-the-art programs to develop the talents of its managers. What was going wrong? Was it poor planning, problems with design, a problem with suppliers? An internal audit was launched to identify the root causes.

The audit indicated that the problems had a common origin on the people side of the business: a lack of mastery of the ability to lead key technical areas. Fast-track managers were moving rapidly from function to function and from one business unit to another. That rapid mobility was producing unanticipated and undesirable consequences; people with responsibilities in new product design, production, and marketing were insufficiently seasoned in the details of their work and unable to execute in accordance with the company's high standards.

Using the audit findings as a starting point, we dug deeper, analyzing ProductCo's internal labor market by using the Internal Labor Market (ILM) Analysis^{SM} tool described in Chapter 5. An internal labor market analysis identifies the causes and consequences of employee movements in, through, and out of the organization. Applied to this case, the goal was to quantify and map the company's selection, mobility, reward, and developmental patterns for managers. We also focused on the causes and consequences of managerial mobility. The analysis reconstructed the record of the actual events, circumstances, and dynamics that managers experienced by "reading" the facts maintained in the company's human resources information system (HRIS) and related databases.

The results of that work confirmed earlier suspicions and added new insights. HR data confirmed high rates of movement in key management positions. Managers were jumping from job to job every two years, with the most highly regarded people moving even more frequently. That "time in position" was very low and was not conducive to achieving technical mastery in the product, design, and marketing areas. Indeed, the rapid pace of talent mobility within the company went to the heart of its quality and product delay problems. People were not developing the specialized skills they needed to do their jobs well. The best and brightest were, as a matter of company policy, being trained as generalists, compromising their ability to develop the depth of knowledge needed to ensure product quality.

Furthermore, since some of the new products for which they had responsibility often took a long time to develop and launch, managers, designers, and engineers who were on board at the beginning of a project usually were gone by the time the outcomes of their decisions were tallied. That limited, if not eliminated, accountability for results. It also contributed to frequent course changes as new managers substituted their own decisions for those made by their immediate predecessors.

How had this situation come about? We found three culprits in ProductCo's talent strategy. In isolation, each was a reasonable practice for developing human capital. In combination, however, they conspired to produce unintended and damaging results.

One culprit was a bias toward firm-specific human capital over generalized human capital. The company pursued a policy of filling most open positions with internal candidates. That apparently commonsense fill-from-within policy inadvertently resulted in an unhealthy volume of movement within the company. Every manager's promotion or lateral move created a vacancy, and that vacancy triggered other personnel movements. A few hires from outside would have neutralized the problem substantially, but hiring from outside was counter to the top management's belief that employees had to grow up inside the company to be fully productive and "understand the business." The facts showed otherwise. Careful analysis of employee records demonstrated that the performance of outside hires was not substantially lower than that of individuals who had been promoted from within. Indeed, new hires quickly caught up to the performance levels of longtime employees.

The second culprit was related to incentives. The company's reward system was closely attuned to where one stood on the hierarchy ladder.

Generalized Versus Firm-Specific Human Capital

Human capital has two essential forms. One is *generalized*; that is, employees have attributes and qualities that are of value not only to their current employer but to potential employers as well. Employees bring this form of human capital with them when they are hired. They increase their generalized human capital when, for example, they pursue a new degree or professional credential through part-time study outside the workplace. The value of that credential can enhance their standing with their current employer or a new employer. People with generalized skills can move easily from business unit to business unit and from company to company.

The other form of human capital is *firm-specific*. This type of human capital reflects the value of employees that is unique to a single firm. It grows with tenure and experience in the firm. Its growth is accelerated by in-house training and structured programs of movement through related jobs. Firm-specific human capital is distinguished by its special value to the employing firm in which it is developed; thus, it is less marketable to other organizations.

Different firms require different combinations of firm-specific and generalized human capital to be successful. Neither one is always best or right. Even within a firm, some jobs may require employees with extensive firm-specific knowledge while other jobs may require a high degree of generalized know-how.

In fact, the reward system was a classic example of a "tournament" career model, in which there is a close calibration between opportunity for advancement and financial rewards.[1] Rewards for moving *up* a level dwarfed pay increases for performance *within* a level, no matter how excellent. Thus managers had much greater incentives to move up than to stay put and do outstanding work. However, the probability of promotion was quite low, making an individual's prospects for reaping financial rewards so low that a "choke point" existed at the lowest leadership levels in the company. Individuals who rose to that level had a very low chance of continuing their rise through the hierarchy.

Faced with that bleak outlook, people looked for ways to improve the odds. They quickly learned that lateral moves would do the trick. Data drawn from internal HR records showed that a lateral move—one that cut across functional areas, for example—was a valuable precursor to a vertical promotion and was far more valuable than a small "in-grade" promotion within one's current area. Staying in the same position for more than two years also drastically reduced the chances of moving up. Therefore, ambitious managers did whatever they could to bounce around the company. That behavior helped them understand broad dimensions of product development, design, marketing, and the like, but did little to develop deep, specialized expertise in any single area.

Finally, we discovered that the existing talent management advisors were inadvertently acting as agents for individual employees. Review boards composed of HR and line representatives had been set up to spot talented people, assess them vis-à-vis open positions, and move them along the career ladder. Over time, however, managers looking for lateral moves and promotions took an increasingly directive role in regard to the review boards, virtually asking them to become their agents. Board members often did just that.

In isolation, none of the practices was unreasonable. Moving talented people around makes sense; it creates a cadre of people with broad knowledge of the company and how it works. Hiring from within also has merit; it provides opportunities for capable and hardworking employees and gives them a reason to stick with the company. Financial rewards for upward mobility encourage people to perform well in their current positions. In some places it is the most efficient, powerful way to encourage high performance and build firm-specific capabilities critical to development, production, and marketing cycles. Also, having HR people act as career facilitators increases employee satisfaction and supports the talent development that every growing company needs. However, taken together in their unique production context, those programs were creating a workforce deficient in specialized knowledge, unaccountable for results, and unable to support goals of product quality and rapid time to market.

Systems Concepts

The ProductCo story underscores the first principle of effective human capital management: systems thinking, that is, an awareness of the connections that link organizational units, people, processes, and behavior.

Organizations are complex systems with many linked elements and subsystems. A change made in one subsystem produces effects in others. Organizations are in turn embedded in larger systems that include customers, suppliers, shareholders, competitors, regulators, and the general economy. Thus, any major change in pricing, products, or internal policies ripples through the larger system.

We conceptualize the system for human capital productivity with the graphic image shown in Figure 1-1. Here an organization—a system unto itself—operates within a large "macro" system of customers, competitors, and so forth: the market environment. This model, which was first developed in 1994 and was refined in the field over the intervening years, is a synthesis of research results on the drivers of human capital productivity. It provides the conceptual underpinning of our analytic tools and the various case studies described in this chapter and later chapters in this book. The model reflects the observation that productivity is not inherent in a practice or program but is a consequence of how that practice or program is aligned with the broader context of the system. A successful human capital strategy is one that is aligned with business needs and is internally coherent; that is, it is made up of mutually reinforcing practices.

Systems thinking is fundamental in environmental science, macroeconomic forecasting, weather studies, the social sciences, business, and many other fields. Although executives understand it intuitively, they don't always apply it when they formulate strategies and practices, including people practices. With that in mind, let's consider a few key

Figure 1-1

A Systems View Of Human Capital Productivity

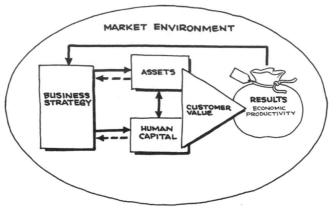

aspects of systems thinking and their applications to the ProductCo case.

Systems Are Made Up of Interrelated Parts

Parts can be "elements" such as individual employees. They also can be subsystems, organized collections of people, practices, and technologies within the larger enterprise. Divisions and business units are subsystems, as are the bundles of practices and individuals that make up purchasing, marketing, legal, and other functions.

The existence of interrelated parts has important implications. One is that the operations of parts may or may not be tightly linked. Hospital emergency rooms are systems with very tightly linked parts. An aircraft carrier in the middle of operations is a system with tightly linked parts. The launch of airplanes is a result of closely coordinated efforts of several functionaries acting in unison to get them off the deck swiftly, safely, in the right order, and properly configured. Other organizations accomplish their missions with much less subsystem coordination. A law enforcement agency, for example, does its work with dispersed units acting relatively autonomously in different areas or in pursuit of different types of crime. Carriers and cops have many things in common, such as strong hierarchies and command and control structures, but the organizational subsystems through which they accomplish their missions operate with different degrees of interdependence.

Interrelated parts operating with varying degrees of interdependence have important implications for human capital. An obvious one is that some people perform better in some parts of an organization than in others. A more subtle implication is that the effectiveness of reward programs will vary with the degree of interdependence among the parts. For example, programs that reward individual accomplishments can be counterproductive when tight coordination and teamwork are required. Placing individual achievement on a pedestal detracts from the willingness of employees to cooperate with others with whom they are tightly linked.

The fact that organizations are systems of interrelated parts is a fundamental principle. Failing to accept its implications creates the risk of mismanagement. Managers must understand how the component parts of their organizations are interrelated and, more specifically, how human capital practices can best be matched to interrelationships.

Changes and Practices in One Part of the Enterprise Can Have Consequences In Others

Because of linkages across component parts, changes in any subsystem often are felt in another subsystem. For example, a change to "mass customization" in manufacturing—that is, building large numbers of products to the differing specifications of various customers—may have consequences for the way a company markets its products. A corollary of this principle is that implementing planned changes in one part of the enterprise without making changes in other, related parts is a recipe for failure.

Consider a change in how the call center employees of a financial service firm do their work. Let's say that under the current arrangements each service rep performs a job with narrowly defined responsibilities. For example, a rep who helps a customer with an automobile loan payoff will transfer that customer to someone else if the customer inquires about her mortgage. The mortgage rep then will hand off the customer to a third employee for matters related to credit card balances.

Let's suppose that this financial services company has created new work arrangements under which each service rep responds to all customer service needs: one-stop shopping. For this change to be successful, changes in several other organizational subsystems are required. For example, changes in technology are needed to provide service reps with quick and complete access to the full portfolio of customer information. Training also may increase in importance as reps will need expertise in a broad spectrum of products and services. Changes in the supervisory system may be required as well. Supervisors will need broader expertise. Further, systems of measurement and metrics also may need changing. Under the current arrangement reps are rewarded for handling each call as quickly as possible. That might not be an appropriate metric under the new work system.

The point here is that a change in any one part of an enterprise usually has implications for other parts. Managing successfully requires recognition of this fundamental principle.

The Potential Causal Pathways Are Many

Every complex system is a web of causal connections and pathways of influence. Consequently, the same end usually can be achieved through different means. Indeed, this is the meaning of the term *equifinality*. One practical implication of the principle of equifinality is that the route to success for one organization may not be the route to success for another. Even companies in the same industry seldom have the same configurations. They have different subsystems, different parts. Thus, a practice that works well in one will not necessarily carry over successfully to another.

Another implication is that it is possible to find an optimal route to success for each system. Although there may be several ways to achieve growth and profitability goals, for example, some ways are better than others, depending on the unique properties of the organization. Thus every organization can—and should—determine the optimal approach to managing its human capital. That optimal approach can become a unique source of competitive advantage.

Causal pathways within systems often contain feedback loops (Figure 1-2). A feedback loop indicates that one organizational practice or condition has consequences for another, which in turn affects the first. For example, the type of people a company attracts and hires today can affect which of the company's veteran employees decide to stay or leave.

Figure I-2

Feedback In A Causal Relationship

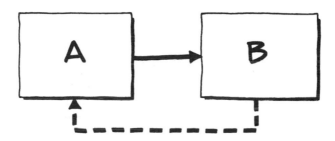

The kinds of people who stay will in turn affect the company's ability to attract other desirable types.

The existence of many causal pathways has another implication: namely, some of them may go unrecognized. When strong causal pathways go unrecognized, managers are left to act on the weak ones. Failures to discern the potent pathways are often rooted in an over-reliance on anecdote or organizational folklore.

Unintended Consequences Abound

Because organizational systems are made up of interrelated parts with multiple causal pathways, new programs and practices can have unintended consequences. Failure to anticipate those consequences explains why many new programs fail to achieve their goals and produce unwanted "side effects."

How can we deal with unintended consequences? One way is to make them less likely. This can be accomplished by understanding the dynamics of the organization's systems and the way in which a planned change will ricochet through the organization. Techniques for doing this with respect to human capital practices are at the heart of this book. Essentially, these techniques bring discipline to the understanding of human capital systems and shift the task of managing from the realm of intuition to the realm of fact.

Our experience with an energy company provides a good illustration. In an effort to reduce costs that company abandoned a pay system with many narrow bands in favor of a broad-band system. The new system meant that there were fewer pay grades. It also provided a means of reducing overall wage and salary costs; for example, a pay adjustment could be made within a band without incurring the costs associated with promoting individuals to new bands. Fewer pay bands also went hand in hand with "delayering," that is, reducing the number of levels of hierarchy and the managers required to staff them. The unintended consequence of this approach to cost reduction, however, was a complete disruption of the career system. The company had at its disposal only two real ways to reward its employees: pay and promotion. The two were closely interrelated. The move to the new system essentially eradicated promotion as a reward and thus removed much of the incentive for staying with the company.

Combined Changes Can Produce Costly Problems or Can Work Exceptionally Well

The nature of systems is such that programs and practices that are implemented in combination may produce different outcomes than they would if they had been implemented separately. That is the lesson of the ProductCo case. Sometimes the combined effects are devastating. The field of medicine provides a useful analogy: Some perfectly safe and effective drugs produce lethal side effects when taken together.

The combined effect of different programs is actually better in some circumstances. For example, research indicates that sophisticated selection techniques can contribute to organizational performance.[2] Training can do the same thing. However, the *combination* of the two can be exceptionally powerful, producing a better result than would be expected if one merely summed the benefits of the two practices in isolation.

In a similar vein, research by one of the authors of this book and his colleagues found that people-centered interventions that aim to improve productivity—objective setting, job redesign, and so forth—often have positive results but that those results are highly variable.[3] This is not a surprise, but that variability was reduced greatly when multiple interventions were made simultaneously. In other words, making several related changes at once reduces the risk of failure. Terms such as *interaction effect* and *complementarity* have been used to describe this combination effect. Finding and then acting on the complementarities among management practices is a sure path to success.

Closed Systems Often Fail to Change and Self-Correct

Although no business organization can isolate itself from the larger business environment, some companies act as if they could. Filling all open positions through internal promotion is an example. Organizations constantly are exposed to influences from the larger systems and the environments in which they are embedded. Technological advances and the entry of new competitors are examples of influences that an "open" organization will respond to, for each of those influences can have major effects on the human capital of the enterprise.

Finding Root Causes in a System

In light of the principles of systems thinking we have described, let's return briefly to ProductCo, the manufacturing company whose story opened this chapter. In cases like this one it is impossible to solve the problem by treating the symptoms. Instead, it is necessary to identify and attack the root causes of the symptoms. But how can they be found? Causation in a complex system has many pathways; those pathways are not always obvious, but they can be identified. In ProductCo's case we approached causation through a mixed strategy of qualitative data and then a deep dive into quantitative analysis.

Gathering Data

Data gathering through interviews with executives and on-line surveys of managers was an important part of the analytic process. The insights gained were wide-ranging and essential. For example, ProductCo's implicit strategy for developing leadership talent emerged from these "soft" methods of data gathering. That strategy was predicated on the development of generalist capabilities through the movement of people through many jobs within their functions and occasionally through jobs outside their functions. That strategy was abetted by the perceived importance of filling leadership positions from within and the respect given to those who played the game.

The soft data were supplemented by "hard" quantitative data obtained by digging into the organization's human resource information system (HRIS). The combination of soft and hard data revealed both what people *said* about the system and how it worked in reality.

The quantitative approach used in this case was an Internal Labor Market (ILM) analysis, a bedrock tool of human capital management that is explained later in this book. From it we learned a wealth of facts about how the system actually operated, including the following:

- The rates of movement through jobs
- The rates of promotion
- The financial gains that employees experienced through lateral moves and promotions
- The (low) number of outsiders hired into leadership positions
- The job performance of those outsiders

These descriptive measures were essential for understanding the system, but they were not sufficient to establish causal connections.

Taking a Deep Dive

What we call a deep dive involves statistical modeling of how events unfold over time. This final step brings one face to face with causal relationships. It tells an analyst which factors contribute the most to the outcomes of interest, the magnitude of their impact on those outcomes, and their ultimate consequences.

The virtues of statistical modeling as a foundation for management action are communicated in more detail in the following chapters. For now suffice it to say that modeling reveals and explains interrelationships among organizational practices, conditions, and consequences. Modeling also helps reveal the unintended consequences of actions and provides a way to recognize complementarities, both positive and negative. In short, statistical modeling of causes and consequences provides a disciplined foundation for both understanding and action.

One of the things revealed by our deep dive at ProductCo was the price tag of its manager mobility strategy: tens of million of dollars each year. Knowing that monetary cost helped the leadership answer two important questions: Does this policy make sense? and Are we getting value for our investment?

Once we had uncovered and determined the impact of the facts, we were in a better position to make recommendations and the company had a solid foundation on which to make decisions about human capital. The data not only supported management's suspicions but also made critical connections between processes and results.

In the end we were able to provide the company's leadership with a concrete plan for redesigning its program for promising managers. Here are the high points:

Changes at ProductCo

CURRENT SITUATION	RECOMMENDATION
Large rewards for promotion	Strengthen rewards for performance in place
	Enhance reward and recognition for those who develop technical depth and excellence
Insufficient time in position	Clarify the required minimum time in position for different roles and functions
	Establish new attitudes, behaviors around time in position
Bias toward developing generalists	Restore a balance of generalist and specialist capabilities through managed career paths
	Focus on business-critical competencies
Quality and performance problems	Monitor implementation of changes and their business impact

Another Systems Tale

Another example that illustrates the value of systems thinking is the case of TechCo (the name is fictitious; the company is real). TechCo is a midsize technology company that designs and produces computer chips used in consumer products and business equipment. The firm constantly creates new components to meet the specific needs of its customers; most of those components are adapted from previously successful designs.

For TechCo delay is deadly. Product life cycles are short, peaking within two to three years and then decaying swiftly. Profitability depends on getting to market quickly with a workable component. The press for speed goes hand in hand with quality, since every failure in the design process delays the introduction of new components and thwarts revenue growth. Because of the importance of quality, the CEO defined the organizational climate as having an "institutionalized intolerance of error."

In the mid-1990s TechCo ran into serious problems. Its revenue growth and shareholder returns were flagging, prompting top management to review operational productivity. Rising turnover among design engineers was identified as the cause of those problems. During the prior seven years the company's overall turnover rate had risen from 6 percent to 15.6 percent. The defection rate among engineers was even more pronounced and more damaging since engineers controlled the development of new parts from past designs. Experienced, able engineers with deep knowledge of the company's proprietary designs and technologies were critical to the achievement of low design error rates and rapid product launches, the twin drivers of TechCo's revenue growth. However, for some unknown reason engineers with the most education and years of service were leaving, as were those with high performance ratings.

The CEO was aware of the problem but was unable to stem the tide: "We've tried everything," he complained, "pay, stock, training, coaching, new managers, hiring different people, screening differently. But nothing works." Indeed, nothing worked because the cause of the engineering turnover had not been identified. The root cause or causes could be learned only by examining the entire human capital system. Using the techniques described in the previous case, this is what we discovered:

- *There was a clear barrier to advancement.* TechCo's best-trained and most experienced engineers were hitting a promotion "wall" roughly halfway up the job level ladder. If one tracked the annual movement of engineers into the firm through hiring, up and down through promotions/demotions, and out through defection, it was impossible to miss the fact that promotions were highly improbable once people reached that wall. That was where most defections were occurring. The best and brightest—the fast-trackers who received early and rapid promotions in TechCo up to this level—created their next promotions by leaving TechCo and taking engineering jobs elsewhere.

- *The incentives were misaligned.* Like many high-tech companies, TechCo counted on variable pay and stock options to spur performance and encourage loyalty. Fully one-third of an engineer's pay varied with performance. These practices are highly suited to entrepreneurial cultures, where risk taking is encouraged and rewarded, but TechCo had no such culture. Its reliance on direct intensive supervision, documentation, by-the-numbers work, and intolerance for errors limited opportunities for entrepreneurial expression. The presumed incentive value of variable pay was in fact being squandered and appeared to contribute to increased turnover. The reliance on stock options also enhanced the risk. Variability in the price of the company's stock was very much driven by general market movements and industry swings rather than by the products and contracts and decisions of the company. Therefore, options acted more like lottery tickets; their value was beyond the control of TechCo employees.
- *TechCo paid twice for supervision.* The company paid above-market wages, presumably to attract and retain self-directed goal-oriented individuals who needed little monitoring. It paid again through intense supervisory and control practices ostensibly exercised in the name of error reduction. Faced with these findings, TechCo's head of technology said, "We hire the kind of people who should be able to think for themselves, but we don't allow them to."

These observations suggested a number of opportunities for solving TechCo's problem with engineer turnover, ranging from changes in management philosophy and organizational climate to changes in the ways employees were recruited and their careers were developed. As this case reveals, viewing human capital management practices from a systems perspective can lead to the articulation of fact-based opportunities for change. Systems thinking, supported by empirical knowledge of how things really are working, is a key principle for managing human capital to achieve business goals.

Key Points

- Systems thinking produces an awareness of the connections that link organizational units, people, processes, and behavior.

- Unexamined changes in one part of a system can produce unintended consequences elsewhere.
- The careless combination of changes or people practices can cause costly problems.
- Many relationships have causal linkages; it is necessary to identify and understand them.
- To understand causal linkages within an organizational system one must get the facts and use them, aided by statistical modeling, to discern which among many possible causes are truly the most potent.

Get the Right Facts

THE SECOND PRINCIPLE of human capital management concerns facts. For decision makers, facts are like candles in a dark place: They illuminate portions of the landscape with a degree of certainty and cast some light onto the murky path ahead. There are, of course, no facts about the future, and so every decision contains some level of uncertainty. However, facts about the past and the present help reduce that uncertainty and increase the probability of desirable outcomes.

Unfortunately, many decisions that are intended to improve the productivity of human capital, some costing hundreds of millions of dollars, are made without sufficient facts or without the *right* facts. For some reason executives who refuse to spend a dollar on a new piece of equipment until they have studied all its costs and potential benefits will make multi-million-dollar decisions about people programs with little more than hunches or irrelevant facts dragged in from other companies to guide them.

Consider your own decision-making approach. If you were faced with a decision about replacing your current e-commerce infrastructure, you'd insist on substantial facts and financial projections. You probably would ask for a net present value analysis of the best-case, worst-case, and most-likely-case outcomes. The assumptions underlying that analysis would be scrutinized or challenged. In some cases you'd go a step further, conducting a "sensitivity analysis" to determine how those forecasted outcomes would change if certain critical assumptions failed to hold. You also would want to know the internal rate of return from the proposed investment. If that rate is positive, does it exceed the returns available from alternative investments? If too few facts were available to support those analyses—and assure a good decision—you probably would ask staff people to chase them down to reduce the level of uncertainty.

Such fact-based rigor almost never is applied to decisions about human capital, even when they involve huge sums of money. More often one sees decisions based on the following:

- *No facts.* "Common sense tells us that our employees will be more productive if they have a stake in the profits of the business."
- *Unreliable facts.* "Employees say that they are more likely to stay if we offer profit sharing."
- *Irrelevant facts.* "We benchmarked three world-class companies with variable pay plans: a bank, a hotel chain, and a defense contractor. All reported good results."

These types of "facts" won't help you. What you need to make high-quality decisions are relevant and reliable facts. And decision quality matters. Think how much better your company would perform if the decisions made by lower-level and mid-level managers improved by just 10 percent. You'd see a notable boost in bottom line results. Now think what would happen if the CEO and other senior executives improved their decisions by 10 percent; you'd see a huge effect on the bottom line. David and Jim Matheson made this observation in *The Smart Organization* noting the leverage that decisions made at the top have on outcomes.[1]

Not all facts are created equal. Some facts are weak or too unreliable for important decisions. Facts drawn from anecdotes fall into this category. Facts drawn from benchmarking (internal and external) and statistical correlation are generally stronger; they can help you form useful insights. As Figure 2-1 indicates, facts about cause-and-effect relationships have the greatest power. These facts not only provide a better understanding of the role of human capital in organizations but allow you to predict the impact of decisions about human capital. Here is an example: "If we redirected bonus pay from group performance to individual performance, the likely result would be a 6 percent increase in workforce productivity and a 10 percent reduction in the turnover rate of high-performing employees."

Establishing causality is always a challenge and seldom assured solely by means of statistical analyses. At a minimum, three conditions must be met to infer causal relationships among variables. The first is simple correlation. The variables must move together in a consistent, orderly way, as occurs when increases in labor productivity are associated with increases in target rates for incentive compensation. Second, changes in the presumed causal factor must *precede* changes in the outcome variable (i.e., when a change in bonus eligibility occurs *before* increases in productivity are observed). Otherwise it is plausible that the chain of causation is actually reversed or reciprocal. Productive organizations tend to have more resources at their disposal for generous pay and benefits. Thus, increased productivity may account for higher bonus payments, not the other way around. Understanding the chronology of events is essential in discriminating between cause and effect.

Figure 2-1

Some Facts Are More Powerful Than Others

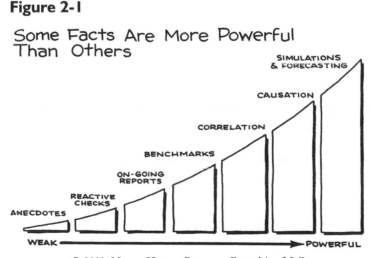

SIMULATIONS & FORECASTING

CAUSATION

CORRELATION

BENCHMARKS

ON-GOING REPORTS

REACTIVE CHECKS

ANECDOTES

WEAK ———————————————————————▶ POWERFUL

© 2003, Mercer Human Resource Consulting LLC

Third, it is necessary to take account of other factors that affect the outcome of interest, factors that may be changing simultaneously with the variable of interest. It is known, for instance, that general economic conditions affect economic productivity and that the correlation between the two is strongly positive. Thus, an observed increase in productivity could well be attributable to better macroeconomic conditions, not to changes in incentive compensation.

In attempting to establish causality, therefore, it is imperative to introduce appropriate "control" variables in any statistical analysis and to do that on the basis of a solid theoretical or empirical understanding of what drives the outcomes of the interests—in this example, workforce productivity. Such knowledge about human capital has grown enormously during the last several decades as a result of research in the fields of economics and organizational psychology. That research has provided a firm foundation for empirically evaluating hypotheses about causal relationships. It provides the basis for selecting appropriate control variables in statistical models to better evaluate whether and how particular human capital factors are influencing outcomes that are of interest to managers. Thus, the "facts" one seeks can be generated through a disciplined process of hypothesis testing. To return to our earlier example, a plausible theory of how tighter labor markets influence pay and employee turnover can enhance the predictive power of a model that relates productivity to bonus pay. Theory-based statistical controls are far superior to the unreliable "data-mining" approach sometimes used in making decisions about human capital.

Several dimensions of facts affect their power to inform. This chapter introduces the four dimensions of facts that are especially pertinent in making decisions about human capital: what we call say versus do, time, magnitude, and inside-outside balance. Each is illustrated by a brief case study.

The Say-Do Trap

During the 2002 U.S. elections pundits, politicians, and the public were shocked by the wide discrepancy between polling data and the outcomes in many key races. Dozens of contests described by pollsters as too close to call ended in a sound drubbing of one of the candidates. The political parties and news organizations that had paid royally for measures of voter sentiment during the campaign were left scratching their heads and wondering what they had gotten for their money. What those politicos and newspeople failed to recognize is that there is often a big difference between what voters say to preelection pollsters and what they do in the voting booth. The same say-do disparity exists in the workplace among both employees and companies.

Like political pollsters, companies that rely on surveys and exit interviews to understand what their employees value and what motivates their behavior often fall victim to the say-do trap. The reason is simple: What employees say is not always what drives their behavior. For example, a person in an exit interview may say that she is leaving because of a higher-paying offer elsewhere, but is that statement a reliable basis for action? Many defectors make this statement because higher pay is a socially acceptable reason to leave. Better still, it will not be challenged and will not make anyone think less of them. In reality, the employee may be leaving because she thinks the company's managers are dimwits or because the workload is excessive. These are the things that actually undermined her commitment to the organization and made her receptive to other possibilities. However, she won't say this for fear of burning her bridges, creating bad feelings, or admitting to something that may be interpreted in an unfavorable light. Who, after all, would say, "I'm leaving because the work is too demanding"? Moreover, it is common for employees to load onto a single factor, such as pay, the complex set of factors that influence how they perceive their jobs and employers. That by no means signifies that that single factor is what the employee most values or is most predictive of actual behavior. It is simply a convenient proxy for the entire employment package. Whatever the reason, in these circumstances the company will conclude erroneously that it may not be paying enough for talent. We'll explain below how FleetBoston Financial avoided that trap.

Companies invest millions of dollars every year in employee surveys to understand what employees value, what they like and don't like about their group and organization, what keeps them on the job, and what would induce them to leave. However, few companies look at the actual record of stay/leave decisions: what employees "do" and the context in which those decisions are made. Few measure the objective antecedents of turnover and use what they learn to anticipate employee responses to policy changes.

This omission is mystifying in light of the way in which marketing personnel in many companies approach customers. Good marketers take a multidimensional approach to understanding customer preferences. Yes, they ask. They conduct surveys, run focus groups, and do all sorts of tests to determine what customers value in their products and services; what product and service characteristics appeal to customers the most; how they would respond to changes in price, quality, and product and service design; and so forth. They do all these things, but they also track and measure actual buying behaviors: what customers do. Point-of-sale data capture in retail stores is just one example. Those data speak loudly and clearly about customers' choices. In short, smart marketers consider both what customers say and what they do. They understand the distinction between "stated" preferences and "revealed" preferences and recognize the value of examining both. They follow the dollar trail and use actual buying patterns to draw inferences about customers' values and to anticipate customers' responses to price and other product changes. They use that information to make decisions about what they will bring to the market and how they will price their products and services.

Benetton, the apparel maker, has been a pioneer in using that customer behavior approach. Instead of just asking which colors customers prefer, it uses its point-of-sales information system to capture the colors of actual purchases on a daily basis and sends the data to the factory floor, where undyed stock is ready for the finishing steps. Within a matter of days those items—in the preferred colors—are on the shelves and in the shopping bags of Benetton customers. In today's information-rich world, what marketer would dream of asking customers what they *thought* without looking also at what they *bought*?

Somehow the marketer's approach to obtaining customer knowledge and anticipating customer behavior seldom finds its way to the realm of decision making about human capital, where knowledge of employee values and preferences is based almost exclusively on what the employees say. Employee surveys are everywhere, but what employees actually do is ignored when people policies are developed despite the fact that companies have vast, easily accessible information on employee behavior. The following case is typical and underscores the potential costs to companies that fail to dig deeper for the facts.

Toyota Avoids the Say-Do Trap

Toyota Motor Manufacturing North America almost fell victim to the say-do trap not long ago. That world-class company conducted an annual employee survey and relied heavily on it in formulating its human capital programs. The company believed that pay and promotion were tied closely to employee performance. It also offered extensive training and career management designed to improve skills and give promising individuals opportunities to broaden the scope of their know-how through moves within the company.

Toyota naturally was surprised when survey data revealed that employees discounted both of those expensive programs. In the collective view of employees pay and promotions were *not* tied to performance, and employees did not see any payoff from training and movement around the company. In light of what the employees said, Toyota was wasting millions of dollars each year on those programs. Once they heard the voice of their employees, company executives considered revamping the performance management and compensation systems, with spending shifted to other programs.

It turned out, however, that there was a major disconnect between employee perceptions and company practices. An analysis of who actually received higher pay and promotions indicated that rewards indeed went to high performers. Payroll and human resources (HR) records provided the proof. Contrary to the employee survey data, pay and promotions consistently were tied to performance in what was an elegantly functioning system. The same thing was true with respect to training and movement within the company. An examination of HR records over several years indicated quite clearly that all else being equal, the people who completed company-sponsored training and those who accepted moves within the organization were being promoted at much higher rates than were those who didn't.

If this company had relied entirely on what its employees were saying, it would have wasted lots of time and money changing or eliminating human capital programs that were essentially sound. However, if the company had not listened through the survey and instead had relied only on HR information systems and payroll records, it would have missed the real problem: a lack of understanding among employees about what the company actually valued, what criteria were used to evaluate performance, and how specific behaviors and results were translated into rewards. The insights came from pursuing both say *and* do data. What Toyota really needed was a relatively inexpensive revamping of its communications with employees. The company needed to communicate the *facts* about performance, training, and movement and their connection with higher pay and promotion. It could then use those facts to bridge the gap between management and employee perceptions (Figure 2-2.)

How to Avoid the Trap

Employees' stated preferences for benefits arrangements, training options, and so forth, do not always reflect how those individuals will behave when faced with real-world trade-offs. They are facts, but not the complete facts for decisions about human capital. This discrepancy often results from the way surveys are designed. For example, a survey that asks employees to rate the importance of pay in their decisions to stay or leave will not always reflect an individual's future behavior. When there is no cost associated with rating a benefit highly, respondents generally will say that that benefit is "very important." The real world, however, requires people to make trade-offs

Figure 2-2

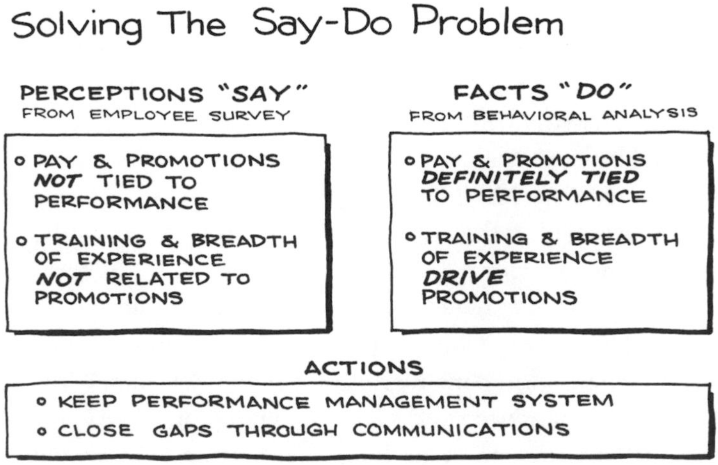

Solving The Say-Do Problem

PERCEPTIONS "SAY" FROM EMPLOYEE SURVEY	FACTS "DO" FROM BEHAVIORAL ANALYSIS
○ PAY & PROMOTIONS **NOT** TIED TO PERFORMANCE ○ TRAINING & BREADTH OF EXPERIENCE **NOT** RELATED TO PROMOTIONS	○ PAY & PROMOTIONS **DEFINITELY TIED** TO PERFORMANCE ○ TRAINING & BREADTH OF EXPERIENCE **DRIVE** PROMOTIONS

ACTIONS

○ KEEP PERFORMANCE MANAGEMENT SYSTEM
○ CLOSE GAPS THROUGH COMMUNICATIONS

between things they value, even things they value highly, such as higher pay and more time with their friends or families. Everything cannot be "very important." In a world of constraints people give up one value to have more of another, revealing their highest preferences through their behavior.

Market researchers have known this for a long time and employ techniques such as conjoint analysis to clarify those trade-offs. Unlike surveys that offer "not important," "important," and "very important" as choices, more modern sensing methods pose questions in a more realistic context that takes into account the fact that limited resources require people to make trade-offs. These methods force choices and allow the researcher to draw inferences about the value of the individual components of a complex offering. Those techniques have been adapted to researching employee preferences. For instance, one can examine how employees with similar characteristics value different components of a pay and benefits package and then use that information to fashion a package that delivers higher utility to employees, perhaps at lower cost to the employer. The value of doing this is clear, but a basic limitation remains: At best, such methods offer better ways to mimic actual behavioral scenarios, but they do not capture actual behavior. The difference is often significant and extremely revealing about the workforce and the organization.

The say-do disparity does not pertain only to employees. Companies also say one thing but do another, usually without realizing it. One well-known high-technology company, which we'll call Digitt, thought of itself as a pay-for-performance organization, offering multiple bonus programs, profit sharing, recognition awards, and various broad-based stock plans. When we read the documents describing the various reward programs, we concluded that pay for performance was certainly the foundation of that company's reward philosophy, but that was what the company said. What did it actually do?

To answer the question, we followed the money trail, evaluating over time who did well in the company and what kinds of performance were rewarded. We discovered several important facts:

- Individual performance was not differentiated substantially. Only 5 percent of total pay was affected directly by individual performance.

- Performance pay was channeled to business units. Lower performers shared equally in the bonus pool by virtue of being in a strong group, receiving over $30 million in the year in which we studied the situation and almost $100 million in total "performance" pay.
- Companywide, people in the lowest quartile of performance were getting 25 percent of all performance pay, more than those in higher quartiles were getting and almost as much as was being received by the company's highest performers (Figure 2-3).
- A low performer in a high-performing group could expect a larger dollar bonus than could a much higher-performing individual who happened to work in the newer business units that had not yet reached profitability.

Without realizing it, this company was shelling out about $13 million each year to employees who had been ranked in the bottom performance quartile *for five years in a row:* about 6 percent of the employee population.

The bottom line was that the company basically rewarded two things: years of service and business unit performance. It mattered

Figure 2-3

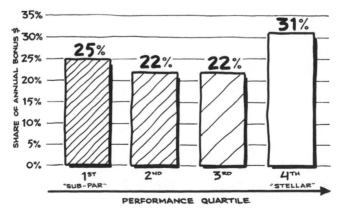

Significant Variable Pay Went To Low Performers

more where employees were in the organization than how they did. Focusing on what the company actually rewarded, *not* its stated policies, made it possible to cut through the say-do problem and identify millions of dollars in misdirected rewards. Those poorly targeted investments were costly, undermined the workforce, and jeopardized the company's competitive position. In the end investors turned on the company with a vengeance, destroying over 50 percent of its share value.

Our prescription for avoiding the say-do trap is to get the "right" facts by rigorously capturing perceptions and observing actual behaviors and company practices, the way Toyota does. In looking at the "say," consider the perceptions of both employees and the company itself. Then uncover actual behavior—the "do"—from com-

The Noise Problem

Capturing facts at a specific moment in time presents another problem for decision makers: the effects of random environmental influences, or noise. In the parlance of statistical analysis, *noise* is the transitory and unexplained variability found in any set of data. If there is significant noise in snapshot data, decision makers can be led astray.

Consider this example. The sales revenue of a bookstore fluctuates from month to month, week to week, and day to day. A substantial portion of that variability is based on known market factors: the seasonality, the year-end holidays, day-of-the-week shopping patterns, and so forth. These variations can be adjusted out of the data. Another part of the variability reflects the actual performance of management and company employees: what they actually do. The variability that remains is noise. Noise in the bookstore's revenues might be caused by temporary road construction near the store, by a large one-time order, or by unknown causes. Thus if one were evaluating the bookstore's performance on the basis of a short-term snapshot, the facts could be skewed by those transitory events.

The remedy for noise is to look at facts over time, smoothing performance to get a clearer picture of the more persistent patterns of performance. This is something that people do in most business analyses but seem to overlook in getting the facts about human capital.

pany records and the behavior of employees in different environments over time. Recognize that learnings derived from the analysis of hard data have limitations as well, since not all programs or events with which the organization and its employees experience are recorded in electronic files. Sometimes it is impossible to find a reasonable proxy or indirect indicator for a program or event of interest. In such cases, there is nothing better than to ask. Once you have the say-do facts, you can assess their business relevance by means of statistical modeling.

Time Matters

Time is a key element in uncovering the root causes of many human capital problems, including turnover. Traditional assessment tools such as employee surveys provide a snapshot of what is going on at a particular moment, but it's more important to see things from a time perspective.

Many of the most important drivers of employee behavior don't even have meaning if they are not measured over time. Consider rewards as an example. Current compensation is of course an important component of rewards. It can be measured at a single point in time, as can its relationship to current market rates for comparable jobs. However, there are other important components of rewards that cannot be measured at a single point in time. The way an individual's pay grows from year to year is an important example. Indeed, in some organizations and for some employees, the *trajectory of pay* may eclipse pay *levels* as a motivator of employee performance and turnover behaviors. Similarly, the *rate* of promotion and other forms of advancement may be critically important. These are inherently dynamic constructs. They have no meaning and certainly cannot be measured unless they are examined over time.

Unless one takes a dynamic view of workforce events, one is likely to miss some of the most important aspects of the employment relationship and of human capital generally. One would be working without one of the most critical pieces in the human capital puzzle.

Time is another dimension in which surveys can be deficient. Too often organizations use surveys to present a static picture at a particular point in time. By doing so, they fail to capture the dynamic aspects that really tell the story of what is happening to their human capital. Although a survey will indicate where people stand in terms of pay, job level, and other static descriptors, a time-based (longitudinal) study will show how *fast* or how *slowly* they are moving upward through the system or broadening their experience. It will reveal the kind of human capital that is being developed and how quickly it is taking shape. In the modern economy this is indispensable information for managing human capital. It certainly proved vital to FleetBoston Financial, as the story on the following pages show.

Applying Time-Based Analysis at Fleet Financial

FleetBoston Financial, a large regional bank with more than 40,000 employees, has grown substantially in recent years, mostly through an aggressive merger and acquisition strategy. In 1998 Fleet, which was then called Fleet Financial, was experiencing a surge in voluntary turnover. Indeed, by some measures its turnover rate was almost twice the industry average, exceeding 40 percent in some occupational groups. Those defections were costly and disruptive to the organization.

The company's HR department had been tracking turnover for some time to determine the scope of the problem. It had relied on exit interviews and employee surveys to determine what kept people with the company and what encouraged them to leave. Those traditional methods pointed to two prime causes of employee turnover: excessive workload and inadequate pay. Fleet responded with policies aimed at relieving stress and adjusting pay where possible. Nevertheless, turnover continued to rise. The company was ready to try something different.

An alternative approach was to examine the actual pattern of turnover *over time* to see whether objective antecedents of turnover could be identified. That approach involved rigorous statistical modeling of turnover behavior among the employees. Every day the employees of that vast organization were making decisions to stay or leave in different but easily observed circumstances. Some were in locations characterized by very tight labor markets; some were in softer markets. Some were in large units; some were in smaller ones. Some occupied jobs in which pay was comparable to market rates; others were receiving pay significantly higher than that in the market, and so on.

Simply stated, the workplace reality on the ground contained distinct variability even though Fleet espoused uniform, standardized HR policies. Those variations in effect created a natural experiment, allowing the company to evaluate how particular factors influenced behavior and measure the relative magnitude of the effects. That revealed a story about the drivers of turnover, which were at odds with what departing employees were telling exit interviewers.

The facts gleaned from Fleet's HR database helped identify and quantify the impact of various workforce characteristics and management practices on employee turnover. To the surprise of many managers, the findings revealed that pay levels had the *weakest* impact on actual turnover; this was in striking contrast to what exit interviews suggested. As an illustration, the modeling determined that a 10 percent across-the-board increase in pay levels would reduce turnover by less than 1 percentage point. Thus, relying primarily on pay adjustments to stem turnover would have required a major commitment of resources with little payoff for the company. The real drivers of retention, according to the analysis, had little to do with pay and much to do with factors related to careers, such as promotions, pay *growth*, number of jobs, and breadth of experience at Fleet. See Figure 2-4.

Clearly, the most powerful deterrent to defection was a recent promotion. Individuals promoted in the prior year were about half as likely to leave, all else being equal. Those who made the specific career transition from hourly to salaried status (i.e., from nonexempt to exempt) were also more likely to stay. Interestingly, they performed better compared with those who came into the exempt ranks from the outside. The analysis also indicated that the highest probability of defection was among employees who had been in the same positions for more than two years. In fact, the likelihood of defection shot up dramatically in

Figure 2-4

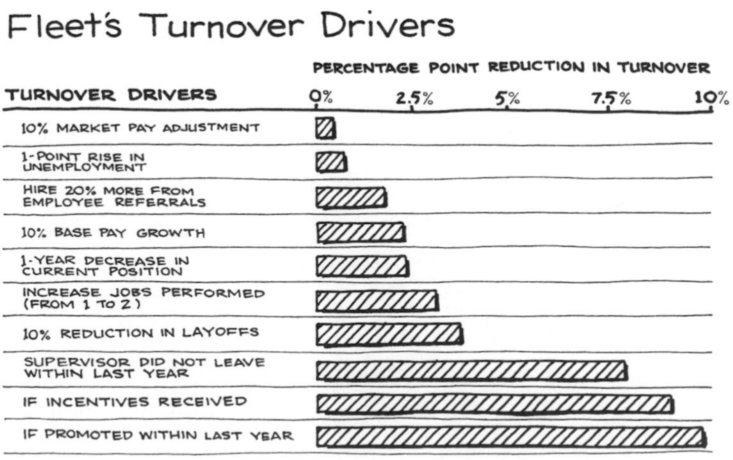

Fleet's Turnover Drivers

TURNOVER DRIVERS	PERCENTAGE POINT REDUCTION IN TURNOVER				
	0%	2.5%	5%	7.5%	10%
10% MARKET PAY ADJUSTMENT					
1-POINT RISE IN UNEMPLOYMENT					
HIRE 20% MORE FROM EMPLOYEE REFERRALS					
10% BASE PAY GROWTH					
1-YEAR DECREASE IN CURRENT POSITION					
INCREASE JOBS PERFORMED (FROM 1 TO 2)					
10% REDUCTION IN LAYOFFS					
SUPERVISOR DID NOT LEAVE WITHIN LAST YEAR					
IF INCENTIVES RECEIVED					
IF PROMOTED WITHIN LAST YEAR					

that group. Simply changing jobs, even without a promotion or a significant pay increase, tended to diminish an employee's propensity to leave.

Stability within the ranks of supervisory personnel also had a substantial effect. Specifically, the likelihood of turnover almost doubled when an employee's supervisor left the organization, but only if that supervisor was a high performer. If the supervisor simply moved to another department, there was hardly any effect, suggesting that this had less to do with the relationship between the supervisor and the employee than with the adverse message that is sent when good people leave an organization.

The facts revealed through this analysis helped Fleet avoid costly and ineffective solutions. They encouraged management to focus on the real drivers of employee retention as the basis of a new retention strategy. Specifically, management made the following choices:

- Focus on high-performing supervisors and managers, emphasizing the elements of the employment package with the largest demonstrated impact on managerial retention, such as advancement and career development. Keeping good supervisors with the bank would have a positive effect throughout the organization; that is, keeping down the defection rate of good supervisors would reduce the overall turnover rate.
- Focus on careers and the programs and practices that help employees develop their skills and experience. Make sure high-performing employees, regardless of rank, have a clear idea of the career opportunities available to them and the financial significance of being successful in the organization.
- Concentrate on career tracks for nonexempts that involve transitions to exempt status. Those tracks were shown to be especially fruitful in enhancing retention and ultimately producing both loyal and productive employees in the exempt ranks.
- Do not allow good people to linger too long in their current positions. Move good people periodically into new and better jobs. Ironically, building an employee's résumé by enhancing his or her experience made people stay, not leave.

- Pay special attention to new hires, ensuring that those coming into the organization are well matched to their jobs, have a realistic understanding of job requirements and the work environment, and can ramp up more deliberately into their full workload. The data analysis showed that the problem of "quick quits" would abate with such actions.

It Worked

Some of those interventions were not easy to execute. Imagine asking supervisors to facilitate job moves by their top performers when their own rewards reflect the performance of the units they manage. Imagine selling the idea that investing in employees and building their résumés will help Fleet as much as if not more than it will help their employees. It took guts to take this on.

Fortunately, courage was not in short supply at Fleet. Under the leadership of Anne Szostak, executive vice president and corporate director of human resources and diversity and chairman and CEO of Fleet Rhode Island, the company launched its retention initiatives. Within eight months Fleet experienced a 25 percent reduction in the turnover of the nonexempt population and a 40 percent reduction among the exempts even in the face of severely tightening labor markets. The company's own estimates of annualized savings exceeded $50 million per year. More than three years later, the results of statistical modeling show that the retention strategy continues to work in spite of all the bank's acquisition activity. (Acquisition tends to spur increases in voluntary turnover.) Retention of top managerial talent has been remarkably successful.

None of the important facts uncovered in the Fleet case could have been gleaned from a snapshot of the company's current employment practices. A snapshot reveals nothing about career progressions, the rate at which promotions occur, the trajectory of total pay, or the development of new skills and the acquisition of new and broader experience. It reveals little about intertemporal linkages between the turnover of supervisors and that of employees. No organization can determine root causes of workplace phenomena without taking into account the element of time. To determine cause and effect, it is necessary to know *what went before*. The past does matter.

Relevant facts such as these depend on the ability to analyze payroll and HR records going back several years. That is why an employee survey should be just one of many tools for learning about human capital.

Magnitude

HR managers and business executives generally have been content to know that their practices and policies are moving people in the right direction. For example, if spending more money on training improves productivity, knowing that the spending produces a positive outcome generally has provided sufficient justification for the added cost.

Unfortunately, good economic decisions must consider direction *and* magnitude. For example, you wouldn't be satisfied if one of your managers said, "Boss, we should invest $10 million in this equipment. It will produce positive cash flow every year." You would say, "It's nice to know that cash flows will be positive, but we cannot make a good decision without knowing *how large* the cash flows will be." And you'd be right. It is impossible to determine the value of an investment or its rate of return without knowing the magnitude of its future cash flows.

Are These Best Practices?

The drivers of retention at Fleet may not be relevant to a different organization. Remember what we said in our introduction: Context matters. Advocates of external benchmarking will say that Fleet's decision to focus on supervisor loyalty and its attempt to move good employees into a new position every two years are two "best practices" that you should adopt at your company. We disagree. These practices worked for Fleet, but they will not necessarily work for you.

The same reasoning applies to decisions about human capital. It is necessary to know the magnitude of a program's effect on who stays and who leaves, the magnitude of the results of a new hiring initiative, the magnitude of productivity improvements from costly training, and so forth. Otherwise there is no basis for choosing from among competing alternatives for a company's considerable investments in people.

Thanks to more comprehensive and accessible HR databases and new tools of analysis, it is now possible to measure the magnitude and significance of the impact of programs on critical workforce outcomes (e.g., attraction/retention, development, individual performance) and business results (e.g., profitability, productivity, quality). That should be apparent in the story of Fleet where the ability to quantify the relative impact of alternative interventions helped the organization avoid tactics that were patently noneconomical and focus instead on those that promised a real return. It also should be clear in the story of the high-tech company described earlier, in which measuring the actual dollar investment in low performers helped the company recognize the previously hidden failure of its "pay-for-performance" reward system and galvanized management support for fundamental change in some long-standing programs.

However, there is another story that illustrates perhaps even more powerfully why magnitude matters and why knowing only the direction of workplace outcomes is of little use to executives faced with expensive decisions about human capital decisions.

Marriott International, Inc., is a leading hospitality company with nearly 2,200 lodging properties in the United States and over 60 other countries. It operates and franchises facilities under 14 brands, including Marriott Hotels and Resorts, Marriott Executive Apartments, Renaissance Hotels, Courtyard by Marriott, and Ritz Carlton Hotels & Resorts, among others.

Among Marriott's 129,000 employees is a cadre of hotel and resort managers. In many respects those managers are the linchpins of the company's success. The company develops those managers in many ways, including moving them from one location to another. That strategy is intended to broaden their backgrounds and give them experience in managing progressively larger or more complex properties. It also is meant to motivate managers to reach the premier properties. The company views this strategy as the best way to groom its managers, develop careers, and produce higher retention of high performers.

Were there potential risks to that strategy? Might not the process of taking good people out of a property and bringing in someone new challenge that business unit's performance? Intuition could not answer these questions with reliability. It was insufficient to sort out the positives and negatives of this development strategy. Marriott wanted the kinds of facts that come from good measurement and analysis. It would have to dig for the facts about the effects of its program (and their magnitude) on managers and on property performance. Marriott needed to know whether the negatives of moving people around offset the positive benefits of developing managers' careers, and it asked us to help.

We gathered internal data on the retention of hotel managers in the program over a period of four years and assessed the profitability of the affected hotels over the same time frame. Here's what we found: The movement of managers contributed not only to their development but also to their retention. Further, their movements produced no measurable loss of profitability in the affected locations: There wasn't even a short-term dip.

It seems clear why movements would enhance managers' careers, but why didn't the movement of Marriott's managers produce negative effects on business results? Intuitively, managers' moves could bring about complications of disruption or discontinuity that would reduce the performance of a property. However, those negatives appeared be offset by the benefits of the new perspective and fresh ideas brought in by the newcomers. Further, the progression of managers from one property to the next was very systematic, designed to move individuals "up" in an orderly way. Indeed, the overall movement of managers between properties appeared to be a well-managed process that served the operational needs of the enterprise while enhancing individual careers.

Inside-Outside Balance

Where do the facts that support *your* human capital decisions come from? If you are like most executives, you draw on facts originating inside and outside your organization. That is always a good approach, assuming that the facts you gather and use are the "right" ones, that is, facts that are appropriate to the situation and to the context of the organization. External facts can alert you to innovative practices that may benefit your organization; they provide a sense of where your industry is heading and often answer the question of how you stack up against rivals on any number of important factors, such as pay, training, and productivity, among others. However, many external facts found through benchmarking and other means are not particularly relevant. In the worst cases they are misleading. Using them to guide decisions can only lead to bad outcomes.

One reason why these external facts may be misleading is that they are inaccurate. Most HR benchmarking studies, even those involving sophisticated statistical modeling, rely on self-reporting. Usually, the senior HR executive or, perhaps more likely his representative, is asked to reply to a survey containing questions about the HR programs and practices. For instance, the respondent may be asked whether the company has a gain-sharing program. Unfortunately, the term *gain sharing* means different things to different people. To some it specifically signifies the original industrial engineering–type plans, such as Scanlon, Rucker, and Improshare, that focused on hard measures of operational performance and tracked performance relative to some historical or benchmark standard. To others it refers to any form of variable pay, including pay based on financial performance, such as profit sharing, revenue sharing, and even shareholder value. These are very different types of programs that have very different implications for human capital management. When they are pooled inadvertently in the summary of survey responses, the informational value is blurred or lost.

External comparisons also raise the problem of say-do. A company may say that it has a particular program even though the reality (the "do") is quite different. Think for a moment about the high-tech firm, Digitt, which thought it was paying for performance. If we had relied on interview or survey responses from the HR department or, frankly, from any company officials, we surely would have characterized the company's reward system as pay for performance. Virtually every generic category of variable pay was in place, and broad segments of the population were covered. However, as we've seen, this was not the reality. Measures of actual pay-performance sensitivity—the year-to-year variation in pay related to changes in different measures of performance—were insignificant compared with those of other workforce attributes, such as years of service and level in the hierarchy.

The most important problem with benchmarking is that it fails to account for context. It thus flies in the face of the systems character of human capital management. If performance is indeed about "fit" or alignment, applications of benchmark data can be seriously misleading for an organization. Here's an example.

TechCo, the computer-chip maker discussed in Chapter 1, discovered the perils of creating a human capital strategy that was based on external benchmarking and so-called best practices. Historically, the company held a solid position in its industry as an efficient, reliable low-cost manufacturer of chips. Its workforce consisted primarily of experienced engineers who knew the company's library of chips and their possible applications, forged strong relationships with customers, and understood the company's sales, design, and manufacturing processes.

This chip maker, however, began to mimic the people practices of recognized technology leaders, firms such as Intel and Apple that made their money through innovation, not efficient process engineering. For example, it began to hire the "best and brightest" engineers at premium pay even though the work would hardly be challenging to top-flight engineers. Also, it made stock options an important part of its total compensation scheme even though the company's stringent command and control management system, which had been designed to ensure process efficiency, precluded the kind of entrepreneurial and risk-taking behavior that such rewards encourage. Those "best practices"— external facts—simply did not fit the organization's business strategy and organizational culture. The result? TechCo found itself plagued by inflated labor costs, declining quality, lower profits, and high turnover among its most experienced design engineers. The new recruits also left because the work was incompatible with their desire to be innovators.

TechCo experienced trouble because it relied on external facts drawn from its benchmarking of other firms in its industry. Some of those facts might have been useful in expanding the range of possible choices for executives, but they did not directly answer whether those choices were a good fit for TechCo. That question could be answered only with facts drawn from within.

The fundamental problem was that TechCo's management failed to recognize the true source of value in its workforce: firm-specific human capital. Whereas the innovators may require the best and the brightest and the leading-edge thinkers, TechCo's business model put primacy on solid homegrown talent, engineers who knew the company's library of chips and could adapt existing designs to new commercial applications quickly. That institutional knowledge made it possible for the company to serve customers with high-quality, low-cost chips in a timely manner. In this competitive business, margins are low and errors in design or production are deadly to profits. Nothing could substitute for the experience of engineers who had grown with the company. The policies TechCo put in place pursuant to benchmarking were geared towards general, not *firm-specific*, human capital. Therefore, they were a direct assault on the core assets on which TechCo's business model was built. It is not surprising that those assets began to erode.

Finally, it is important to note that TechCo's command and control management system was incompatible with the more participative reward system that the company was putting in place. Benchmarking failed to capture the systemic nature of practices in other firms and led TechCo to put in place practices that were fundamentally incompatible with each other.

The TechCo story is a cautionary tale about focusing too intently on external facts while ignoring internal data. In most cases internal facts are the best guide on human capital issues. Careful examination and analysis of a company's own data (e.g., employee and customer surveys, financial data, accounting data, operations data) will produce critical facts and insights about that company's workforce. Those facts and insights will lead to better decision making and the development of an effective human capital strategy. What accounts for profitability and growth? Who gets hired, who stays, who advances, how are rewards distributed, and how is talent developed? How frequently should managers cycle through positions? How broadly should incentives be distributed? How much should the organization staff up for a busy season, and how does turnover affect the organization's performance metrics?

The answers to questions like these form the backbone of fact-based decisions about human capital. When they are joined to disciplined, sophisticated analysis, they can help you identify (1) the human capital factors that drive business performance in your organization and (2) the combination of people practices most likely to optimize the productivity and value of your human capital.

Gathering internal facts about human capital used to be laborious and often unproductive. Pertinent data about pay, benefits, time in position, rapidity of promotions, and so forth, had to be pieced together from individual employee files. Thanks to advances in information technology those data are now readily available in enterprise resource planning systems, payroll databases, and human resource information systems (HRIS), all of which are becoming standardized across industries. Many companies have spent tens of millions of dollars on these information systems, yet most sit on the data they contain, maintaining and tapping into them mostly for compliance purposes. This is unfortunate because when properly used, these systems tell the human capital story of an organization. They are the ultimate source of facts that can and should inform decisions about human capital management.

Finding the Right Balance

If both external and internal facts are needed for good decisions about human capital, what is the right balance? Because business strategy generally drives human capital strategy, it is necessary to create a workforce that is capable of making the strategy work. Thus, to the extent that your business model is truly unique, internal data should dominate. You should know the most relevant facts about your internal labor market and develop metrics to track its most critical dimensions. However, don't ignore external facts. Your internal labor market does not exist in isolation; it is in constant interaction with a larger and competitive labor market. As a result, external facts are needed to determine how successful your policies and practices are likely to be in the face of competitive market conditions. Obviously, your company must be competitive in pay and benefits if it hopes to attract and retain good people and make its strategy work, but you can be competitive in different ways. Should you focus on matching pay and benefits to market levels or emphasize advancement? Will learning and career opportunity do the job? Only the internal lens can shed light on these choices. Unfortunately, for too many companies that lens isn't even in the tool kit.

Sources of Internal Facts

We find that the best approach to obtaining internal facts is twofold:

1. Gather qualitative facts through surveys and interviews, which will yield perceptions about how the organization functions and "expert opinion" about current realities and future needs.
2. Gather quantitative facts through measurement and statistical modeling. Our key tools for measurement are Internal Labor Market (ILM) Analysis and Business Impact Modeling. You will be introduced to them in later chapters.

Key Points

- The *right* facts—particularly causal facts—are the foundation of good decisions.

- What people say is often at odds with what they do. One can avoid the say-do trap by also tracking critical events and actual behaviors.
- Employees are not the only ones who sometimes say one thing but do another. The behavior of companies is sometimes at odds with their doctrine. For example, a company may say, "We encourage entrepreneurial behavior," but then punish people who deviate from prescribed methods. It may publicly embrace teams and extol cooperation yet reward only individual performance.
- Time is a key element in uncovering the facts about and root causes of many human capital problems. Only by looking at certain events over a period of years is it possible to determine the pace of employee advancement, pay improvement, and the actual causes of employee behaviors.
- Neither the value of a human capital investment nor its rate of return can be determined without an estimate of the magnitude of its impact. Knowing only whether the impact is positive or negative is insufficient for making economic decisions.
- It is necessary to strike a balance between internal and external facts.

Focus on Value

THE THIRD PRINCIPLE of human capital management concerns value. Value is generated when revenue exceeds costs (including the cost of capital). When one focuses on value and the many activities and decisions that create it, one is focusing on the right things.

Like any asset, human capital is an investment with a stream of economic returns. When those returns are positive—that is, when the benefits produced exceed their costs—that asset has produced real value. It produces a current return and some level of future return. Every alteration in the asset has an effect on those returns. Therefore, rotating people through positions, investing in training, reconfiguring pay and incentives, and so forth, change this asset's potential to produce value.

The type of human capital that is developed through managerial decisions also affects value. The global manufacturing company case described in Chapter 1 showed how decisions about career development produced a cadre of managers with skills that were too general for the company's good. In another organization those general skills might have produced greater value, but this company needed more specialized talent along with its generalists, especially managers who knew in detail how to move new product concepts from the design stage through manufacturing to on-schedule product launches.

The personal choices of employees—to stay or leave, to increase their skills or allow those skills to become obsolete—also shape the value-producing power of a company's human capital. Company policies and practices can influence those decisions but in the end cannot control them. Thus, the human capital asset of an organization is always in the process of becoming something else, with greater or lesser power to create value for shareholders and customers.

Regrettably, most executives are inclined to view human capital as a cost rather than a value-producing asset. They manage it accordingly, as something to be minimized, reduced, reined in. This view of human capital is supported by traditional accounting practices which expense rather than capitalize workforce investments that build capability and motivation such as training and financial incentives. Unlike fixed costs that do not vary with the volume of production (e.g., leases, interest expenses), variable costs are charges that increase and decrease with the level of production. Thus, when sales slacken and production decreases, fewer overtime hours are worked, employees are furloughed or laid off, and wages may be frozen or even cut. It is a short step from regarding a workforce as a variable cost to regarding it as something that can be increased or decreased with the ebb and flow of customer demand.

One also can speculate that executives manage human capital as a cost because they manage what they can measure and know how to measure people as costs. Indeed, most companies know to the penny the costs of their human assets in terms of base pay, variable pay, benefits, and support services. What they haven't been able to measure until now has been the *value* of those assets, and managing anything one cannot measure is bound to be problematic.

Managing human capital as a cost is often unavoidable during periods of business distress, but it is a strategy with clear limits: There is a point below which there are no costs left to cut. Gordon Bethune acknowledged this in reflecting on his struggle to pull Continental Airlines out of its death spiral in the mid-1990s.[1] The company, he noted, had managed costs so aggressively that it had very little left to offer its customers. Gertz and Baptista made the same observation when they wrote that a company "cannot shrink to greatness." Further, they noted that cost reduction is "a game that anyone can play," not a viable strategy to achieve a sustainable competitive advantage.[2]

Cost reduction has a natural floor. However, there is no ceiling on the potential value of human capital. For example, a company might save a grand total of $55,000 by canning the lethargic-looking drone in the research and development (R&D) lab who never appears to be doing anything useful, but that quiet individual might be the unrecognized genius who is halfway to creating the company's next great hit: a product family worth hundreds of millions of dollars in revenue every year. This example may stretch the point, but it underscores the fact that a focus on cost management eventually leads to a dead end, whereas managing human capital for value has no theoretical limit. This point is recognized by investors who pay attention to the intangible worth of employees when pricing company shares.

Ironically, the executives who manage the people side of a business as a cost problem do not approach the costs of other assets in that way. When they get out the checkbook for other assets, they don't talk about cost as much as about expected future returns *net* of costs. In the best cases they balance costs against returns over time, producing a single number—net present value—that encapsulates the cost of the investment, the cost of capital, and all the anticipated cash flows from the investment. When the net present value is sufficiently high relative to alternatives with similar risks, concerns about costs take a very different and more positive form: "Where can we find the cash?"

The Case of the Struggling Health-Care Company

To better appreciate the kinds of problems that result when companies focus on people strictly as a cost, consider the story of a health-care provider we refer to here as HealthCo. That organization was struggling to reduce its costs. Like other companies in its industry, it was being squeezed. Insurance and government payouts were reducing reimbursements even as the cost of operating was going up every year. The only way HealthCo could maintain profitability was to hold the line on some costs and reduce others. One of the ways it aimed to do that was by reducing its employee outlays, a major segment of its total cost structure. For example, the organization focused on how it staffed its facilities, especially with regard to the use of part-time employees, the amount of overtime worked, and managerial headcount.

After some deliberation HealthCo decided to look for every opportunity to reduce overtime. It also reduced the number of managers in its facilities. Further, it decided to replace many full-time employees with part-timers who cost less per hour in base wages and received fewer or no benefits. This tactic was abetted by the practice of obsessive benchmarking, which encouraged HealthCo to compare its ratio of part-time to full-time employees with those of others in its industry. That comparison told HealthCo management that it could save money by having a higher percentage of part-timers.

The choice to rely on more part-time employees appeared to give HealthCo both greater flexibility and lower costs. The work schedules of part-timers could be shifted with rising and falling patient censuses, and their pay and benefits would be measurably less than those of their full-time counterparts. This strategy appeared to be a workable solution to the company's financial problems.

Unfortunately, the company understood only half the equation. It knew its wage costs but had no information about the value generated

---

Asset Scrapping

The notion of people as a variable cost may have outlived its usefulness, particularly in knowledge-based enterprises in which the skills, customer relationships, and inventiveness of employees are the primary source of competitive advantage. In those enterprises people are the obvious source of value creation. In contrast, the enterprise's buildings, computers, and filing cabinets are commodities that provide only moderate value and no competitive differentiation. In these companies laying off people is analogous to a farmer dumping his seed corn in the trash or a steel producer leveling part of its production operation. Both actions sacrifice future earning power and don't even recoup the "scrap value" of what they've thrown away.

What is the scrap value of the furloughed people a company has trained and developed at great expense over the years?

The growing recognition of the value of human capital undoubtedly explains why knowledge-based companies such as Schwab, the U.S. financial services giant, was so reluctant to furlough people during the most recent recession. Forced by shrinking customer demand to reduce headcount, the company nevertheless went to great lengths to keep discharged people in its orbit through six-month leaves, the use of rehiring bonuses, and other mechanisms. It recognized that layoffs were robbing it of firm-specific knowledge it had spent heavily to develop and would need again as soon as customer demand returned.

by its staffing policies. Consequently, HealthCo initially celebrated the cost savings produced by its new workforce. However, when it ultimately assessed the impact of the new scheme on value creation, it found that excessive use of part-timers was hurting overall productivity, as is shown in Figure 3-1.

Our analyses revealed that the organization's interests were not well served by its growing reliance on part-timers. At the time of the analysis roughly 45 percent of HealthCo's employees were full-timers, far short of the optimal level identified through statistical modeling. Through that modeling, the influence of other variables that could affect productivity was controlled, including differences in facilities, labor markets, wages, capital investments, case mix complexity, employee turnover, and percentage of total hours worked as overtime. By measuring and plotting the relative productivity of full- and part-time employees at this company, as shown in Figure 3-2, we established the optimal mix of part-time and full-time employees as slightly over 60 percent full-time employees and slightly under 40 percent part-time employees. By deviating from that optimal mix, HealthCo unwittingly destroyed revenue worth *five times* the anticipated savings, an amount equal to 3 percent of the company's annual revenues.

Figure 3-2 is a result of what we call *Business Impact Modeling*[SM], an

Figure 3-1

The Most Productive Units Used Full-Time Employees

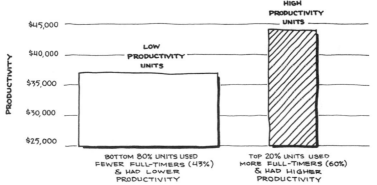

Figure 3-2

Too Few Full-Timers Reduced Productivity

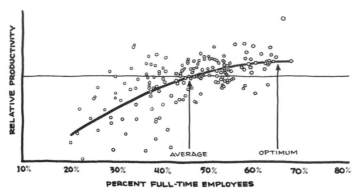

approach that is described more completely in Chapter 6. The heart of the approach is the disciplined analysis of how key business outcomes such as productivity are affected over time by human capital attributes and practices.

Why did having too many part-timers hurt productivity? One factor may have been the impact on long-term career incentives for full-time employees. As the number of part-time employees in a facility increased, full-time employees experienced slower earnings growth, fewer promotions, and in some cases higher turnover. The reduction of full-time people also cut into the development of the firm-specific know-how HealthCo needed to operate effectively, especially in its tertiary-care hospitals that provided more complex services.

Further analysis showed that part-time employees were not being deployed in ways that created the hoped-for flexibility. The evidence indicated that short-term changes in caseloads were not matched with commensurate changes in the use of part-time employees. The potential gains expected from part-time employees did not materialize because HealthCo deployed them as if they were full-time employees.

Still further analysis showed that the cost-cutting strategy of reducing overtime also had backfired. Intuitively, reducing overtime hours seemed like a sure way to reduce personnel costs, but that commonsense idea didn't hold. We found that productivity at HealthCo actually increased 3.3 percent for every 1 percent *increase* in the ratio of overtime to regular hours worked by current employees. Apparently, HealthCo managers were using overtime to get more value out of their full-time employees, an increasingly scarce resource. Of course, overtime hours cannot be increased without limit, but within the range of "normal practice" in this system overtime appeared to represent a very effective utilization of spending on human capital.

This case vividly displays the systems concept of unintended consequences. Here a company's noodling with one people practice produced consequences in other, related practices. Indeed, facts about the complementary effects of staffing and overtime needed to be understood in order to get the right practices in place.

Lessons

In summing up the HealthCo case, the company made three mistakes in its human capital strategy that one sees repeated in different companies and different industries:

1. *Placing too much reliance on benchmarking.* Many companies purchase data that, among other things, indicate such things as the average ratio of full-time to part-time employees at so-called high-performing companies. The implication is that (a) that ratio has a causal relationship with high performance and (b) other companies should follow suit. Because of contextual differences, however, there is no reason to believe that mimicking the practices of other companies will help your company.
   Lesson: Use external benchmark data to stimulate thinking and further investigation; don't use those data to make decisions, especially strategic decisions.
2. *Basing decisions about human capital on intuition.* It seemed that reducing overtime and raising the proportion of part-timers in the workforce would reduce spending on employees. However, that intuitively appealing idea did not take into account the complex dynamics of the workplace.
   Lesson: What appears intuitively obvious does not always hold true in a complex system such as a workplace. Sort out important causal relationships before making any decisions.

3. *Measuring costs but not value.* HealthCo's decision makers missed a big one here. Full-time employees cost more, but a dollar spent on them produced more value than did an equal amount spent on part-timers. The reason: higher productivity among full-time people.

Lesson: In measuring costs, also measure the value that is received in return.

How People Practices Affect Value

HealthCo learned the hard way that several of its key people practices were inadvertently destroying value, but its experience is not unique. Other companies have done the same thing, though not always through a myopic focus on costs. In many cases decision makers focus on value but implement practices that fail to optimize it. Our experience with First Tennessee National Corporation made that clear.

First Tennessee National Corporation is a nationwide financial services institution with a history dating back to 1864. With over 10,000 employees, it ranks among the 50 largest bank holding companies in the United States in asset size and market capitalization. Its goal is to provide "all things financial" to its customers.

When we first met the managers of that organization, we were struck by their intense dedication to understanding their customers and by their use of research methodologies. This bank routinely employed sophisticated tools of market analysis to understand customer needs and measure key indicators of customer response such as the number of new accounts, the size of accounts, customer retention, the "share of customer wallet" captured by the bank, and market share. For any specific time period managers knew where they stood on those measures and where trends were taking them.

The bank also was very clear about what set it apart from its rivals. Through extensive market research, it had identified customer service quality as the foundation of its competitive position. That was what accounted for its current success and differentiated it from the many other retail-oriented financial services companies against which it competed. Since service quality was dependent on interactions between customers and the bank's many customer-facing employees, senior management naturally wanted to know more about its employees.

Indeed, it wanted to understand its employees as well as it understood its customers. This is a great idea that most companies overlook.

By tapping both employee and business performance data and using statistical modeling techniques, the company was able to discern how business outcomes were driven by people practices and employee attributes. For example, it found that all else being equal, the locations with the longest-serving employees performed best in key customer and financial measures such as customer retention, growth of premium accounts, net earnings, and market share. No other factor came close to the importance of years of service. People who knew the bank's products, procedures, and customers were demonstrably more effective in producing the customer satisfaction on which First Tennessee's competitive position rested—and the business result that would satisfy shareholders. On the basis of that finding, the bank concluded that increasing the average years of service of customer-facing employees by just one year would have the following two effects on companywide revenue:

1. Revenue per customer would increase by 4 percent, or $15 million, per year.
2. Market share would expand by 2 percent, resulting in revenue gains of $25 million annually.

In addition to this $40 million revenue increase, eventual alterations in its people practices would reap another $20 million in savings from reduced turnover, greater operating efficiency, and lower payroll expenses.

With employee years of service being the key to higher revenue, the next step was to determine the effect of current people practices on longevity with the bank. Were those practices encouraging customer-facing employees to stick with the company or pushing them toward the exit? Company leaders, accustomed to making data-driven decisions in other areas, knew that credible information on that issue could not come from conventional human resources (HR) benchmarking or best-practice approaches because the bank's environment was unique. Facts and solutions would have to be developed from within, and that was where the company's leaders began looking.

Analyses based on several years of employee, financial, and customer data yielded three important facts. First, in an effort to expand its breadth of service offerings, the bank had been hiring new people with new skills and experiences in investment counseling, marketing, and information systems. Of course, the newcomers lacked the firm-specific know-how they would accumulate over time. In the meantime, every new person hired diluted the bank's depth of firm-specific service and product knowledge. Second, because of the tight labor market at that time, outside hires were receiving top-dollar pay packages. That practice had the effect of tipping the rewards balance in favor of newer employees with general skills and against longer-service employees with the firm-specific and customer-specific knowledge that data had identified as the key drivers of value. In other words, direct experience with the bank's products and customers and years of service in First Tennessee's unique business environment didn't matter a great deal when paychecks were handed out. Third, the bank's incentive pay scheme left most customer-facing employees out in the cold. Pay for performance rewarded executives and commission-based salespeople but touched very few of the frontline people on whom the bank's competitive strategy depended.

Not surprisingly, experienced employees, including a high percentage of top performers, were leaving the company at increasing rates. In effect, the company's people practices were undermining the value of its human capital. Could the loss of customer value be far behind?

Recognizing the risk to its strategy, the bank moved quickly to realign its people practices with what it had identified as the key driver of customer service quality. That meant focusing on career development and rewards. Specifically, the bank took steps to do the following:

- Ensure that high performers had a clear path for growth (and long-term service)
- Extend pay-for-performance opportunities to more customer-facing employees
- Invest more in training to broaden the capabilities of the existing workforce

Most importantly, the company institutionalized ongoing measurement of its human assets and practices. Today it applies as much rigor to understanding workforce needs and characteristics as its marketing researchers apply to understanding customers, a claim few organizations can make.

Lessons

The First Tennessee case underscores two important lessons:

- Find the drivers of competitive advantage and then align people policies and practices with them.
- Be as diligent in understanding the workforce as you are in understanding the customers: What attracts them to your company? What encourages them to stay or leave? What produces the greatest and least value?

Length of Service Versus Cost

Unless they've been asleep at the wheel, employees with more years of service have greater firm-specific knowledge. That knowledge often makes them more productive than newcomers, and the productivity differential can be measured objectively. However, at any given career level long-serving employees generally cost more than do people hired off the street; that is another fact that is easily checked.

The question that many companies want answered is this: Is the greater productivity of long-term employees worth the added cost? In other words, they are asking, "Are we getting what we pay for in terms of added value?" Perhaps you've been asking the same question. In the First Tennessee case actual measurements of productivity versus cost were made at different levels of years of service, all of which indicated positive value: The company was getting greater value for higher pay. However, what was true at First Tennessee is not necessarily true at other companies, including yours. The only way to know with certainty is to dig out the facts, as the following example shows.

A Value Gap

This story is based on an actual case. ConstructCo is a subcontractor in the highly competitive commercial building market. Its executives knew that profitability and growth depended on its being very competitive on price. Since labor was a major component of their total cost structure, the company's building crews had to be highly productive.

ConstructCo's executives believed that length of service increased productivity. However, long-term employees performing jobs with high physical demands also tended to be costly in terms of health claims, disability, and absenteeism. Those highly tenured employees were paid considerably more than people with less experience or years of service were. What was the economic value of long-term service to the company after overall employment costs were accounted for?

The only way to answer that question was to dig out the facts by using ConstructCo's HR and payroll records and measures of productivity. After controlling for other influences, such as location and on-the-job training, the answer became clear: Employment costs eventually outpaced tenure-related productivity. Every one of the job levels examined reached a crossover point at which pay and benefit costs *exceeded* productivity gains. Overall, after the eighth year on the job the typical crew member's productivity growth stalled even as his or her costs of employment continued to rise. This produced a value gap that threatened to blow a hole in ConstructCo's future profitability. The increasing age of its building crews made that threat extremely serious. These findings encouraged the organization to design reward and skill-building initiatives aimed at boosting individual productivity in an employee's later years. A number of jobs were redesigned with that end in mind. Collectively, those actions were projected to produce annual savings of about 22 percent of average crew members' annual earnings, an amount sufficient to close the value gap.

Key Points

A key principle for managing human capital effectively is the importance of focusing on value. It is easy to measure workforce *costs*. It is decidedly more difficult and unfamiliar to measure the *value* created by human capital attributes and practices. Difficult and unfamiliar as it may be, measuring value is now possible. Facts, not assumptions or expectations, are the key to discerning which people practices and attributes drive value. With such knowledge managers can make wise choices about where to invest and what to do and ground those choices in the unique system that is their organization. Remember the following points:

- Cost is not the same as value. Organizations are adept at measuring the costs of their human capital, but few have a precise sense of the value it creates.
- Sources of value include human capital attributes such as tenure, experience, and professional credentials and organizational practices such as reward systems, supervisory and control processes, and staffing practices.
- Tools and procedures exist to get the facts about which human capital attributes and practices most drive value in an organization.
- Facts about the value created by human capital enable an organization to manage that intangible asset with greater sophistication and effectiveness than previously was thought possible.

Tools

Defining Human Capital Strategy

THE FIRST THREE chapters described the principles on which an effective human capital strategy must be based: systems thinking, decisions based on relevant facts, and a focus on the workforce characteristics and management practices that create value. The next step is to integrate those principles in the form of practical tools that every executive can use to understand his or her organization's current workforce and determine the type of human capital needed to support the business. This chapter defines human capital strategy more concretely and presents an overview of the process that can be used to develop such a strategy. The next two chapters describe in some detail two critical tools—Internal Labor Market (ILM) Analysis^{SM} and Business Impact Modeling^{SM}—that support the process by providing the factual foundation for decision making. But first a true story.

A national consumer services chain had made a dramatic change in its business strategy. That company operated in a very old-line business. Tradition drove customer and employee behavior, and the services the company offered were essentially no different from those of its competitors. Competition in the industry consisted of a handful of other national chains and thousands of small proprietorships with long-standing ties to their communities.

Management was concerned that the company's declining financial performance was in large part the product of a secular decline in the demand for its core services and a shift toward lower-end, low-cost offerings. And it was right. Exhaustive research confirmed that demand for traditional services was declining. However, the same research detected latent demand for highly customized services in which customers would play the lead role in service design, with the service provider acting as an adviser. The latent demand appeared to be so powerful that the company decided to recast its business in a bold gamble to satisfy it.

Redesigning the business required many large and costly changes. For instance, the company's facilities could not accommodate the new delivery model without significant alterations. Further, putting customers in the driver's seat would require educating them about many alternative services and options and the related costs. Like architects experimenting with different design features and different materials, customers would want to know how the pieces would fit together. An information technology consultant was engaged to develop a customer-friendly computerized approach to the problem. Since technology played virtually no role in the old business design, major investments were required. Perhaps the biggest challenge involved brand identity. Success would require a "rebranding" of the company; it had to shed its image of tradition and reliability and project a more modern and dynamic vision that emphasized creativity and customer involvement. This transformation would require changes in the design of their facilities, but also would require a major marketing initiative. Potential customers had to know that the service and the company were new and different.

With coordinated initiatives involving physical plant, technology, and marketing in place—and with financing to support them—management felt that its transformation plan was complete. But was it really ready? What about the human capital implications of the new service model? Wasn't it likely, if not certain, that the new business design would require changes in human capital as well?

Important questions had to be addressed. Did the current workforce have the right skills and experience to deliver the new services? Could employees switch from selling standard products to acting as advisers? Would they—could they—work collaboratively with customers? What combination of training and rewards would effect the necessary changes? Should the company change its hiring profile? Should it change its reward systems to attract a different type of employee and encourage new behaviors among current ones?

These were just a few of the human capital questions that management had to ponder in revamping the business design. Yet this company, like most others, neither asked nor answered those questions. It had a blind spot for human capital and assumed that human resources (HR) would magically align the company's people assets and practices with the new business requirements. That wishful thinking imperiled the company's ability to execute the new business design. What the company needed was a human capital strategy that matched the job.

What Is Human Capital Strategy?

Every company needs a human capital strategy that supports its business strategy, but what exactly does that term mean? Let's start by revisiting the concept of human capital.

People Are Not Things

Describing human capital as an asset, as one would describe equipment or the cash in a bank account, may sound manipulative and cold-blooded, and it would be if one failed to recognize the qualities of human capital that other intangible and physical assets do not have.

For starters, human capabilities can and do change. In effect, the human capital asset is altered as it is employed. People grow through on-the-job learning and experience. More important, they have volition—that is, a will to make choices and pursue their own interests, an ability to improve if they choose to, and spirit. Also, human capital is never separable from its owner, as are other assets; the company does not own the asset.

These qualities set human capital apart but do not negate the fact that a workforce is a manageable asset that can and must be integrated with the strategy of the organization. Further, research has demonstrated sufficient regularity in the links between human capital and business outcomes that executives would do well to bring a disciplined, investment return–oriented approach to the management of this asset.

By definition, *human capital* is the accumulated stock of skills, experience, and knowledge that resides in an organization's workforce and drives productive labor. Since human capital is an asset, it follows that human capital strategy is a form of asset management: a plan for securing, managing, and motivating a workforce capable of achieving business goals. We think of it as a blueprint that specifies all workforce requirements and the management practices needed to secure them and to optimize business performance. In our lexicon, the key workforce characteristics have three dimensions:

1. *Workforce capabilities.* These are the mix of knowledge, skills, competencies, and experience that determine what the workforce *can do*.
2. *Workforce behaviors.* These are the specific actions of the workforce as reflected in work intensity, diligence, cooperation, teamwork, and adaptation to change, among other things. These behaviors are what the workforce *does*.
3. *Workforce attitudes.* We use the term *attitudes* loosely to refer to psychological propensities concerning risk taking, initiative, commitment, teamwork, flexibility, and so on: what the workforce *believes and values*.

Together, these characteristics define the workforce of an organization and drive its productivity. Because companies try to distinguish themselves from their competitors, it stands to reason that their workforce requirements reflect the uniqueness of their business goals; that is, a unique business strategy will have a direct counterpart in a unique human capital strategy. Copycat tactics have little chance of delivering a workforce and motivating behaviors precisely tailored to a business's needs.

HR policies and practices such as reward systems, employee training, and diversity programs alone do not constitute a strategy. They are simply instruments for influencing workforce characteristics: a means to a higher end. To be effective, those policies and practices must be consistent with each other; in the best of circumstances they are mutually reinforcing. The test of the value of those practices and policies is their impact on the workforce, not how well they conform to what others are doing.

As noted in the Introduction, the management practices that drive human capital strategy define the following:

- How people are selected and developed
- How their work is organized
- How they are supervised or directed
- How information is developed and shared
- How critical decisions are made
- How people are motivated and rewarded

Each of these factors, alone and in combination, ultimately affects the workforce and its ability to deliver value.

The relationships among workforce capabilities, behaviors, and attitudes are complex and difficult to measure. Moreover, they are contingent on the broader business context and environment (i.e., system) in which they play out. Fortunately, major strides have been made in understanding these interrelationships and in developing practical tools for measuring them (facts).

Most organizations lack an explicit human capital strategy: They cannot show anyone a blueprint. However, this does not mean that they do not have a strategy; every organization has one, if not by design, then by default. Those strategies arise as concatenations of discrete people management decisions made over the years, often forming an incohesive patchwork of practices that limits the full potential of the business.

The practices that influence human capital extend beyond the domain of traditional HR. Indeed, many are within the control of line managers and even top executives. For instance, HR often has little to do with how work is organized or how technology is deployed, yet both influence workforce productivity and have important implications for the design of more traditional people management practices, such as recruitment, training, and rewards. They must be considered in any plan to build and manage the workforce. Similarly, the structure of decision making, particularly for decisions that involve strategic issues, is a fundamental management concern, not a traditional focus of HR. However, there are few areas of management that have a greater impact on the behaviors and performance of the workforce. Clearly, this area has to be a part of any human capital strategy that purports to serve the business. The point is that many parts of the organization are involved in building and managing human capital, but their activities with respect to that asset seldom are coordinated with care. The result is that human capital management is often fractured and inconsistent. Companies that avoid this misalignment and develop coherent people strategies have a decided advantage.

What is needed is a coherent and explicit human capital strategy that (1) produces the right workforce for the business and (2) manages it in ways that optimize its economic productivity.

Does your company have an explicit human capital strategy or a mixed bag of uncoordinated polices and practices? If it has a strategy, is that strategy producing the workforce you need to be successful? Are its components aligned with each other, or do they work at cross-purposes? Is the strategy understood and accepted by key stakeholders? Is it adaptable to changes in the business environment? Is it backed by measurement so that management can track how well it is being executed and be accountable for the results? These are important questions that can guide the development of an organization's human capital strategy. Answering them invariably involves making a comparison between current workforce capabilities and what they ideally *should be* and between current and potential workforce performance. The next two chapters describe a disciplined process for making those comparisons involving two core tools. The first is Internal Labor Market Analysis^SM, and the second is Business Impact Modeling^SM.

Would you like to understand your workforce and what it will look like three to five years from now assuming no major changes in policies and practices? Would you like to know how particular interventions are likely to change your workforce or workforce outcomes, such as experience and skill mix, leadership development, turnover, and diversity? Internal Labor Market Analysis can provide the answers.

Would you like to know which workforce attributes and which people policies and practices have the greatest positive effect on performance and profitability and which ones hold you back? Would you like to know how a particular intervention is likely to affect workforce productivity or customer retention? Business Impact Modeling can tell you.

Bring the output of these two tools together and you will be on the way to creating a human capital strategy that is aligned with higher-level business goals. We'll explain how to do that in the next two chapters.

Key Points

- As a company develops a strategy or a new business design, it must pay appropriate attention to the human capital strategy that supports it.
- Human capital is the accumulated stock of skills, experience, and knowledge that resides in an organization's workforce and drives productive labor.
- Human capital strategy is a form of asset management: a blueprint for securing, managing, and motivating the workforce needed to support the organization's strategic goals. To be effective, the management practices that influence the workforce should be consistent with each other and mutually reinforcing.
- Business leaders should compare what workforce capabilities *are* and what they ideally *should be*. They also should compare current and potential workforce performance. New analytic tools allow these comparisons to be made on a strong factual foundation.

Understanding Your Internal Labor Market

THE STARTING POINT for a human capital strategy is a clear understanding of the workforce, both what it is today and what it is becoming. Like a living organism, a workforce evolves constantly as new people enter, others leave, and employees acquire new skills and experience. Thus at any moment in time an organization's workforce is the outcome of the following three interrelated labor "flows" and the effectiveness with which they are managed:

- *Attraction.* Who comes into the organization? How successful is the organization at drawing in the kinds of people it needs to achieve its goals?
- *Development.* How do people move through the organization, through different assignments, jobs, and levels of responsibility? How successful is the organization at growing and nurturing the kinds of human capital it needs to execute its business strategy?
- *Retention.* Who is staying and who is leaving? How successful is the organization at retaining people who have the "right" capabilities and produce the highest value?

Attraction, development, and retention interact in a dynamic process that over time determines the characteristics and effectiveness of the workforce. The dynamics are influenced by both management practices and external market conditions. In other words, they operate in an open system. Because that system governs labor transactions *inside* an organization, we call it an internal labor market, drawing on a concept that is well developed in the research literature. We will return to that concept below.

As in any system, changes in one component produce changes in others. For instance, changes in labor market conditions, such as local unemployment rates, typically produce changes in an organization's retention rate, although the degree of change varies from organization to organization. So if labor markets tighten, turnover is likely to rise to some degree as employees take advantage of growing opportunities elsewhere. Changes in retention in turn affect the pace and pattern of hiring as well as the rate at which incumbents are promoted. These outcomes also may affect the ways in which those incumbents develop and the kinds of experiences they acquire in moving from job to job. This chain of events also is influenced by the level and pattern of rewards, which signal the capabilities, behaviors, and attitudes the organization truly values. These affect how employees value the employment relationship, and so on.

The point we are making should be clear. The workforce is always in flux, always in the making. The way a company manages these dynamics determines the kind of workforce it will have and how that workforce will perform.

The Role of Rewards

Rewards play a critical role in a firm's internal labor market dynamics. We use the term *rewards* to mean more than money. Rewards include compensation, benefits, and career-related opportunities and experiences. Understanding how those elements come together to energize internal labor market dynamics is essential to managing them successfully.

Rewards affect more than employees' motivation on the job. They affect *who* is in the workforce: both the kinds of people attracted to the organization and the kinds who stay with it. Rewards also influence the way human capital develops in an organization. Indeed, rewards and development are linked inextricably. For one thing, development opportunities are rewards in themselves: a form of in-kind payment. Development expands an individual's capabilities and enhances his or her prospects for future earnings. If you doubt the financial significance of this statement, think about how often people take a lower-paying job because of the experience or special training opportunities it provides. Employment in the military is a classic example.

Rewards also influence employees' choices about their learning and development. They signal what an organization ultimately values. Let's recall the manufacturing company discussed in Chapter 1. That company knew that it needed technical specialists to ensure product quality, and it extolled their contributions. However, capable engineers, observing how much farther and faster generalists progressed, could not misconstrue what the company's actions said about its values. They did not need to look at their colleagues' paychecks to learn the truth. They only had to look at where individuals were moving in the career hierarchy. That was why so many tried to get on the generalist development track. The company rewarded generalists, and that was precisely what it got, to its chagrin.

Over time, an organization *becomes* what it rewards. Thus, any attempt to measure and model the dynamics of an internal labor market must include a careful evaluation of the drivers of rewards. Prices and quantities are always linked. Translated to the terms of an internal labor market, this means that rewards (price) and labor flows (quantities) define the system *together.*

Foundations of Internal Labor Market Analysis

Obviously, a necessary step toward managing the dynamic process in the internal labor market is to understand it. At a minimum, that means describing it accurately. Better still, understanding means knowing *why* the internal labor market operates as it does and what the consequences are for an organization.

The dynamic process we have described is complex but not inscrutable. New analytic tools and the wealth of data in modern human resources (HR) information systems make it possible to measure and model these labor flows and rewards, decipher their patterns, identify the forces that drive them, and gauge their consequences. That knowledge can be used to forecast what the future workforce will look like in response to changes in external conditions or management practices. The knowledge gained also provides the basis for implementing the right measures to track progress toward achieving the most desired internal labor market dynamics.

The analytic tool we've devised for these purposes is the Internal Labor Market (ILM) analysis. The concept of an internal labor market dates back to the 1950s, although the idea was developed most fully in the early 1970s in the work of Peter B. Doeringer and Michael J. Piore. Their seminal book, *Internal Labor Markets and Manpower Analysis*, was concerned with labor transactions within organizations, which those authors tried to characterize and understand.[1]

Doeringer and Piore actually used the term *internal labor market* to describe institutional practices that supplant the external market. Those practices reflect and encourage long-term commitments between the employer and the employee and include, for example, reliance on formal career paths, a tendency to hire only at lower levels within each career path, and the convention of linking pay to jobs within a rigid hierarchy of jobs rather than to the attributes of individual employees. The effect of those practices is largely to insulate an organization from the influences of outside labor markets.

Our use of the term is not limited to a particular organizational form or set of employment practices. Instead, we use it to encompass the entire range of management practices that govern transactions between employer and employee inside the organization. To us, the most important and practical implication of Doeringer and Piore's work is that every organization is running a form of labor market, usually without realizing it. Decisions made by executives affect the efficiency with which that market operates and the results it produces. By managing their internal labor market astutely, executives can shape the workforce to the specifications of the business and leverage human capital investments far more effectively.

In the years since Doeringer and Piore's book was published researchers in economics and organizational psychology have tended to focus on particular aspects of internal labor markets, such as the drivers of turnover and compensation and patterns of response to vacancies created by employees leaving an organization. A vast research literature has emerged that provides valuable information and insights that can be used to interpret findings about one's own internal labor market dynamics.[2] (See Appendix B.) However, until now no one has provided a *holistic* view of the way internal labor markets operate or characterized the dynamics of this system through the use of a set of integrated statistical models. That is what ILM analysis is all about. It can be used to understand what makes a company's internal labor market tick, the processes by which it creates the company's human capital and applies it to business objectives. That understanding can help leaders manage the microeconomy of their organizations to deliver the workforce and practices their business strategies require.

The three principles of human capital management—system, facts, and value—come together in an ILM analysis. That analysis views an organization and its environment as an interconnected *system*. It uncovers *facts* relevant to decision making and determines where *value* is being created and lost. ILM analysis is systematic in the sense that it looks at the different pieces of the human capital puzzle and the ways they interact. Rather than relying only on employees' and managers' opinions or what company policy manuals state, ILM analysis establishes the facts by observing and measuring critical workforce events and behaviors over extended periods and identifying what drives them. Finally, it concentrates on *value* creation by forecasting how human capital will grow and where value is created.

What Internal Labor Market Analysis Does

ILM analysis provides a fact-based platform for making many essential decisions about human capital. At the most basic level it examines the flow of people into, through, and out of an organization by using HR data and answers fundamental questions about a firm's workforce, including the following:

- Who gets hired?
- Who stays?
- Who advances?
- Who performs well?
- What actually gets rewarded?
- How are rewards distributed?
- How is talent developed?

At a higher level ILM analysis provides critical insights into the operation of the human capital system, reflecting actual practices and their consequences. It focuses on causal links between critical workforce events and behaviors *over time*; thus, it can be used to forecast the effects of specific changes in management practices and market conditions. ILM analysis combines simple descriptive counts and sophisticated statistical modeling techniques that we and our associates have been perfecting through research and work with companies since 1994. It draws on an organization's HR and payroll databases and other relevant sources, including external labor market data. It can be applied to the entire workforce or to particular occupational groups and business segments.

Mapping Human Capital

The point of departure for an ILM analysis is the creation of an *internal labor market map*, a graphic, quantitative picture that describes key dynamics related to the flow of people into, through, and out of an organization over time. The map is a flexible, highly detailed description of the way an organization's internal labor is operating currently. To best understand the current state, of course, it is useful to understand the recent changes that have brought it about; thus, ILM analyses typically capture facts from the preceding three to five years.

The map tallies and displays things such as the average annual number of people entering and leaving an organization at various career levels. It quantifies the movement of people within and between career levels. The map also is used to display where various attributes of human capital—experience, selected skill sets, and so on—are concentrated. An ILM map can do this for the entire organization, for each of its business units or functions, and for different segments of the employee population. In summary, an ILM map provides a concise picture of an organization's human capital.

Every organization has a unique ILM map. Figure 5-1 shows the ILM map for TechCo, the chip-making company whose business problems were introduced in Chapter 2. How does one read such a map? Let's begin with the horizontal bars in the center of the figure. Each bar represents a different career level. Each level clusters a number of jobs and titles and shows the relative proportions of employees at that point in the hierarchy. Those levels are not just markers of salary grades; they

Figure 5-1

TechCo's Internal Labor
Market Map

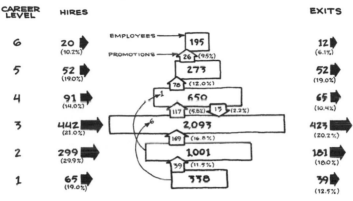

© 2003, Mercer Human Resource Consulting LLC

represent major points of career advancement at which the level of responsibility, authority, scope of job, and pay change fundamentally. The numbers in the horizontal bars represent the number of people in the level.

Now note the arrows between the boxes. Upward-pointing arrows indicate the average annual number of people promoted to the next higher level during the period, with fast-track promotions shown by arrows that skip a level. The numbers next to each upward arrow show the associated probability of promotion. Downward-pointing arrows indicate the rare instances of demotions. For example, on average 15 people were demoted from level 4 to 3. Some of the demotions are performance-related, and some are the product of negotiated arrangements between employer and employee, such as helping employees make the transition to retirement or deal with pressing issues of work-family balance.

The left-hand column of arrows in the map indicates the number of people entering at each level per year. Those average numbers also are expressed as a percentage of the total employees in their respective career levels. The number of individuals (and percentages) leaving the company from each level per year are shown in the right-hand column of arrows and numbers.

All calculations for an ILM map must be based on a consistent unit of time, such as a year, to be meaningful. Maps, however, can be constructed for shorter or longer periods, depending on the organization's needs. The map in Figure 5-1 is only one example of the kinds of facts that can be displayed. Other maps might highlight the number and rates of lateral moves within a career level. Still others might represent the proportions of employees at each level by employee segment, such as gender or high-potential standing. Maps like the one in Figure 5-1 are flexible and accommodating to each organization's circumstances and needs.

ILM maps come in a number of different shapes (see the sidebar following). Obviously, the shape reveals how hierarchical an organization is and how employees are spread throughout the organization. It also indicates something about the likely role of career advancement in the overall reward structure of the organization. By looking at patterns of entry and promotion throughout the hierarchy, one can tell whether an organization is prone to buy or build its talent. Build-from-within organizations tend to limit hiring at the middle and upper levels in order to concentrate on the development of homegrown talent and keep promotion opportunities for incumbents strong. A proportionately large number of middle-level hires is inimical to both objectives.

Finally, the pattern of entry and exit can indicate something about the organization's sensitivity to changes in outside labor market conditions. Doeringer and Piore note that in some organizations inflows and outflows of employees are concentrated at certain levels only, what they call "ports" of entry and exit. These are touch points with the marketplace where the company has the greatest exposure to outside influences.

Organizations that build talent from within might have the most entry points at certain lower levels and exit patterns that are more diffuse. Organizations that tend to buy talent have many touch points with the market, as evidenced by diffuse patterns of entry and exit. In a build-from-within organization, reward systems may be hierarchical as well, strongly linked to job level and/or length of service. Hence, employees are locked quickly into the organization as the cost of leaving becomes prohibitive. This creates a degree of insulation from the outside labor market. Indeed, changes in labor market conditions have little or no impact on turnover for a build-from-within firm. The advantage is more stability in the workforce and greater opportunities to invest in people and build firm-specific human capital. The disadvantage is loss of flexibility and a distancing from market realities. This can be especially hazardous at times of fundamental change in competitive conditions.

The Story Behind the TechCo Map

What specifically can be learned from the TechCo map shown in Figure 5-1? Quite a bit. First, it can be seen that the employee population bulges near the middle. Highly hierarchical companies are shaped like pyramids, with a handful of people at the top and more and more people filling each lower career level. This is true of TechCo within the leadership levels of the organization, levels 4 and above, but not below.

- The map reveals a large population (of engineers) congregated in level 3. Level 3 is a career bottleneck or "choke point." As the percentages associated with the upward arrows indicate, employees at levels 1 and 2 have a high probability of promotion. The probability of moving beyond level 3 in a particular period (a year in this case), however, is low: 5.8 percent. It is even lower for engineers.
- Level 3 employees are leaving in large numbers. On average, almost 20 percent of employees at this level left the organization each year during the period in question.
- TechCo's hiring practices are at odds with the need for firm-specific knowledge. How does the analyst know this? The ILM map indicates that the largest number of outside hires occurred at level 3, but a substantial percentage of new hires were coming into the management ranks at levels 4 and 5. By definition, those individuals arrived without the firm-specific knowledge, on which the company depends. Clearly the company is not developing its managerial talent from within.

Beyond Description: Modeling Internal Labor Market Dynamics

Maps are the foundation of the ILM analysis, but they are only the beginning. Far more revealing are the facts unearthed through statistical modeling of the dynamic process behind a map. It is the statistical modeling that reveals *how* and *why* internal labor markets actually work. This is where the true human capital story of an organization emerges, and with it the detail every organization needs to manage its internal labor market successfully. Let's see how the analysis is done.

ILM analysis consists of an integrated set of core statistical models that cover the following areas:

- Drivers of turnover
- Drivers of promotion
- Drivers of lateral movement
- Drivers of compensation, usually pay levels and pay growth
- Drivers of individual performance

These models often are supplemented by an analysis of the patterns of entry to determine what kinds of people are joining the organization, which recruitment sources are utilized most intensively, and which are most effective in delivering the right kinds of people. The analysis also can show how successfully an organization is tapping external labor markets whether those markets are defined geographically or occupationally. Other models, such as the determinants of incentive compensation, sometimes are created and tested to fit an organization's specific situation.

Modeling is all about understanding causes and consequences in a constantly changing system. The analyst wants to see how management practices and employee attributes bring about the movements, events, and changes observed in a company's internal labor market. Modeling also is about priorities. We want to identify which of the many potential causes (rewards, selection, etc.) of key events (quitting, career success, etc.) are the most important drivers of those events so that managers can prioritize actions to address problems. Deciphering causes and consequences requires an examination of system dynamics over time. It also requires the ability to account for competing influences.

The statistical models in an ILM analysis have a certain symmetry in that they rely on a common set of independent (or predictor) variables and statistical controls that fall into three categories:

- *Employee attributes*—indicators of demographic and job-related characteristics measured at the individual level. These include age, gender, race, education, job, credentials, and labor market experience, and performance history, among other things.

- *Organizational attributes and practices*—characteristics of the immediate environment in which an employee works and the management practices that affect those measures. These attributes include measures such as the size and heterogeneity of a department or work group, the turnover rate within the group, the manager's span of control, and workload, to name a few.
- *External influences*—characteristics of the market environment in which the facility operates, including local unemployment rates, product or service market share, and location. These influences often function as statistical controls in the models.

Clues from Map Shapes

One can learn a lot about a company by looking at the shape of its ILM map. Maps with a clear pyramid shape indicate a strong hierarchical situation. The majority of employees occupy the lower job levels, and populations fall precipitously as one moves up the pyramid, along with opportunities for advancement. Other companies have maps with more of a diamond shape, such as TechCo, with employees clustering in the middle layers. In those organizations populations tend to be more homogeneous, at least in terms of occupation. Still others have more of a block shape, with employees distributed more or less evenly across levels. In these cases those at the top are still actively involved in the "production process" and are not focused exclusively on managing functions and other employees. Professional services firms sometimes have this structure.

Figure 5-2

Sample Map Shapes

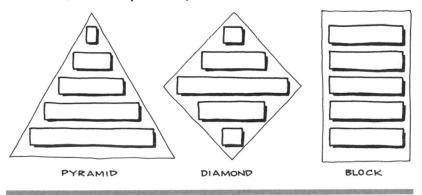

PYRAMID   DIAMOND   BLOCK

The statistical models that make up ILM analysis produce an account of what drives the dynamic flows that characterize internal labor markets. A core turnover model, for instance, would provide an estimate of how factors such as an employee's length of service in the firm and educational attainment, to name just two, affect the likelihood that that employee will leave in a particular year, all else being equal. The promotion model might provide an estimate of how an employee's performance rating or past performance history affects that employee's chance of being promoted in a particular period after accounting for all the other relevant factors (e.g., job, operating unit, identity of supervisor). The compensation models can be used to assess the extent to which changing labor market conditions influence pay levels of both incumbents and new hires or to measure differences in total compensation for those with different specializations. The models together provide a rich and comprehensive picture of the kinds of human capital the organization is securing and valuing. (See Appendix B for models.)

It also is possible to measure the way different causal factors work together. One might hypothesize, for instance, that all else being equal, the effect of unemployment rates on turnover is greater among technically skilled employees. One can test whether this holds true within a specific workforce. If the data support the hypothesis, one can say that an interaction exists between technical skill and unemployment rates; that is, the impact of unemployment rates on a company's workforce depends on the employee segment (in this case, employees are segmented according to technical skills). Knowledge of these interdependencies can prevent an organization from wasting resources on one-size-fits-all solutions and help it direct interventions to the areas where they are most needed. That knowledge can even help a company detect complementarities between management practices that can be exploited to increase the impact of a particular intervention.

In summary, ILM analysis not only describes but also explains. By isolating the attributes or circumstances associated with employee movements and experiences through modeling, the tool delivers the unvarnished facts that executives need to make good decisions about the people side of their businesses.

Case Illustration: MoneyCo

Let's examine some outputs from the ILM models and see how the results from ILM analysis come together to shed light on an organization's internal labor market. We'll use the case of an organization we call MoneyCo, a financial services organization with operations in several regions of the United States. Its core business serves a specialized segment of the financial market. Many of its competitors offer almost identical products and services.

MoneyCo competes on service quality and to some extent on price. Financial results indicated that MoneyCo was not faring well on either dimension. However, upon its acquisition by a larger regional bank, MoneyCo sought to expand its range of services and exploit linkages with its parent company, including opportunities for cross-selling. This represented a significant shift in its business strategy.

Difficult times had forced MoneyCo to go through several rounds of layoffs, a shakeup in the senior management team, and reorganization. Those dislocations had produced an unstable workforce and weakened its management system. The chief executive officer (CEO) recognized these problems and knew that MoneyCo had to tend to its human capital if it hoped to succeed.

The executive team agreed that certain human capital requirements were paramount. To avail themselves of cross-selling opportunities, they would need a workforce that could play more of an advisory than a purely selling role. That workforce had to be customer-focused and equipped with excellent relationship-building skills. In addition, customer-facing employees would need expertise in a full range of products and services, both those of their own company and those of their parent, and have the perceptiveness and discipline to match them to customer needs. This combination of capabilities could neither be created overnight nor "bought." It represented firm-specific human capital that could only be built from within. Finally, the company would need to expand its workforce's ability to support a broadening of its product portfolio.

An ILM analysis was conducted to determine whether MoneyCo's internal labor market as it was managed currently would produce the workforce needed to achieve the company's objectives. Some key results of our analysis of rewards at MoneyCo are summarized in Figure 5-3.

The grid shown in the figure—a key output of ILM Analysis—represents the combined results of statistical modeling of the drivers of (1) promotion, (2) year-to-year pay growth, and (3) pay levels at MoneyCo. It encapsulates what the organization *actually* rewards. It identifies the factors (individual, organizational, and environmental) associated with

Figure 5-3

MoneyCo's Rewards

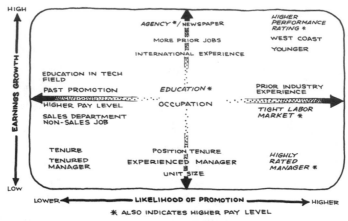

© 2003, Mercer Human Resource Consulting LLC

individual success in a particular company. At the individual level it is a success profile. Viewed from the organizational perspective, it is something of a culture map, representing the characteristics that the organization most values in its employees as evidenced by actual reward patterns. Yes, there is more to organizational culture than rewards, but the grid provides insight into aspects of an organization that strongly influence its culture.

Here is how to read this rewards grid. Promotion likelihood is on the horizontal axis; annual pay growth is on the vertical axis. Italicized factors are associated with higher pay levels. The center of the grid, where the lines cross, is the origin. Factors near the origin add nothing to the probability that an employee will be promoted in the next year and do not influence pay increases.

Consider these examples. In the upper-right-hand corner one sees "higher performance ratings" in italics. This indicates that all else being equal, an individual with a higher performance rating is more likely to be promoted, is experiencing larger pay growth, and tends to be more highly paid overall. In other words, when one compares like people in like jobs and like locations, those rated higher tend to do better across all the reward dimensions than do their lower-rated counterparts. Thus, MoneyCo's performance management and rewards systems clearly differentiated employees according to individual performance. Because of the way work was structured at MoneyCo, that seemed to be a good thing. It would encourage high performers without obstructing the cooperation required for cross-selling and referral activity. And it would encourage high performers to stay.

Now let's look at the elements in the center of the grid. Note that "education" is located there, in italics. This means that education contributed positively to pay levels. That finding is not surprising. Employers typically recognize the increase in human capital that arises from an increase in education and reward it with higher pay, and MoneyCo was no exception. To hire someone with a higher degree, it had to pay more. Note, however, that education contributed nothing to the other components of rewards. All else being equal, annual pay growth was not higher for the more educated employees, and neither was the likelihood of promotion. In other words, once employed, those with higher degrees were not doing any better than were their less-educated counterparts.

There are two possible interpretations of this finding. The first suggests inappropriate matching of workforce capabilities to company needs. Perhaps formal education did not contribute incremental value to the firm even though it increased the market value of the individual employee. Because of the nature of this business, other factors not associated with educational attainment may have outweighed education: people skills, experience, selling skills, even street smarts. We've encountered this phenomenon many times before. The second explanation is that the current rewards and performance management systems were failing to recognize the real value attributable to education. Either because of the way more educated employees were utilized or because of the failure of supervisors to evaluate performance properly, the more educated people were not getting their due. How could the company expect to keep those people if it failed to value them?

The CEO of MoneyCo didn't care which of these explanations was accurate. He wanted a more educated workforce. He and his team were convinced that the ability of the workforce to take on an advisory role, match products and customers, and build productive relationships with the parent company was enhanced by education. "Yes, perhaps it was true in the past that an individual's performance had little to do with what degree that person had," he said. "But that won't be the case under our new business model. We really need more educated employees. I want to see education take its place alongside individual performance as something we value in this company. Let's make this happen!"

A final observation concerns MoneyCo's rewards grid. Note that length of service (tenure) is in the lower left corner. Simply put, it had a negative impact on all the dimensions of rewards we measured. A negative relationship with pay *growth* and promotion came as no surprise. It is known from labor economics that although pay typically grows over an employee's work life, its rate of growth begins to decline on average when the individual reaches his or her late thirties. Tenure is not the same as age, and depending on the organization's human capital strategy and the way it structures rewards, the observed relationship between pay growth and tenure can vary. In most cases, however, it follows a trajectory similar to that of the pay-age relationship. That is what we have observed in the vast majority of organizations for which we have done this kind of work.

This negative relationship between length of service and pay *levels* is rare. It usually occurs when companies hire aggressively in tight labor markets, something MoneyCo was doing. Those companies pay such a high premium to new entrants that they end up devaluing their incumbent employees. The "return to tenure," as it is called, declines, sometimes even turning negative. In these cases an additional year of service in the company is worth less than a year working outside it. Apparently, employees at MoneyCo caught on to this.

Greater clarity about this problem emerged when we looked at the results from the analysis of turnover. The results, based on drivers of turnover over a five-year period, are depicted in the bar chart shown in Figure 5-4 where stronger drivers have longer bars.

One thing to note right away is that MoneyCo was extremely vulnerable to conditions in the external labor market. A one-point change in unemployment rates in its geographic areas of operation was associated with at least a four-point change in annual turnover, all else being equal. This was high by any standard, higher than what we've seen in most organizations for which we've estimated this relationship. This was the case for two reasons. One, already discussed, is that the value of employment at MoneyCo was at or below market alternatives, and so employees were quick to leave as outside opportunities increased. The

Figure 5-4

Turnover Drivers At MoneyCo

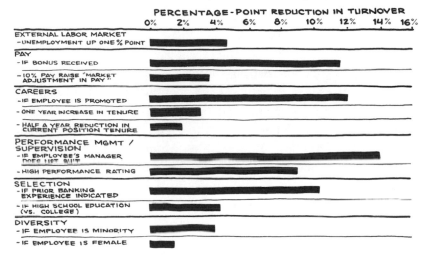

PERCENTAGE-POINT REDUCTION IN TURNOVER

0% 2% 4% 6% 8% 10% 12% 14% 16%

EXTERNAL LABOR MARKET
- UNEMPLOYMENT UP ONE % POINT

PAY
- IF BONUS RECEIVED
- 10% PAY RAISE "MARKET ADJUSTMENT IN PAY"

CAREERS
- IF EMPLOYEE IS PROMOTED
- ONE YEAR INCREASE IN TENURE
- HALF A YEAR REDUCTION IN CURRENT POSITION TENURE

PERFORMANCE MGMT / SUPERVISION
- IF EMPLOYEE'S MANAGER DOES NOT QUIT
- HIGH PERFORMANCE RATING

SELECTION
- IF PRIOR BANKING EXPERIENCE INDICATED
- IF HIGH SCHOOL EDUCATION (VS. COLLEGE)

DIVERSITY
- IF EMPLOYEE IS MINORITY
- IF EMPLOYEE IS FEMALE

other is that there was little or no "backloading" of rewards at MoneyCo, no glue to bind employees to the company for the long term. Many organizations backload rewards by tying certain benefits to length of service. In others backloading is achieved through the carrot of valuable advancement opportunities. The mere prospect of significant financial rewards—if they are credible—encourages employees to forgo other opportunities and stay with the organization. Neither of these incentives was at work within MoneyCo.

This pattern would not have been a problem if the company's business strategy required mostly general human capital, but it didn't. Its strategy depended on firm-specific knowledge and experience, which was undermined by MoneyCo's exceptional vulnerability to labor market forces. That vulnerability was reinforced by what we learned about the retention effects of compensation at the company compared with longer-term career rewards.

It can be seen in the bar chart that MoneyCo's employees were highly responsive to short-term incentive compensation. Employees who received it were about half as likely to leave the company as those who did not, all else being equal. They clearly responded to money. Employees also were responsive to promotion and the trajectory of pay.

At first blush that might suggest that MoneyCo employees had a strong career orientation after all. A deeper look, however, cast doubt on that interpretation. The effect of promotion was shown to dissipate very quickly. Only a promotion within the year reduced the likelihood of turnover, and the same thing was true of past pay increases. Employees seemed to respond only to the most recent pay actions, not to how they were faring over the longer haul. It seemed as if employees looked on promotion not as a meaningful career event but simply as MoneyCo's mechanism for delivering more money.

The company had established a "show me the money" culture, and that had created a serious danger. Unless MoneyCo's financial performance improved quickly, it would be unable to enhance its pay position relative to the market for the incumbent workforce. New hires, whose pay levels better reflected market rates, would continue to outpace longer-term employees, eroding the value of service with the company. If that pattern held, how could the company retain its seasoned, high-performing employees? How would it develop the firm-specific skills that its business strategy required?

The turnover drivers chart shows that those with more years of service were more likely to stay, a behavior we have observed in most companies we have analyzed. However, while directionally correct, the effect was notably small and disappeared after three years with the company.

The analysis confirmed another critical vulnerability: Employees with only a high school education were significantly more likely to stay than were similarly situated employees with a college degree. The more educated employees deemed essential to the new business strategy were walking out. This was by no means a problem unique to MoneyCo: The educated generally have more opportunities and often are more mobile. However, some organizations are able to retain them more readily than others can. The way they utilize and reward those employees is often the key. In light of what we learned about rewards at MoneyCo, was it any wonder that they were leaving at significantly higher rates?

The findings we have revealed here paint a dismal picture, but not everything in MoneyCo's human capital system was misaligned. The rewards and performance management systems appeared to differentiate well between high performers and low performers. Voluntary turnover was much higher among low performers than among those who performed well. Employees with the industry experience needed to enhance MoneyCo's product/service portfolio and expand its customer base were both rewarded and retained. Also, the company had avoided reward disparities for women and minorities, an outcome that supported management's diversity goals.

Still, the ILM analysis revealed that MoneyCo's human capital strategy was not fully aligned with its business needs and market environment. That analysis helped the CEO and his team get a handle on the company's internal labor market, both where it was and where it was heading. Because it quantified the critical dimensions of the workforce situation, management could more easily prioritize its agenda for change. On that basis, MoneyCo developed a new human capital strategy that aimed to achieve the following:

- Reduce its vulnerability to external labor markets
- Restore a credible career structure
- Align rewards, performance management, and supervisory practices with new human capital priorities
- Adjust recruitment and selection criteria to better match the required workforce profile
- Improve retention among employees with critical experience and skills

The tactics used to advance MoneyCo's agenda were selected on the basis of modeling results that allowed the company to prioritize actions and forecast effects. The ILM analysis also positioned the company to create a scorecard of metrics for tracking changes in key components of its internal labor market, assuring accountability for results. Those actions set the company on the road toward building the workforce it needed.

The Value of ILM for Looking Ahead

ILM analysis helps an organization understand both what its workforce is now and what it is becoming. Thus it offers the foundation needed for effective workforce planning that is capable of supporting business strategy, a point we examine more closely in the next chapter.

ILM analysis can be used to simulate the effects of alternative strategies for achieving desired ends. A particularly powerful application of ILM analysis for looking forward is in the area of workforce diversity. Many organizations have formal diversity programs designed to achieve an appropriate level of representation of women and minority group members. Hiring often is seen as a quick way to meet diversity goals. However, this tactic may or may not produce a sustainable solution. The interrelated influences of hiring, development, promotion, retention, and pay that are unique to each organization ultimately determine a company's success in achieving workforce diversity. In other words, a company's internal labor market needs to be geared to support those objectives.

The facts learned through ILM analysis inform a company's choices about how best to meet its diversity goals. For example, a company may find that it has inadequate representation of women and minorities at middle or upper management levels. One solution to this shortcoming is to increase hiring directly into those levels. An alternative is to increase hiring into the jobs and levels that prepare individuals to perform successfully at the middle and upper levels, that is, to improve the pipeline of candidates.

Which solution or combination of practices is most effective depends on the ILM patterns. It may be that what is most important is the innate ability and market experience of individuals—general human capital—and so hiring directly into areas of deficiency is the appropriate solution. However, if firm-specific experience is critical to success, strategies focused on building the pipeline may over time be more effective and financially sound. After all, if the job candidates hired lack this institutional knowledge, they will be less likely to perform well and more likely to leave. The company will do all the right things in hiring and still be left without the diverse workforce it seeks, and the investments made will yield little or no return.

Companies used to guess about these things, but that is no longer necessary. Using ILM analysis, they can measure employees' responsiveness to different factors, such as rewards, internal mobility, and career development programs. These quantitative measures make it possible to project into the future to identify the quickest, surest, least expensive ways of meeting longer-term human capital objectives, such as those related to diversity. This analytic tool also reveals the right measures to track and tells managers when to make course corrections as conditions change.

ILM analysis is critical to understanding current workforce dynamics and projecting what workforces can become. Finding methods to determine what the workforce *should be* is the subject of the next chapter.

Key Points

- An organization's workforce is the outcome of a dynamic process that involves the attraction, development, and retention of employees. That process takes place within the internal labor market of the organization and is influenced by both management practices and external market conditions.
- The starting point for a human capital strategy is a clear understanding of an organization's workforce: both what it is today and what it is becoming. Internal Labor Market (ILM) analysis is the key to that understanding. It brings together the three principles of human capital management: systems thinking, facts, and value.
- The concept of the internal labor market expressed in this book encompasses the entire range of management practices that govern transactions between employer and employees inside the organization. Every organization is running a form of labor market, usually without realizing it. By managing the dynamics of their internal labor markets astutely, organizations can shape their workforces to meet the needs of the business and optimize performance.
- The internal labor market map is a foundation output of ILM analysis. It describes key dynamics related to the flow of people into, through, and out of the organization over time in graphic form.
- ILM analysis provides a fact-based platform for making decisions about human capital. It examines the flow of people into,

through, and out of an organization and the drivers of those movements. In so doing, it answers fundamental questions about a firm's workforce, such as who is hired and who advances. It is forward-looking, allowing organizations to simulate the effects of alternative strategies for achieving desired ends. Statistical modeling makes all of this possible.

CHAPTER

6

Building Your Strategy

UNDERSTANDING INTERNAL labor market dynamics is the starting point for building a human capital strategy. Like the business strategy it serves, a human capital strategy is all about the future. It is a plan for creating future value through the right workforce and the right workforce management tactics. Building these things depends on the answers to three questions:

1. *Where are we now?* What is our workforce, what internal labor market dynamics is it experiencing, and what are our most influential workforce management practices?
2. *Where do we want to go?* The business strategy seeks to achieve a specific vision. What are the implications of that vision for human capital?
3. *What creates value?* What workforce attributes and what human capital practices drive business success?

Knowing where a company is now and where it needs to be while closing the gaps between the two is what the process of building a human capital strategy is all about.

Knowing the Current State

As was discussed in Chapter 5, Internal Labor Market (ILM) analysis provides a wealth of facts about the current state of an organization's workforce and the management practices that influence it. It also provides insight into the future. It does these things in two ways: by documenting workforce-relevant trends that can be expected to continue and by using statistical models to forecast the future state of the workforce in light of those trends. Those models help identify the causes and consequences of workforce dynamics. Hence, they can be used to predict the results that are likely to follow a change in one or more of the causes of those dynamics. Let's say an organization knows through ILM analysis that the education and early job experiences of its new recruits strongly influence the rate at which those individuals advance into management positions. The model behind that knowledge can be used to answer questions such as the following:

- How many new recruits will advance into management positions within five years if the number of new hires with advanced degrees is increased by 25 percent but nothing else changes?
- How much will the company's retention rates and compensation costs change as a result of the new hiring policy?

The modeling part of ILM analysis provides a complete picture of how the human capital system can be expected to change as a result of a single policy change such as a new hiring practice. Organizations can be a lot smarter about the future when they are equipped with strong facts about the present.

Of course, not everything about the current state can be known through quantitative ILM analyses. Those analyses have to be supplemented with other facts and insights from a number of sources, such as focus groups, surveys, and interviews of employees. Those sources produce facts that human resources (HR) information systems and other databases are unlikely to capture and reveal.

Defining the Desired Future State

Defining the desired future state has been largely a qualitative exercise that relies on expert opinion and experience. Those who are most knowledgeable about the business are asked to think through the workforce implications of their current or soon to be implemented business strategy. Interviews, surveys, focus groups, and structured planning meetings are familiar ways to obtain those qualitative data. Further, selected customers and suppliers may be asked for their views on how the organization ought to be and what they seek from the workforce. Due diligence on competitors' tactics and strategic intentions also can represent an important qualitative input.

A second approach to defining the future state is quantitative. As was just discussed, quantitative ILM analysis can provide clear cues about what a desired state would look like from the perspective of workforce management. However, another quantitative approach is germane to specifying the desired future state. We call that approach Business Impact Modeling[SM].

Finding Value through Business Impact Modeling

Business Impact Modeling is a quantitative method that analyzes the running record of business performance with the goal of identifying the workforce characteristics and management practices that are the strongest drivers of a company's most desired and most important business outcomes: productivity, profitability, quality, and customer retention, among others.

Knowing the human capital drivers of value is essential to effective strategy making. For one thing, it prevents mistakes. For example, a change in business strategy may seem to dictate certain changes in workforce management practices, but what if those practices are the same ones that are most responsible for high performance? In that case would it not be a big mistake to change them? Without a formal assessment of the impact of human capital practices on business performance, organizations remain in the dark about the likely impact of their changes no matter how reasonable those changes appear to be. Getting all the facts, including facts about the business impact of human capital attributes and practices, is essential for good strategic decision making.

Business Impact Modeling is also useful in anticipating the future because, like ILM analysis, it involves statistical modeling. Whereas ILM models focus on workforce outcomes, business impact models focus on business outcomes. They enable decision makers to anticipate the likely effects of changes in workforce practices and characteristics on business performance. For example, a company might ask: To what extent will customer retention be hurt if we accelerate the rate at which our employees rotate through customer-facing jobs?

The next section provides more detail about the Business Impact Modeling approach. That is followed by an in-depth case study illustrating its application to the broader process of building a human capital strategy.

Don't Rely Exclusively on One Approach

Although qualitative and quantitative approaches to defining the future state of a company can be used independently, they are best used in combination. Indeed, throughout the strategy-making process qualitative and quantitative data complement each other to provide the most fully informed strategic decision making.

Business Impact Modeling: A Closer Look

Business Impact Modeling is a family of statistical tools that can identify the effects of specific human capital practices and attributes on business performance. Although the statistical modeling in this approach is not very different from that used in ILM analysis, the sources of data are broader. Like ILM analysis, Business Impact Modeling makes use of data in HR information systems and payroll systems. However, it also uses data kept by the finance, quality control, marketing, and operations departments. Those data provide the measures of business performance.

The Production Function

What techniques constitute Business Impact Modeling? The following is a high-level overview of a few techniques. One fundamental technique is based on the production function, a core construct in microeconomics. The production function is a mathematical expression of the relationship between inputs and outputs in the production process. In its classic form, the left-hand side of the equation (the "outcome" or "dependent variable" side) is represented by the quantity of output produced during a particular period of time. This also may be represented in financial terms as value added: the difference between net revenues and material input costs. On the right-hand side (the "predictor" or "independent variable" side) appear measures of capital and labor.

In traditional microeconomic analyses, the right-hand side of the equation has represented labor (that is, human capital) too simply, all too often using a single measure such as headcount, hours worked, or compensation expense. For the production function to become a useful management tool, those simple measures have to be replaced with a greater number of specific measures of workforce attributes and management practices that influence labor productivity, precisely the type of information captured through an ILM analysis. Indeed, there is a long list of human capital attributes (length of service, diversity, education, prior work experience, etc.) and practices (hiring, base pay, variable pay, training, rotation through job assignments, etc.) that can be influenced or fully controlled by management, making the results of the analysis useful in setting strategic priorities. The relative weight of these factors can then be estimated through multivariate regression analysis. More detail on this approach is provided in Appendix B.

We adopted the production function approach to help determine the effects of workforce attributes and human capital practices at HealthCo, the hospital system discussed in Chapter 3. Using eight years of employee and performance data, covering 20 hospitals and facilities in their system, we were able to apply the production function to identify the key human capital drivers of workforce productivity, after accounting for differences in the capitalization of the hospitals and the patient mix they served. The analysis showed that over 60% of the differences in workforce productivity (measured as value added per employee) were explained by factors relating to human capital. Of these, the single biggest factor was how the facilities staffed their operations, particularly the mix of full-time versus part-time employees and use of overtime. You may recall Figure 3-2, the scatterplot diagram relating workforce productivity to the percentage of full-time employees in the workforce. This is a classic output of a statistical analysis based on the production function. In this instance it revealed that, all else being equal, the facilities that relied more heavily on part-timers experienced significantly lower productivity than those with a larger full-time staff. In its efforts to reduce expenses, the organization had overshot the optimal level of part-time staffing, because it failed to account for productivity in its cost calculations. The disciplined comparison of productivity within their system, made possible through this form of business impact modeling, exploded some myths about the drivers of labor cost at HealthCo that had serious policy repercussions.

Granger Causality

Another member of the Business Impact Modeling family of tools is Granger causality analysis. This method is especially powerful when one is focusing on the business impact of one or a few human capital issues. Employee turnover is an excellent example.

Most organizations blithely assume that turnover is bad. That untested assumption usually is expressed in a spreadsheet that attaches a dollar cost to each activity associated with employee turnover: time spent processing terminations, interviewing and screening applicants, adding new people to the payroll, and so on. Direct costs such as advertising and recruiters' fees also are included. Those estimates are tallied and multiplied by the number of instances of employee turnover, resulting in a statement such as "Employee turnover cost this company $16,090,423.31 last year." Note that this exercise is *guaranteed* to come up with a dollar figure, although that figure may contain lots of guesswork. This is also an exercise that implicitly assumes that (1) all turnover is costly and (2) all turnover affects the business negatively.

Quest Diagnostics is a company that did not settle for the usual assumptions about turnover. It wanted to know if turnover really mattered and if so, to what degree. Did it truly affect important business outcomes, or was it just a normal, if annoying, part of business? To get the answer the company undertook a Granger causality analysis of the impact of turnover on a number of measures of business performance, including quarterly operating margins for the company's laboratory facilities.

The Granger approach rests on the observation that the best predictor of an outcome variable, such as operating margin, is the same variable in earlier time periods. Thus the operating margin in a current quarter should be relatively well predicted by the ongoing rate of prior quarters' operating margins. Mathematically, this means that the right hand side of the model (the predictor side) also contains the operating margin. In evaluating the cost of turnover, the real test for this technique is to ask whether turnover in a prior period contributes significantly to the accuracy of predicting the current operating margin. If adding turnover to the right-hand side of the equation indeed increases the accuracy of prediction, one can be confident that turnover has a business impact. If that impact is large, turnover is clearly a problem that merits attention. Figure 6-1 illustrates the results for Quest Diagnostics.

Turnover was indeed a business problem. Further, the value of reducing it became known. More specifically, the financial return of actions and investments required to reduce turnover could be estimated because the model showed how much operating margin (and other outcomes) would improve for every percentage point reduction in turnover.

The next step in solving the problem required identifying the drivers of turnover; this task was accomplished

Myth Busters: Employee Turnover Is Not Always a Cost

Contrary to what most people believe, turnover can have many positive consequences. It provides an escape hatch for poor performers and creates vacancies for new and possibly outstanding employees. Turnover is also a means for improving the match between employees and their jobs and organizations. Without turnover, many workers would be stuck in jobs for which they are ill suited and companies would be saddled with employees who are not positioned to contribute maximally. Turnover also creates opportunities for advancement, especially when an organization is slow-growing. Indeed, it is a linchpin of career planning; companies in no-growth situations need turnover to open slots for high performers who are ready to advance.

Perhaps the most positive effect of turnover concerns the nature of human capital. Turnover allows companies to retool and replenish their workforces and thus to prevent stagnation. New ideas, new capabilities, and new experience from the outside generally are required if an organization hopes to remain competitive.

Any method used to estimate the costs of turnover has to account for potential positive effects like these, which traditional calculations do not do. It is far more useful to ask, "Is turnover really affecting the business?" and "Is there an optimal level of turnover for the company?" than to think that all turnover is bad.

through an ILM analysis. All in all, a powerful business case for change was created. According to a report in *People Management* magazine, the company was able to reduce turnover and realize returns that were quite close to forecasts.[1]

Other techniques that fit under the label of Business Impact Modeling include various forms of structural equation modeling, a powerful approach for establishing the direction and magnitude of effects over time, as well as formal evaluations of the business impact of selected

Figure 6-1

Turnover's Impact on Quest Diagnostics

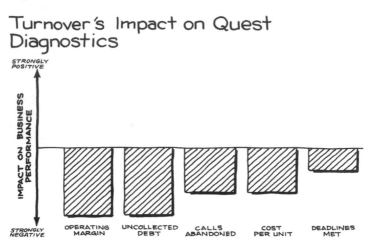

management programs. Many of those evaluations are in effect evaluations of organizations' experiments with new practices or programs.

National City Corporation, for example, evaluated the impact of a new training and on-boarding program designed to enhance workforce skills and customer service to support its new business strategy. The investment in the program was substantial. The evaluation of the program involved several components, including how much trainees learned and changes in their on-the-job behavior. The most compelling element was an assessment of the program's impact on measures of business performance. Using a number of statistical modeling techniques, the company determined that the program raised business performance substantially, particularly the growth in the number of new checking and savings accounts and sales of annuity products. National City's approach earned it the Corporate University Best-in-Class Award as well as the Optimas Award for Financial Impact given by *Workforce* magazine.

Building a Human Capital Strategy: Case Study

ProCo is a global and diversified consulting company with strong positions in many areas. The company was enjoying stable profitability because of its traditional service offerings in mature markets, but times were changing. The chief executive officer (CEO) and other executives were concerned about limited growth. They also faced the challenge of developing new growth areas without jeopardizing their successful businesses.

The top management team concurred that in addition to accelerated global expansion, the greatest opportunities for growth required (1) strengthening relationships with the company's large, profitable customers and (2) more aggressively tapping synergies across service groups and business segments. Those synergies included both cross-selling and developing new services that would provide customers with integrated solutions to business problems. At the core, synergy involved a shift from a product orientation to a customer orientation. That strategy could give ProCo an unassailable competitive advantage for many years and put it on the road to double-digit growth.

Applications of Business Impact Modeling

Business Impact Modeling provides facts about the human capital drivers of business success. It can address a wide range of questions, including the following: Does productivity rise with years of service? What is the impact of customer service training on sales? Is the incentive pay program producing the desired effects? Does employee turnover affect the company's bottom line? Are the spans of control optimal? What is the impact of part-time employees on the business? Is the leadership development program raising business performance?

Informing a company's management is exactly what Business Impact Modeling does. It brings new, powerful information to decision makers about human capital attributes and practices. The statistical modeling inherent in the approach gives decision makers greater certainty about what drives business results and what does not. The statistical models also help decision makers anticipate the future, especially the returns (i.e., improvements in business performance) that can be expected to result from a change in a human capital policy or practice. The insights that result from applying this approach significantly improve the ability of an organization to settle quickly and objectively on the strategy and tactics best suited to achieving the desired business objectives.

From Business Strategy to People Strategy

ProCo set out to develop a human capital strategy that could support its new business strategy. As a first step its executives took a hard look at the current workforce and asked, "What are our key skill sets?" "How effective are we at developing them and retaining the people who have them?" "What attracts the right kinds of people to us, and which practices drive them away?" "How strong is our leadership pipeline?" and

"How well are we tracking performance and differentiating rewards for top performers?"

The company conducted an ILM analysis to answer those and other workforce questions about its current state. Next, it addressed the future state: "What kind of workforce do we need to make our growth strategy work?" "What would it look like?" The firm's leadership determined that ProCo needed people with specialized skills to maintain its existing position in traditional service lines. To capitalize on synergies and develop integrated solutions, however, it required something very different: People who knew how to work *across* specialized functions, get things done through the use of cross-functional teams, and expand customer connections. People with those more general business skills and entrepreneurial attitudes would be needed at all levels, and employees who fit that description would need a long leash and a suitable set of rewards.

Finally, the strategy would require a shift from having a "hiring talent" orientation to having a "building talent from within" orientation. Previously the firm typically had hired experienced talent and let those employees operate as they saw fit as long as they upheld the highest professional standards. The new strategy had very different people implications. Employees would have to unite around distinctive offerings and new proprietary techniques. They would have to be trained in those techniques and broaden their experience within the firm. In a word, the growth strategy called for increasing amounts of *firm-specific* human capital.

When management compared the desired employees' qualities with those of the current workforce, several gaps stood out. "If you look at how we're hiring and promoting people," said one manager, "it's clear that we're attracting and retaining people who want to become technical specialists. People who come to us with generalist skills are not highly rewarded or promoted. They are most likely to leave us. That's a problem if we want to adopt this new business strategy." "We need more risk takers," said another. "But how will we attract and motivate such people when the evidence shows that they're not rewarded in our company?"

Others chimed in to identify other gaps that would have to be addressed. Indeed, a comparison of the current versus desired the state revealed significant alignment in some areas but important gaps in others. For one thing, the company was hiring significant numbers of experienced midcareer professionals, people who generally did not remain with the company for long. That signaled a problem because of the sums spent on recruiting and selecting such people. Worse, that pattern was inconsistent with the new business strategy, for which homegrown talent was the linchpin.

Another drawback of hiring experienced professionals was the effect on up-and-coming junior talent. ILM analysis indicated that many of the younger people were leaving, especially in units with significant senior hires. Perhaps those less-experienced professionals saw few opportunities for promotion. The facts, however, showed that this was not the case. Promotions were valuable but had no effect on retention among promising young professionals. Pay alone seemed to matter. This was a shock to senior management in light of the considerable attention given to advancement in the organization. In short, the company inadvertently was creating a pay culture rather than a career culture, the exact opposite of what it needed if it was going to build homegrown talent successfully. In fact, many of the essential human capital requirements of the firm's strategy were not supported by the rewards system.

On the basis of those assessments, a team of managers, executives, and HR specialists met to create a new human capital strategy, a coherent set of recommended changes in the company's employee policies and practices. Those changes included new hiring objectives and plans for targeted retention, training, and rewards.

Major shifts in management practices are difficult to make when a company is successful and has a deeply engrained culture. In the case of ProCo, the existing businesses were doing well but the newer parts had yet to establish their economic viability. How could one argue in favor of substantial reallocations of resources from those who clearly drove the current business to those who *might* drive the business in the future? This is a conundrum for many businesses. Everyone is prone to rest on his or her laurels, and with boards looking over one's shoulder, building human capital for future needs can be very risky if it comes at the expense of current performance.

ProCo, however, took the plunge, but not before taking one more step to ascertain whether its vision of the future was valid. It wanted to know which human capital attributes and management practices were critical to the success of its new strategy. Of particular interest was the staffing of client service teams. Were certain staffing arrangements better than others? To answer that question the firm brought together revenue data maintained by the finance department and HR data for the most recent 12 quarters. Business Impact Modeling then estimated the impact of different staffing configurations on revenue growth. Control variables such as differences in individual team members' performance levels were included in the analysis.

The results were powerful and often counterintuitive. For example, there had been an unquestioned belief that teams staffed with the most experienced members of the firm were the most effective. Business Impact Modeling indicated something very different: Teams of highly experienced employees were not nearly as effective in growing revenue as were teams made up of employees with varying years of service and experience.

Other findings confirmed existing beliefs but also quantified and prioritized their links to results. Turnover among team members, a source of discontinuity in client relationships, clearly detracted from revenue growth. The impact of turnover on revenue growth was greatest among the more tenured employees. Also, the greater the "dedicated" staffing in service teams—that is, team members spending a majority of their time serving a single client—the greater the ability of the team to increase revenue. Although the directionality of this effect was long assumed by management, the magnitude of its importance was unknown. In fact, the magnitude of the effect of dedicated staffing far exceeded the effect of employee turnover.

Finally and perhaps most important, teams composed of employees from different service groups were far more likely to expand client relationships than were teams that focused exclusively on a single service segment. Revenues increased faster when the first staffing model was in effect. Thus, the economic potential for blended service teams became visible within current patterns of performance. The business case for the new strategy of broader client relationships was there for all to see, and human capital was at its center.

The ILM Analysis/Business Impact Modeling Combination

The approach described in the ProCo case confirms the value of combining ILM analysis, Business Impact Modeling, and qualitative assessments of the current and desired states. A clear picture of current workforce realities derived from an ILM analysis and the identification of drivers of value derived from Business Impact Modeling provided new facts and dispelled old myths. Leaders who get involved in the details of the design of a human capital strategy understand their organizations at a much deeper level. They become more acutely aware of the human sources of competitive advantage. They also discover metrics they can use to track progress on the people side of the business.

Models Versus Experience

ILM analysis and Business Impact Modeling emphasize the importance of facts and their inter-relationships as expressed through statistical models of workforce and business outcomes. Could models ultimately replace the role of personal experience in management? Atul Gawande's book *Complications* provides an illustration of what can happen when a model is pitted against experience.[2] The example centers on electrocardiographic (ECG) tests. Those tests record and print out electrical impulses from heart muscles, whose patterns can reveal the difference between a healthy heart and, say, one that has experienced a heart attack. The patterns are not simple. The test output includes multiple waves. Further, each wave has many attributes, such as height and disturbance, and there are almost innumerable combinations of waves and attributes, all of which must be recognized and interpreted appropriately.

In Gawande's example, one of Sweden's most experienced cardiologists, a professional who read the ECGs of over 10,000 patients every year, was pitted against a statistical model. In that contest 2,240 real ECG results were presented to the expert. Half were known to be associated with healthy hearts, and half with cases of heart attacks. The cardiologist correctly identified over 55 percent of the heart attack cases. A computer-based mathematical model of ECG patterns, however, correctly identified just over 66 percent of heart attack cases, a significant improvement over the results with the experienced doctor.

Was this a quirk? Not at all. As far back as 1954 the psychologist Paul Meehl demonstrated that statistical and actuarial models consistently showed greater accuracy in diagnosing patients than did experienced clinicians. Robin Hogarth points out that these results hold up in other areas as well, such as predicting the prices of securities, the longevity of cancer patients, and success in graduate school.[3]

What does this say about the role of statistical models in strategy making? Should executives' experience be discounted or replaced by formulas? Before answering these questions let's look briefly at why models are often more accurate than experienced professionals.

Part of the reason for the accuracy of models is that they efficiently reduce complex relationships to formulas—sets of rules for weighing and combining facts. The process of finding those formulas is designed to weed out irrelevant facts: those which are not consistently related to the outcome, for example, or those which are redundant. The process itself disciplines thinking and establishes an order of importance among relevant facts. It also helps identify the combinations of facts that best predict outcomes.

There is also a degree of consistency and objectivity in models that human experts generally lack if only because of the fact that they are human. Models benefit from being unthinking; their rules for recognizing and combining facts are used over and over and in the same way. Humans, in comparison, are less consistent. Their attention wanders. They sometimes rush to judgment or overemphasize certain facts. Cognitive limitations may prevent them from processing complex patterns accurately.

What is the role of experience? Simply put, experience is critical but insufficient. When practical models are available to inform strategic decision making, there is no reason for modern organizations to rely exclusively on experience and qualitative facts. It is necessary to use those things in the strategy-making process, but it is important to supplement the power of experience with fact-based models of workforce and business outcomes.

Steps for Building a Successful Human Capital Strategy

This chapter and the previous two have described the importance of aligning human capital strategy with business strategy. They also have provided empirical tools for uncovering the facts about the existing workforce and measuring the impact of people-oriented practices on business results. These tools represent a new science for building and managing human capital.

You can put this new science to work for the benefit of your company by taking the following steps. In reality, the process of building a human capital strategy through these steps is unlikely to unfold in a tight order. There is likely to be an iterative process involved that is characterized by some "cycling back" and "leaping forward."

1. *Know where you are.* Use ILM analysis and qualitative data to ascertain the facts about the current workforce and workforce management practices. Ask such questions as: What are our workforce capabilities? Are we building or buying them primarily? What are our special areas of strength and weakness? What are we actually rewarding? What are the characteristics of those who leave the organization?

2. *Project the future.* Use interviews, surveys, focus groups, structured planning meetings, and the like, to build a picture of where the organization should go. How will the business be different? What changes can be anticipated in technology, processes, and customers? What are the human capital implications of changes in strategy?

3. *Find the value.* Use Business Impact Modeling to identify the human capital attributes and practices that are creating the greatest value for the enterprise. Where possible, test and validate the qualitative data that have been gathered from executives and unit leaders. Prioritize attributes and practices in accordance with their importance. Identify the combinations of practices and attributes that create the greatest value.

4. *Close the gaps.* Identify the most important differences between "is now" and "should be." Test alternative solutions such as new combinations of practices and new workforce attributes to identify the ways of closing the gaps that are most likely to be successful. Protect and enhance the sources of value identified through Business Impact Modeling.

5. *Design the interventions.* Design the specific features of changes that will be made in the workforce and ways to manage them. Use the models created by ILM analyses to simulate what-if scenarios to help identify which alternative solutions will be most viable. Use the models created in Business Impact Modeling to estimate the investment returns of interventions.

6. *Implement with accountability.* Use metrics to focus implementation efforts. Metrics will indicate when course corrections are needed and serve as a basis for assessing progress.

These steps can get an organization moving quickly toward the development and implementation of a human capital strategy. Resistance and skepticism will be reduced because the strategy will be based on facts specific to the business. Targets can be set that are demonstrably realistic and specific. The dreaded "initiative of the month" syndrome is avoided because clear estimates of return on investment can be made to show why changes are being implemented. Trust in leadership grows because the facts behind strategic decisions can be communicated clearly. Line managers and employees are energized by seeing, often for the first time, the real impact of human capital practices on business results. Isn't this much better than doing something because General Electric or some other company is doing it?

In Part III of this book you will see how the principles and tools set forth in this section can be applied to important business issues that many companies now face.

Key Points

- Once management understands the facts about the current workforce, it must determine what that workforce should be in light of the company's business strategy. Gaps between the current reality and the ideal workforce then must be closed.
- Business Impact Modeling is a family of quantitative tools that establishes the impact of human capital practices on business results.
- The statistical models of ILM analysis and Business Impact Modeling are useful tools for strategy making because they give fact-based, company-specific answers to what-if questions about the future.
- The best human capital strategies result from the integration of ILM analysis, Business Impact Modeling, and qualitative data.

Applications

The People Side of Strategic Shifts

ONCE COMMANDER Jean-Luc Picard decided on a course of action, he simply told his starship crew, "Make it so," and they did. If only implementation in business were that easy. Clearly it is not, as evidenced by the dismal history of corporate change efforts in both strategy and culture over the last several decades. Michael Beer and Nitin Nohria of Harvard Business School estimated that almost 60 percent of change initiatives fail.[1] Among mergers and acquisitions the results are equally disappointing.

What is the cause of these failures? Is it poor strategizing on the part of executives? Is it failure to build a suitable financial foundation for change? Do disturbances in the marketplace undermine these corporate efforts from the outside? Are countermoves by competitors the cause? Some strategies are jeopardized by these problems, but more often the source of failure is on the people side of the business. The strategy may have shifted, but most of the management practices are still aligned with the old model, effectively working against leadership's intent.

Managers complain that employees are unable or unwilling to play along when in fact the employees are responding rationally to practices that are in conflict with the new strategy. It is tempting to characterize employee behavior as resistance to change, but a closer look will show that most organizations have institutionalized practices and incentives that discourage people from moving in the latest strategic direction. These "baked-in" practices and incentives are a valuable asset when they fit the strategy, but they become high hurdles when they are at odds with needed changes.

The frequency of failure in strategic change initiatives has led the Stanford business professor Jeffrey Pfeffer to observe that strategy is less important than the ability to execute. At a time when most consultants and academics were obsessed with creating winning strategies, he wrote, "It is more important to manage your business right than to be in the right business."[2] This may sound heretical to a generation of executives raised on the strategy doctrines of Michael Porter and other business gurus, but as Pfeffer put it, "Success comes from successfully implementing strategy, not just from having one. This implementation capability derives in large measure from the organization's people, how they are treated, their skills and competencies, and their efforts on behalf of the organization."[3] Simply put, success in strategic change is accomplished primarily through human capital management. This means that a shift in business strategy must be mirrored by an appropriate shift in a firm's human capital strategy.

The people part of strategy is not reflected adequately in the literature of corporate strategy. Strategists are concerned primarily with customer segmentation, barriers to entry, cost advantages and disadvantages, product differentiation, government regulations, economies of scope and scale, capital spending, and that old will-o'-the-wisp synergy. Except for an occasional reference to "skill transfers," people factors largely are ignored. Indeed, human capital has no place in traditional strategy formulation; it is merely an "input" that comes later, in the implementation phase. Traditional economists weaned on "production functions" tended to consider labor a homogeneous input to production, treating an hour of labor as having as much uniqueness as a cubic meter of cement.

Scholars who deal with organizational change, in contrast, recognize the centrality of people. They universally hold that change is bound to fail if people factors are not given their due. John Kotter, for example, emphasizes the importance of creating a sense of urgency among employees, organizing a guiding coalition of key individuals, empowering people and providing them with a vision and strategy, and encouraging organizational learning.[4] However, although people are at the core of change literature, the importance of having the "right" people and management practices in a change initiative largely are ignored.

Experience indicates that strategic shifts are most likely to succeed when management complements its strategy with people practices that can make the strategy work. Few cases make the point more clearly than the battle for market share in California air travel in 1994.

Air War over California

Stung by losses of market share to Southwest Airlines (SWA) in the lucrative California air travel corridor in 1994, two major carriers shifted their strategies to match those of their rival. Each brought a new low-cost "lite" offering to the California market. Those operations mimicked Southwest's frequent-departure, short-haul, low-fare, point-to-point (versus hub and spokes) strategy, but both failed. Why?

The strategies of the three airlines were essentially the same, as were their customer propositions—at least on paper. The big difference was on the human side. Although the older carriers changed their business strategies to mimic SWA's, they made no corresponding changes in their people practices and policies. Company-employee relations at those two airlines were downright hostile. Management treated flight attendants like angry adolescents, and flight attendants responded in kind. The pilots and mechanics unions were at odds with management when they weren't fighting with each other. Neither carrier took steps to resolve those problems before launching their new airline-within-the-airline strategies. They assumed that they could recapture market share through marketing alone.

SWA, in contrast, complemented its strategy with a workforce that was eager and able to make it work. Indeed, most observers attributed that company's 20 to 30 percent cost advantage over its rivals primarily to the productivity and flexibility of its employees. At the time of the California confrontation SWA handled nearly three times as many passengers per employee as United did. Southwest's people also served travelers better in terms of every key measure of performance: on-time departures, flight turnaround times, lost baggage, and customer satisfaction.

Southwest's integration of strategy and human capital was not a lucky coincidence. Customer-facing personnel were selected and trained deliberately to support the company strategy. They operated as a team and would do whatever it took to get their planes loaded and into the air as quickly as possible. In fact, flight turnarounds took half the time required by United and the rest of the industry. SWA employees also reinforced the company's reputation for friendliness and fun through their behavior and interactions with travelers. Their rivals, in contrast, changed their strategies and relied on their warring parties of mechanics, pilots, ticketing personnel, and cabin attendants to make those strategies work.

The outcome of the air battle over California was practically preordained: The majors failed to regain market share in the nation's most heavily traveled air corridor.[5]

This example underscores the first principle cited in this book: system thinking. Strategy and people are part of a larger system. It is impossible to change one without considering the other. The outcome would not have been different if they had simply tried to copy the management practices of the market leader, since those practices would not have fit their existing management practices and workforces.

A new strategy is bound to have an effect on how people work and how they perceive their interests. Similarly, the behaviors and know-how that people bring to the table surely have an impact on strategy implementation. The traditional airlines' approach to winning back market share did not appear to recognize these system implications. Those airlines followed a traditional approach to strategic change in which executives defined the business strategy and employees were told to "make it so."

That seemed very logical, but it failed to recognize the "stickiness" of human capital. By that term we mean that changing people is often difficult and takes time. A handful of crack strategists can go off to a mountaintop lodge for two weeks and return with a first-class blueprint for strategic change with all its requirements mapped and measured, including an incentive system aimed at aligning people with strategic goals. This blueprint may satisfy the analytic mind but usually fails the test of practice. Why? Because the strategy and incentive design may be opposed by other practices, such as structure, the decision-making process, and the human assets on which the new strategy depends. The employees may have the wrong balance of general versus firm-specific skills. They may be too entrepreneurial or the opposite: too "by the book."

Some people may find change antithetical to their interests and become resisters or saboteurs. The organizational system may contain incentives that motivate people to act contrary to the strategy. For example, many pension plans create penalties for staying beyond a specific age or length of service—sometimes, in effect, reducing earnings for each year they choose not to retire. Does this make sense for a company that may depend on scarce skills or that gets dramatically higher productivity from its more tenured older workers?

Factors of human capital are not immutable: They can be changed, but changing them takes time that a new strategy may not have. For example, an organization can reshape its human capital through recruiting and training. It can use normal personnel turnover to bring in new people with the competencies required by the strategy, and it can generate new skills internally through training. Years may pass, however, before the impacts of those efforts are felt. In this sense human capital can be a constraint on an organization's ability to grow or to pursue a different strategy. Similarly, a firm's human capital strategy may enable certain strategic responses that are not available to competitors. These things should be considered at the outset of strategy formulation. Strategy and the organization's unique human capital must be coordinated from a systems perspective. That coordination is generally absent when companies launch new strategies, with the airlines case being only one example.

The status of human capital in the consciousness of U.S. executives rose sharply during the tight labor market of the late 1990s. The supply and demand relationship for labor changed dramatically during that period, and many companies found their growth hamstrung by a shortage of people with critical skills. Nevertheless, most executives continue to formulate and pursue new strategies without giving human capital its due, as can be seen in the following case.

A New Strategy for Digitt

Digitt, a leading technology manufacturer, which was considered one of the world's best companies and one of the best places to work, shifted its strategy. Responding to increasing global competition and revolutionary technology, the company decided to base all new products on digital technology.

Digitt's new focus on digital technology made it possible to develop and launch a steady stream of new products built on a core technology platform. That stream of new products stood in contrast to the very stable product line that had characterized the company over the previous decades. The new strategy was the result of careful planning by senior executives and R&D, marketing, and manufacturing managers. The early results were promising: The new equipment produced by Digitt received high marks from users. The only things the company strategists had not considered were the company employees responsible for sales and service. The new product line seemed to call for employees with different skills.

The Problem

Digitt relied heavily on its teams of highly trained service personnel, who understood the company's limited product line down to the smallest component. Turnover was low, and that was a good thing for the company since it invested heavily in formal and on-the-job training. Incentives favored business units or groups over individual performance, fostering teamwork. The organization defined itself as having a team culture.

The company's strategic shift to digital technology had implications for the workforce—and vice versa—that no one had anticipated. In the past, human capital practices had rewarded what the company needed most: a stable workforce, teamwork, and deep firm-specific skills. However, those qualities mattered much less in the new era of digital equipment. Here's why:

- The company's new digital equipment was much more reliable than its old products, making the fix-it mentality less important.

- Mastery of digital technology and emerging technological areas superseded the value of expertise in the old-line analogue systems.
- Individuals, not teams, were given responsibility for specific accounts as part of the new strategy.
- With a broader product line it was more important to help customers identify which equipment would solve their problems than to demonstrate a depth of knowledge about any single product. This required an understanding of a customer's business and a different balance of firm-specific and general know-how.

Like many companies, Digitt had launched its strategic shift without making changes in the workforce charged with executing it. It clearly needed new skills, new behaviors, and new attitudes in its workforce but did little to create those changes. It had stepped into the future with one foot while leaving the other firmly rooted in the past. Deeper study revealed the extent to which that clash was undermining the success of the new strategy.

Although the strategy encouraged reps to act as individual entrepreneurs and look for cross-selling opportunities in their assigned accounts, the reward system sent a different set of signals. The lion's share of pay continued to be based on years of service, a legacy of the old system that was intended above all to retain the training and experience needed to service a complicated but unchanging product line. Bonuses had been aligned effectively to encourage teamwork by basing awards on the group one was in. Individual performance mattered very little when bonus checks were passed around: A poor performer in a high-performing group would receive a much larger bonus than would a high-performer on a low-performing team. Those high performers, who often worked in newer businesses in the ramp-up stage, had to rely on the unit's ability to fund the bonus pool. Under the existing reward system, the best strategy for low-performers was to attach themselves to a high-performing group and "hang in there" for as many years as possible. That practically would guarantee an annual pay raise and a good bonus. In effect, high performers in the up-and-coming business units were subsidizing poor performers in the traditional businesses.

Not surprisingly, Digitt got more of what it subsidized—low performers—and less of what it effectively taxed: top performers with the newly required capabilities. An analysis of performance indicated that Digitt was retaining low-performing employees at an alarming rate. While many of the best employees in the new areas moved on to greener pastures, the worst employees wisely stayed put until retirement. Who else would hire and reward them so generously? Thus, at a critical time in the firm's evolution, marginal performers in the cash-cow businesses were taking home bundles of cash, but the best people in the new ventures—the future of the company—were receiving little or nothing. That practice strangled the motivation of Digitt's best and brightest. Also, since the low performers stayed put, Digitt had few opportunities to reshape its workforce through recruiting because there weren't many vacancies to fill.

Investors eventually figured out what was going on, and the company's stock price took a big hit. All those things happened because the organization clung to the old ways and missed new opportunities. In short, its human capital strategy badly lagged its business model. A company that wouldn't dream of allowing its technology to lag behind that of competitors inadvertently was allowing obsolescence to affect critical parts of its workforce. Its historical emphasis on teams, loyalty, and longevity had served it well but now was causing stagnation, inhibiting the acquisition of the new talent that its technology shift required.

The Solution

Using data obtained through Internal Labor Market analysis, Digitt's executives eventually developed a plan to harmonize their human capital practices with their new business strategy.

Recognizing that some employees would not choose to develop the new skills they needed and that subpar performers would have to make way for new blood, those executives removed the incentives historically passed along to everyone regardless of skills or performance. Their approach was to establish a minimum individual performance threshold for participation in team-based rewards. In other words, simply being a team member did not create an entitlement; anyone not pulling his or her weight no longer would share in team rewards. That change did not scuttle the team concept: It simply meant there were now minimum membership requirements to share in a team's rewards. That solution had the secondary aim of encouraging voluntary turnover among low-performing employees. Each vacancy created through turnover created an opportunity for Digitt to hire a person with the right stuff for the new strategy.

The new human capital strategy was aimed at complementing the business strategy. It enabled workforce transformation over time and created a performance system that saved the company over $150 million each year.

InCo Looks Before It Leaps

Occasionally a company will examine its human capital capabilities *before* it sits down to create a new strategy. One case of this occurred in 2000, when the executives of a large financial services company asked us to apply our methodologies to their operation.

The impetus in this case was senior management's concern that the business environment was changing and the company would have to alter its strategic approach to creating value for cus-

Myth Buster: A Strong Culture Is Always Desirable

A company's culture identifies what the leadership and workforce value and how people at all levels approach organizational goals. A strong culture is an important component of organizational success, but only when it is compatible with strategy. For example, a business strategy based on product innovation for a volatile market would be well served by a culture of entrepreneurship and employee empowerment, but a culture of entitlement would not support that strategy. The annals of business contain many examples of organizational cultures that have undermined good strategies or blocked efforts to pursue strategic change.

Consider the case of Encyclopedia Britannica, whose venerable history goes back more than two centuries. Its 32 volumes were considered the ultimate repository of knowledge from art to zoology. When digital technology emerged in the early 1980s, the company began experimenting with educational software, and in 1989 it introduced one of the earliest multimedia CD-ROM encyclopedias, *Compton's MultiMedia*. Thus Britannica was well positioned to make the strategic transition from bound books to knowledge software.

The culture of the company, however, stood in the way. That culture was dominated by a nationwide force of direct-to-home salespeople, the very force that had made Britannica a trusted household name. No one dared to tinker with the traditional sales format on which his or her livelihood depended. The sacredness of the direct sales force business model was the company's Achilles' heel.[6] As a result, Britannica failed to develop a serious strategy for electronic products until it was too late. Annual unit sales collapsed from a high of 117,000 to about 20,000. It took the intervention of an outside investor and the abandonment of the direct sales approach to save what was left of the company.

tomers and shareholders if it hoped to maintain its leadership position. The managers wanted an answer to two questions, "Are we vulnerable to technology-driven changes in the market?"and "If the facts dictate that we change our strategy, do we have the right kinds of people and practices to make that strategy work?" The second is a question that all executives should ask before making a commitment to a new direction.

During the late 1990s InCo's senior management observed the growth of e-commerce in the financial services segment with concern. On-line agent-free sales to both consumers and businesses were increasing rapidly, but InCo was not structured for that type of distribution. Thus, on-line distribution represented a significant risk to growth and profitability.

The company had long operated with the assumption that it was in a relationship business: Customers purchased and maintained products because of their relationships with trusted brokers. The company's human capital structure reflected that assumption. At the core of that structure was a large group of highly paid individuals in the senior ranks. Most had been with the company for many years, if not for their entire careers. Personnel policies were aimed at keeping them loyal, since every employee defection risked breaking a profitable bond between InCo and the departing broker's many customers.

On-line sales challenged that assumption and represented a threat to InCo's approach to the business. If on-line sales represented the future, as many contended, financial services would become a commoditized business. InCo's main asset—its small army of brokers—would become a liability. Burdened with personnel costs, InCo would become the high-cost provider in an industry with razor-thin margins.

Company executives took that risk seriously. They wondered whether their human capital policies and practices were preparing them to compete profitably in a world of commoditized transactions. If that world came to pass, they would need people with a different set of skills in order to differentiate the company. In their judgment, the broker of the future would be less of a salesperson and more of a value-adding adviser, someone adept at evaluating a customer's objectives and risk management requirements and matching them with the appropriate products. These were important qualities that on-line sales could not deliver. This individual would need more than expertise in financial services; he or she would need broad business training and deep analytic skills. Valued information would be the new source of profitability and customer loyalty.

The Problem

InCo's leaders wanted to know, "Do our policies and practices attract and retain people with the skills and experience they need to act as value-adding advisers?" The best way to answer that question was to analyze the company's internal labor market and determine what actually was happening and which skills and behaviors were being rewarded. That analysis revealed that the highly paid customer-facing employees demonstrated mastery of their craft but that few had broad business skills. Turnover within that group was very low, supporting the old assumption that brokers provided the profitable relationship link with customers. The human capital asset and practices were well positioned to support InCo's current business strategy.

What about the potential new strategy? The facts assembled through Internal Labor Market (ILM) analysis revealed substantial risk. New employees with financial training, consulting-advisory experience, business degrees, and general business backgrounds were joining the company, but they were among the employees who were most likely to leave. Worse, high performers in that group were leaving at roughly the same rate as were low performers. Thus, the company was not holding on to the kinds of people management viewed as critical to a future in which value-added analysis and advice would be the source of competitive differentiation.

A second thrust of the analysis was to cast a spotlight on InCo's assumption about the broker-customer relationship. The company's human capital strategy was built on that assumption, but did relationships really matter? Would higher turnover among the brokers put profits at risk? Through the use of a simple form of Business Impact Modeling, employment histories of brokers taken from the company's PeopleSoft system were combined with three years of office-level financial results to determine statistically the causes of account growth and profitability. Through the measurement of the relationship between broker turnover and customer retention, the fundamental assumption behind InCo's strategy could be tested.

To everyone's surprise, analysis revealed that customer turnover and broker turnover *over time* were essentially unrelated. In other words, customers' decisions to do business with the company seemed to have very little to do with the stability of the sales force. The analysis also revealed that the small number of new individuals with broad business backgrounds who *did* break into the club were doing a better job of developing client accounts and were keeping those clients for longer periods.

Those findings confirmed that the company had been operating on a false assumption with respect to longevity, an assumption that had never been examined empirically. Although customers may have enjoyed their personal relationships with individual brokers, in fact they were buying the capabilities and resources of the firm. Thus, the high compensation the company lavished on long-term employees appeared to be an unnecessary expense that did not necessarily lead to greater value creation. Further, the findings suggested that the company was unprepared to tackle the future competitive environment it anticipated. Its human capital policies and practices were supporting the status quo and doing little to make the company attractive to the kinds of people it needed to execute the new strategy. In a word, the company had a serious problem of human capital risk that could jeopardize the business.

The Solution

On the basis of empirical findings, we offered management a number of suggestions for creating human capital that could support a new strategy:

- Push more incentive dollars down to the lower ranks to encourage high-performing newcomers to stay.
- Create career ladders that would move people with new skills into higher levels.
- Provide for more differentiation between high performance and average performance in the rewards structure, especially in the upper ranks. That would encourage voluntary turnover among low performers within the "club" and create vacancies for people with new skills.

It is worth noting that our analysis of InCo did not extend to management's concern that the business environment was changing in response to e-commerce or the notion that consulting-advisory services would be the new source of value. Those things simply were taken as the starting point for inquiry. We were saying in effect, "If these things come to pass, here's where the company stands and here's what it should do in terms of human capital." In the end those people issues became the centerpiece of InCo's review of the threats and opportunities it faced in the coming years.

Some Practical Advice

Once human capital becomes an essential part of strategic decisions, two good things happen:

1. Strategic options become more realistic.
2. The organization will be better prepared for changes in the competitive environment.

Thus, if you are contemplating a shift in strategy or if the competitive environment is changing around you, get the facts. Uncover the facts about your human assets and practices and you'll view the situation with new eyes. The facts may cause you to view human capital as a constraint on the business strategies you can pursue realistically, for example, how fast you can grow, which geographic area you can operate in successfully, and what you can offer customers. A fact-based view of internal human capital also may suggest strategies for which the organization is exceptionally prepared: people-driven strategies that differentiate the firm and give it a clear competitive advantage.

Key Points

- Strategy and people are part of a larger system. It is impossible to change one without considering the other.
- It is quicker and easier to create a new strategy than to reformulate the skills and behaviors of the existing workforce.
- Every strategy requires an optimal balance of firm-specific

and general skills. A company should consider this as it thinks about its current or potential strategies.

- It is important to challenge both strategy and human capital practices when the competitive environment shifts: Tried and true legacy practices may not fit the new reality.
- A company should never make strategy decisions before gathering and analyzing the facts about the current human assets.

Making Acquisitions Work

MODERN BUSINESS LEADERS are optimistic about strategic acquisitions, but their optimism seemingly is not rooted in reality. Depending on whose research is cited, 50 to 80 percent of acquisitions never deliver the anticipated benefits. Michael Porter's study of 33 large U.S. corporations between 1950 and 1986 indicated that those companies eventually divested more than half of their acquisitions in new industries and more than 60 percent of their acquisition in entirely new fields.[1] Research by Mercer Management Consulting revealed that most deals fail to deliver shareholder value greater than average industry performance: Between 1987 and 1991 only 43 percent outperformed the industry average for total shareholder return. That figure rose only to 48 percent during the boom years 1992 through 1997. When broader criteria are applied, such as the attainment of financial, strategic, and operational synergies, failure rates are estimated to exceed 80 percent.[2]

Some of the biggest deals have produced the worst outcomes, with the AOL–Time Warner merger being a recent example. In most cases the real beneficiaries appear to be the investment banks, which earn big fees for arranging these marriages and harvest still more fees for break-ing up the ill-suited partners.

Acquisitions are driven by many legitimate business purposes: to achieve profit growth, achieve advantages of scope or scale, acquire complementary skills or resources, enter a new market, or capture an important technology, distribution arrangement, or competency. How-ever, they often fail to deliver the promised gains. Could these disap-pointing results be due to faulty pre-deal due diligence? Due diligence mostly concentrates on measurable "things" such as the valuation of inventory and contracts, financing options, balance sheet impacts, exist-ing labor agreements, supplier contracts, and product and distribution issues. If due diligence is at fault, perhaps that is because it fails to account for the human capital of the acquired entity. Traditional finan-cial valuation methods fall short in this regard. The human capital of the acquisition target seldom is evaluated or addressed until after the deal is closed.

Reasons for the failure rates also are found after the deal, when problems of integration first appear. In fact, the most frequently cited reason for the lack of success is failure to integrate. By *integration* we mean the harmonization of structures and processes and the alignment of two organizations with common goals.

A survey of financial executives—individuals who have a great deal to say about acquisitions—indicates that almost half of all chief financial officers (CFOs) view human capital as at best only moderately impor-tant in acquisition pricing (Figure 8-1). Perhaps this reflects the fact that the motivations for acquisitions usually center on gaining economies of scale, dominating markets, or filling a gap in a product line. When financial executives look ahead, however, they report that human capital will become increasingly important in acquisitions. Per-haps the rationale for acquisitions is changing. Perhaps human capital will become *the* reason for future acquisitions as pursuits of scale and the like take on a less central role.

In light of the superficial attention paid to human assets, is it any wonder that so many costly and organization-wrenching deals produce disappointing results? Acquirers would get better results if they paid serious attention to the human capital of target companies, its value, and its potential for integration. That attention should be given before a deal is made and again as soon as the deal closes and integration looms.

Figure 8-1

How Financial Executives Rate Human Capital In Acquisition Pricing

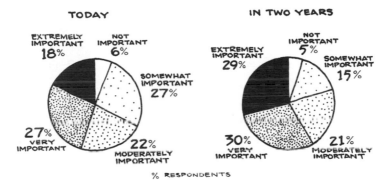

TODAY

EXTREMELY IMPORTANT 18%
NOT IMPORTANT 6%
SOMEWHAT IMPORTANT 27%
27% VERY IMPORTANT
22% MODERATELY IMPORTANT

IN TWO YEARS

NOT IMPORTANT 5%
EXTREMELY IMPORTANT 29%
SOMEWHAT IMPORTANT 15%
30% VERY IMPORTANT
21% MODERATELY IMPORTANT

% RESPONDENTS

Source: *Human Capital Management: The CFO's Perspective* (Boston: CFO Publishing Corporation, 2003), 29.

To Integrate or Not to Integrate

Integration is always a matter of degree. It can be complete, partial, or minimal, as in cases in which the acquired organization is operated as a stand-alone "portfolio" company.

- *Complete integration* occurs when the acquired entity fully takes on the properties of the acquiring firm, including that firm's styles of operating, infrastructure, identity, brands, and so on. Functions and lines of business are melded into one.
- *Partial integration* occurs when some but not all of the acquired firm's systems, practices, and policies are merged with those of the acquiring firm. For example, the acquirer may handle all accounting and financial functions, leaving the acquired company substantial independence in product development, marketing, and so forth.
- *Portfolio* refers to an acquired company undergoing no or very little integration, as occurs when it is held as a subsidiary. There are few examples of "pure" portfolio companies: Acquirers usually exert some influence on an acquired firm's practices.

Full integration is not always appropriate. In some cases the acquired company's business and human capital base are so different that it should be left to its own devices as a portfolio company. Some operational redundancies usually can be combined, lowering costs, but full integration might create a huge mess and sap the unique qualities of the acquired firm. We believe that a substantial number of acquisitions fail to return value because integration is pursued that never should have been attempted.

Berkshire Hathaway is undoubtedly the world's best exemplar of the portfolio approach. Chairman/maestro Warren Buffet acquires exemplary companies with outstanding management and holds them under the Berkshire Hathaway umbrella. He gives portfolio company managers and employees remarkable independence in pursuing their goals. Any other approach to managing subsidiaries in such diverse fields as shoemaking, carpets, chocolates, home care, and insurance probably would fail. Buffet's confederation of companies has produced highly satisfied shareholders, and satisfaction is also high among portfolio company managers. As Buffet reported to shareholders in Berkshire's 2001 annual report: "We have as fine an array of operating managers as exists at any company. . . . The ability, energy and loyalty of these managers is simply extraordinary. We now have completed 37 Berkshire years without having a CEO of an operating business elect to leave us to work elsewhere." This remarkable lack of turnover contrasts sharply with the record of executive retention after most acquisitions. According to one study, 47 percent of the executives of acquired firms leave within the first year, and 75 percent within the first three years.[3]

Sara Lee, in contrast to Berkshire Hathaway, has taken a partial portfolio approach to its acquisitions. Its pattern has been to pool marketing and retailing strategies but leave other aspects of a portfolio company's operations independent. Operating models from one profit center (e.g., hosiery) are not imposed on another (e.g., foods). Decentralized management structures partition the corporation into distinct business centers, each led by an executive with a high degree of authority and accountability.

The portfolio approach is not applicable to all acquisitions, for example, when one airline acquires another or one retail banking corporation acquires another in an adjacent geographic region. These unions typically require full or partial integration of operations, management, and personnel if the goals of the deal are to be achieved.

A Decision Framework

How does one know which level of integration is optimal for success? Should integration be full, be partial, or take a portfolio approach? If integration is called for, should it proceed rapidly or be done in a piece-meal fashion? These are important questions. To help executives answer them, we have developed a practical framework (Figure 8-2) that can help decision-makers do three things:

1. Know themselves, their target, and the difference between them
2. Estimate the potential scope of integration
3. Recognize the pace at which integration should proceed

The horizontal axis in Figure 8-2 refers to "forces for integration," the factors that push the acquirer and the target toward each other. Those forces may be strategic intent, human capital requirements, core business process requirements, or any combination of the three. The stronger those factors, the stronger the need for integration. Since our principal interest is the people side of acquisitions, let's focus here on human capital requirements.

In terms of human capital, the forces for integration are low when an acquisition does the following:

- Meets a need for the product, patent, location, and so on, but not the employees

Figure 8-2

An Integration Framework

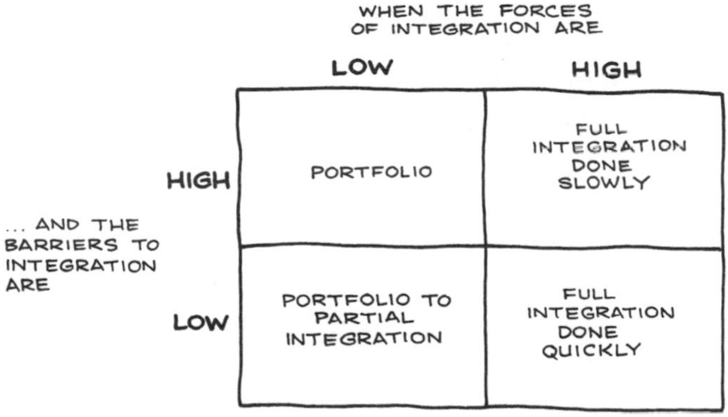

- Brings with it employees who are easily substituted for by new hires (i.e., employees with low firm-specific skills)

Conversely, the forces for integration are high—again from a human capital perspective—when the acquisition does the following:

- Creates opportunities to leverage or join various people-driven capabilities, such as sales and research and development (R&D)
- Requires collaboration on projects or contracts
- Presents significant new opportunities to attract, retain, and develop talent through integration

These are precisely the factors that often are overshadowed by traditional concerns about the price of the deal and the identification of physical assets to keep and to sell.

As is indicated on the vertical axis of the decision framework matrix in Figure 8-2, barriers to integration can be high or low. Life is full of human capital barriers to integration. They come to varying degrees with every deal. Some of those barriers arise because of differences between workforces; others arise because of differences in the way workforces are managed. In terms of human capital, those workforce barriers to integration are high when the acquired company does the following:

- Has a very different demographic profile (age, gender, ethnicity)
- Differs culturally or linguistically
- Has a different skill base

Barriers in the form of differences in workforce management practices exist when, for example, the acquired company does the following:

- Defines jobs with a different degree of breadth
- Differs in terms of the access to autonomy and information given to employees
- Uses different methods of selection, training, and development
- Locates authority for decisions at different levels (degree of decentralization)

- Differs in pay practices (e.g., pay relative to market, the mix of fixed and variable pay, the use of stock options)

That's a long list of integration hurdles, but each is important and should be pondered as part of pre-deal due diligence. The same list should be revisited when a deal has been consummated and people are ready to move forward with integration.

Applying the Integration Framework

The framework shown in Figure 8-2 is a guide for structuring thinking about the integration of acquired firms and business units. It identifies a wide range of human capital issues to consider. The framework raises issues that should be addressed as part of the due diligence work of scouting the acquisition. Typically during this period the acquiring firm does not have access to all the data about the target company that it needs to resolve uncertainties about what barriers to integration exist and how strong they are. However, the issues should be considered as explicitly as possible to prevent wishful thinking. The framework is especially applicable as soon as the deal is completed. That is when the integration team—perhaps consisting of representatives from both companies—can truly go after

Myth Buster: Quicker is Better

The conventional wisdom holds that acquirers should move very quickly to integrate their acquisitions. Some people make an analogy to pulling off an adhesive bandage, which is painful. Drawing out the process makes the pain last longer, and so it is best to do it quickly.

This advice may be well suited some cases but not to others. The best approach to full integration depends on the strength of the barriers arrayed against it. When those barriers are high, slow integration (upper-right-hand quadrant of the Figure 8-2 matrix) is generally more likely to succeed. Only when the barriers are low (lower-right-hand quadrant) should quick integration be pursued. Consider these examples:

- *Nortel Networks and Bay Networks*. These firms had many reasons to come together, but the barriers were high because of major differences in their cultures. Those barriers suggested a go-slow approach. Nortel moved with caution; for example, major changes in compensation did not take place until after a year had passed. Slow integration served the integration objectives well.
- *Union Pacific and Southern Pacific Rail*. The 1996 merger of Union Pacific (UP) and Southern Pacific created the largest U.S. railroad. At the time promised economies of scale made the deal appear sensible, but high barriers turned Union Pacific's rushed integration into a train wreck. Union Pacific should have integrated more slowly with more thoughtful planning.

the facts needed to make informed decisions about the extent and speed of integration. Human capital barriers to integration should be identifiable through a comparative Internal Labor Market analysis (see Chapter 5) of the acquired company and the acquiring company. Business Impact Modeling also can be used to identify similarities and differences in the ways human capital drives value.

Integrating Two Cultures

Like many in its industry, a large and well-known public corporation ("Company A") made several acquisitions in the past decade in both its core and related businesses. At one point, it acquired another large institution ("Company B") with operations in several of the markets that it served. This transaction was driven by a desire to expand its geographic presence and operational scope, capture the other's operations abroad, and achieve still greater scale advantages in a highly competitive industry.

In light of these goals and the similar operational characteristics of the two institutions, this combination was a nearly perfect candidate for full integration that would require the following:

- Uniformity of processes to create value
- A common set of products and/or services capable of meeting customers' needs
- A single public face

However, the merger could not be expected to be easy. The companies had been rivals for some of the same turf; Company B's brand had even eclipsed Company A's in some areas. The two corporations had different information systems. Just as daunting, they had different people policies and practices whose integration could be both painful and risky. However, as a result of its experience with acquisitions, Company A had great confidence in its ability to bring the new entity into the fold. Over the years it had developed an approach to integration that was based on (1) speed and (2) adapting the acquired company's systems, practices, and procedures to its own. The size of this transaction, however, caused it to pause and reflect on its integration practices. It asked: Is this the best way in this case?

Our involvement in this situation came about at the behest of Company A, which was eager to understand similarities and differences in the human capital systems of two organizations *before* making any drastic changes.

We began, as always, by gathering the facts from the two entities. What were the rates of movement of employees into, out of, and upward in the two organizations? How were rewards structured and what did they value: years of service, performance, movement from job to job? To answer such questions as these, we conducted Internal Labor Market (ILM) analyses for both companies, starting as usual with the basic ILM maps of labor flows. The maps themselves tell a story (Figure 8-3).

The ILM map of Company A reveals an organization with a steep hierarchy with many employees in the lower levels and dramatically fewer people at higher levels. Company B, in contrast, is relatively less hierarchical. Its map indicates a more equal distribution of employees through the various job levels and much less thinning out toward the top.

Investigation revealed that the two firms had very different reward systems attached to their respective job levels. At Company A, moving up through levels produced sizable financial rewards that rose at ever increasing rates – what we called in Chapter 1 a "tournament" reward

Figure 8-3

Internal Labor Market Maps: Company A & Company B

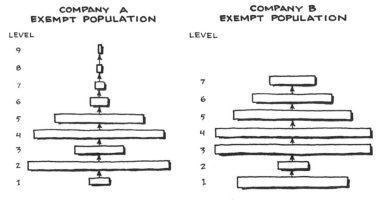

COMPANY A
EXEMPT POPULATION

COMPANY B
EXEMPT POPULATION

structure. That practice encouraged a career orientation among Company A's employees, who apparently understood that simply doing satisfactory work and sticking with the company would not be rewarded anywhere near as much as moving up the career ladder would. Although in most lower- and middle-level jobs they were paid somewhat less than were their counterparts at Company B, their upward "pay trajectories" were more dramatic, encouraging retention and a willingness to develop careers with the company. Company B's employees actually could advance more rapidly, as the high numbers of individuals above the mid-mark of job levels testified, but advancing up the ladder produced less dramatic pay increases. Company B's employees could be consoled by the fact that they were nevertheless paid at or above market rates. Above-market pay encouraged retention.

The bottom line was that Company A had a *career culture* while Company B had a *pay culture*. Which was better? That did not matter as long as (1) the companies were independent and (2) the workplace culture served the respective company's strategic goals. Integration changed this. Management had to determine which culture would best serve the strategy of the combined entities. That determination was made more interesting by the fact that some key executives from Company B were retained in high-level positions in the combined entity. Being accustomed to an environment with fewer job levels and a more market focused, pay-oriented culture, they urged Company A to move in that direction. Those features, they believed, were easier to manage and produced good results. However, Company A's management understood the singular importance of their career culture for retaining top-flight employees. They also recognized that such a culture could better serve the strategic goal of strengthening and growing relationships with customers because it fosters longer-term commitment to the organization among employees. Not surprisingly, the new combined organization maintained a strong career orientation.

Staying on Track

A large technology company offers another example of how measuring internal labor market dynamics can help executives who are faced with post-deal integration. In this case the executives of this global company had to evaluate the effectiveness of post-deal integration to see whether they were on track toward achieving their integration objectives.

This company was a major acquirer of smaller companies and their human assets. In some years as many as one-third of its new employees joined through acquisitions. The acquired companies were purchased largely because they had developed or were about to launch niche technological products that complemented the offerings of the acquiring company. The patents conveyed by those acquisitions were critical, but so was the human capital that generated them. It was hoped that the expertise of the acquired employees would complement the expertise of the acquiring company, potentially accelerating the pace of new product development. Thus, the strategy called for integration of the technical personnel of the acquired companies.

An analysis of the acquiring company's internal labor market dynamics over time revealed the extent to which integration was being achieved in terms of human capital. The results were disappointing. Incumbent employees (those already employed in the acquiring firm) fared differently than did acquired employees in several important ways, with one being turnover. Acquired employees were leaving the company at higher rates than incumbents were, particularly in some units. This signaled integration difficulties.

Employee turnover is one of the more commonly tracked indicators of integration difficulties. ILM analyses involve many additional indicators. In this case, for example, the facts showed that the rate of pay growth of acquired employees was equivalent to that of incumbents, suggesting that integration was on track. However, the two groups differed significantly in several other ways, including promotions. Incumbents were 1.5 times more likely to be promoted than were acquired employees after accounting for differences in performance ratings, job, level in the organization, and other relevant factors. Internal mobility also set the two groups apart. In general, the parent organization had relatively high rates of movement between jobs, mostly within functional areas but sometimes between them. That rate of mobility was well suited to the project nature of much of the work and to the development of skills and expertise in related technical areas. However, it was the incumbents who were doing most of the moving; acquired employees rarely changed jobs. When they did move, they tended to remain in the same functional area. In fact, there was little evidence of integrating talent into the broader workforce. Table 8-1 summarizes our key findings.

Table 8-1
ILM Analysis: Incumbent Versus Acquired Employees

Employee turnover	On average acquired employees left at higher rates, although large differences existed by area
Base pay growth	Equal
Promotion rates	Incumbents were 1.5 times more likely to be promoted
Job changes within area	Substantially higher rates for incumbents
Transfers into different areas	Incumbents moved freely across functional lines; only one acquired employee did that

The story told by this ILM Analysis is one of opportunities lost and a need to get back on track. Acquired employees lost the opportunity for upward or lateral mobility in the parent organization. The acquiring organization lost the opportunity to benefit from collaborative product development efforts. The ILM Analysis did, however, identify where in the organization integration was going well and where it was not and helped prioritize the actions needed to get integration back on track. Further, it provided a dashboard of metrics that executives could use in monitoring the success and shortfalls of its integration efforts.

Lessons on Acquisitions

The two cases presented above underscore the point that rational decisions are made only when executives observe the three principles of human capital strategy:

- *Systems thinking.* The acquiring company must be very clear about the purpose of the acquisition and the strategy to be pursued. The human resources of the acquirer and the acquired are parts of a larger system whose purpose is to execute the chosen strategy. Whether the acquirer accepts the human capital practices of the acquired company or bends them to its own way of doing things, they will have an impact on the system.

- *Base integration decisions on relevant facts.* Many integration decisions are based on hunches or a superficial understanding of the facts. These often lead to disappointing results. A company can avoid disappointments by taking the time to dig out the facts about the workforces that will be integrated. ILM Analysis can be used to get the facts.
- *Select the course of action that will create the greatest value.* A company should not get hung up on the issue of cost; instead, it should focus on value.

Key Points

This chapter has focused on the human capital aspects of acquisitions and their integration. There obviously is much more to the success of acquisitions than what has been presented here, but getting the people issues right is an important first step toward a successful deal. Indeed, as we reported at the beginning of this chapter, human capital is becoming increasingly important in acquisitions.

- Look at the combined organizations and common goals as a system.
- Uncover and evaluate the relevant facts about the workforces that will be brought together. These facts should inform the acquiring company's decisions.
- Determine the type of human capital the company's business strategy will require to create value. Does the human capital strategy of the acquired company support the acquirer's business goals? Will it attract, develop, and retain people with the skills and attitudes needed to get the job done?
- As the acquired entity is integrated, it is necessary to consider the forces that encourage integration and the barriers that will derail it. The acquiring company must consider those forces as it determines the extent and timing of integration.

Better Linking to Customers

F EW AREAS OF business have brought science and practice together as extensively as has the realm of customer behavior. What drives customers' initial purchases? What instills loyalty? How can a company's relationship with current customers be expanded to achieve a larger "share of wallet"? These are value-focused questions that businesses have learned to answer through the use of facts and systematic analysis.

Two approaches help explain customer behavior. The first begins with knowing *who* the customers are: the kinds of people they are, where they come from, and what interests them. The second approach focuses on *how* goods and services are provided. Here the emphasis is on things such as having efficient sales and support systems and designing a process to ensure glitch-free and pleasing customer interactions.

The depth of analysis of the who and how questions with regard to customers almost always exceeds the depth of analysis given to the who and how of human capital. What attributes of the workforce—for example, general experience, interpersonal skills, technical depth—are most valued by customers? How can a company best manage its workforce to optimize customer satisfaction, loyalty, and spending? Careful analysis that establishes the links between customer outcomes and a company's human capital attributes and practices is the way to answer these questions. The facts that result become the guideposts for managing the workforce strategically to achieve the desired customer outcomes.

This chapter examines successful customer relationships from the perspective of the three principles of human capital management: systems, facts, and value. We begin with a brief look at the process of understanding who customers are. That sets the stage for an examination of the linkages between human capital and customer outcomes.

Knowing the Customer

Most companies engaged in the retail sale of services or products know a great deal about who their customers are through the analysis of demographic data. Demographic data include a customer's age, gender, estimated income, and area of residence, among many other things. These are descriptive facts that marketers use to segment customers with the goal of better tailoring marketing messages and product attributes. Some age-based (generational) segments are well known: baby boomers, yuppies, GenX'ers, and slackers among them. Actually, those labels imply more than age. They imply something about personal values and lifestyles, and that is where psychographics comes into play.

Psychographics is the practice of learning about the personal values, interests, and activities of current and would-be buyers to further segment customers into finely tuned groups for even more specific product or message tailoring. Relevant psychographic data typically come from surveys and focus groups. Those data are combined with demographic data to create profiles of like-minded customers. The profiles typically define nonoverlapping "types" of buyers and potential buyers. Differences between those types become the basis for specifying marketing tactics, product or service attributes, service levels, and so on.

Many sources of data can be used to conduct demographic and psychographic analyses. Some of those data, particularly demographic data, are publicly available; one example is census data. Psychographic data are more likely to be the proprietary property of marketing services firms or opinion polling companies and are sold to interested parties. Some data, however, are the unique province of a single company. Specifically, companies that provide goods and services have facts about their customers that no one else can know. Important details about customer behavior reside in such data, including how much customers spent on the most recent transaction, their spending patterns over time, and their loyalty. Taking advantage of this data has been central to the process of knowing the customer.

Discerning important facts about customer behavior is invaluable. For example, at one time it generally was believed that a firm's market share is positively related to its profitability. Data analyses have shown that this is not always the case. Building market share entails customer acquisition costs that, depending on the company and industry, may undermine profits for many years. Others believe that customer loyalty matters more than market share, as Frederick Reichheld postulates in *The Loyalty Effect*.[1] Loyal customers do hold down acquisition costs, but loyalty may pay off in other ways: by increases in spending as customers' incomes rise with age, by referring new customers, and so forth. Further, certain current customers may be more profitable than others because they spend more, require little support, and pay their bills on time. A company with a small market share but with these types of customers could be far more profitable than a market leader with a less desirable clientele. Indeed, a great deal of customer behavior analysis today focuses on identifying a company's most profitable customers.

"Knowing the customer" is essential for successful marketing and product or service specification. It is also essential in creating the human capital system that is best able to serve those customers. Different workforce attributes and management practices, for example, may be required to serve different customer segments effectively. We turn now to the linkages between customer outcomes and human capital management systems.

Connecting Employees with Customers

Although analysis of consumer behavior with respect to durable and nondurable goods such as automobiles and breakfast cereals continues to be done, much recent investigation on the consumer front has been targeted toward services. Because services often are delivered through direct contact with employees, considerable attention can be directed toward understanding the nature of service delivery and the role of employees.

One of the more influential concepts coming out of this work is the *service profit chain* offered by James L. Heskett, W. Earl Sasser, Jr., and Leonard A. Schlesinger in a book by that name.[2] Another model—*the employee-customer-profit chain*—is a closely related alternative developed by Anthony J. Rucci, Steven P. Kirn, and Richard T. Quinn that was anchored in work done at Sears, Roebuck and Company in the mid-1990s.[3] Behind both models is an intuitively appealing hypothesis that employee satisfaction and positive employee attitudes more generally are sources of happy, spending customers. Figure 9-1 expresses the cornerstone hypothesis.

In reality, the connection between the way an employee feels and the profitability that can be realized from customers is not as simple as this hypothesis suggests for at least three reasons. First, the weight of the research evidence indicates that employees' satisfaction does not have a strong direct effect on their job performance. How, then, do employee attitudes affect customer behavior? Second, the causal influence actually may run in the other direction; that is, employee happiness may be a result of interacting with satisfied customers. Third, the very business practices and processes that make for good customers also may bring about positive employee attitudes. In the paragraphs that follow we take a closer look at these possible employee-customer connec-

Figure 9-1

Positive Employee Attitudes Produce Happy Customers

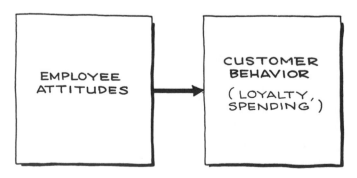

tions. These three are not the only possible ways of proposing links between employee attitudes and customer behavior. But they are the prevailing points of view in practice.

The direct connection between employee satisfaction and job performance implied by Figure 9-1 does not hold water. The first comprehensive, research-based assessment of the direct relationship between employee attitudes and job performance was made half a century ago. A. H. Brayfield and W. H. Crockett reviewed the evidence up to 1955 and found a substantial body of research on the topic; that research was based on a wide variety of employees and types of jobs and indicated that the relationship between employees' attitudes and their performance was weak.[4] That was a surprising and counterintuitive finding and remains so today, yet it has been borne out by several subsequent accounts of newer research evidence. Scholars have revisited Brayfield and Crockett's findings every 10 years or so, only to find that their conclusions still hold.

Despite long-standing weak evidence supporting the concept of a direct connection between employee's attitudes and job performance, which is the core of Figure 9-1, the concept has been extended into a "chain" that links employees to customer profits. Here's how it works:

Positive employee attitudes ➔ more spending by customers ➔ greater profits

No one will contend that the last link in that chain is invalid. The first link, however, is the less supported one. Could it be that employee attitudes and customer behavior are indeed linked, but in a different way? Figure 9-2 offers an alternative formulation.

Recently, one of the authors of this book was engaged in a discussion with an airline employee who after many years of service announced that she soon would be quitting her job. When asked why, she explained that grumbling customers had made her unhappy at work. Heskett and colleagues explicitly recognize that customer satisfaction affects employee satisfaction, invoking the concept of a "satisfaction mirror" to indicate that the attitudes of employees and customers reflect back to each other during person-to-person service encounters. The mirror is an appealing concept, but the evidence offered in its support is nonspecific.

More powerful support for the directionality of influence shown in

Figure 9-2

Happy Customers Produce Positive Employee Attitudes

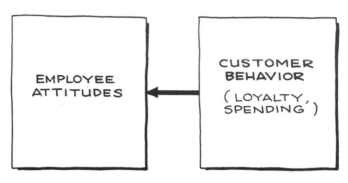

Figure 9-2 comes from the work of Anne Marie Ryan, Mark J. Schmit, and Raymond Johnson,[5] who examined employee attitudes, customer satisfaction, unit performance, and other factors over a two-year period in a large automobile finance company. Their causal analyses indicated that customer satisfaction leads to positive employee attitudes. They also tested the hypothesis underlying Figure 9-1 (positive employee attitudes produce satisfied customers) and found it to be unsupported.

Why fuss about whether Figure 9-1 or 9-2 is more correct? Because it makes a difference in practice. From a manager's perspective, if employee attitudes drive customer results, the task of managing effectively is one of improving employee attitudes and morale. In this case measures should be put in place to monitor employee attitudes since those attitudes are predictors of future changes in the business. In contrast, if Figure 9-2 is correct, all the measuring of morale and efforts to raise employee satisfaction will be misspent. Efforts aimed directly at improving customer satisfaction will generate a higher return and raise employee morale in the process.

Perhaps there is room for both hypotheses under the same tent. That could be the case if one makes a substitution of sorts. If one returns to Figure 9-1, takes out the words *employee attitudes*, and substitutes the words *employee capabilities or skills*, the hypothesis becomes more tenable. That is, knowledgeable employees (knowledgeable about the company's services, products, and customers) who have the right job and customer interaction skills (for example, problem-solving skills and social skills such as listening and negotiating) can drive customer response. Another way to accommodate the two hypotheses is to put them in a larger context, as in Figure 9-3.

Figure 9-3 emphasizes the contributions of company practices and conditions to employee and customer behavior. It asserts that those contributions are the prime determinants of how employees and customers respond. It also acknowledges that employee attitudes—and capabilities—and customer behavior are related. In particular, customers influence employees' attitudes and vice versa. The implication of this set of relationships is clear: Management should focus on getting the *system* of company practices right. Success with customers and employees will result.

Benjamin Schneider and David E. Bowen emphasize the importance of getting the system of human capital practices right in *Winning the Service Game.*[6] Those authors recognize that human capital practices such as effective hiring, adequate training, and appropriate rewards are critical to the delivery of excellent service. Nevertheless, they recognize that those traditional human resources (HR) practices are not by themselves sufficient. Schneider and Bowen speak to the necessity of creating a service culture: an entire system that coordinates nitty-gritty operational issues such as managing customer queues

Figure 9-3

A Third Alternative

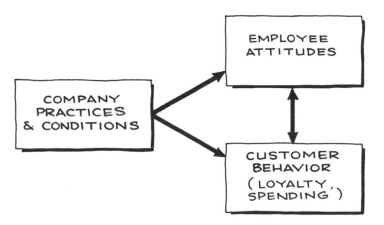

(whether standing in line or calling in by phone) with people practices. Heskett, Rucci, and their respective colleagues also recognize the contribution of system practices to employee attitudes and, ultimately, customer spending.

Common prescriptions for getting the system right include empowering employees to make customer service decisions and building training and reward systems that motivate employees appropriately. The intent is to create the kind of customer experience that wins loyalty and revenue.

Human Capital and the Customer Experience

What is the desired customer experience? Many who try to answer this question focus on customer expectations and the importance of meeting them. The idea here is that customers have expectations about both the goods and services they purchase *and* the purchasing process. Meeting or exceeding those expectations is regarded as the key to customer spending and loyalty. The U.S. auto industry has had a long and often losing struggle with customer expectations. People have product expectations of reliability, comfort, a price that represents good value, and so forth. They also have expectations about the car-buying process. Even when their product expectations are satisfied, many, if not most, buyers view their visits to auto dealers as a mild form of torture. How many car buyers enter the showroom fearing sales pressure, haggling, hard-to-understand pricing of optional equipment packages, and long waits at the credit officer's desk? Automobile dealers have attempted to overcome many of those fears and meet customers' expectations through courtesy, no-haggle pricing, clear information displays about optional equipment, and so on.

How are expectations formed? Frankly, they are shaped by all manner of influences, from prior experience, to word-of-mouth accounts from others, to written reviews in sources such as *Consumer Reports*, to the physical appearance of a Web site or storefront. Some expectation-shaping cues are controllable by the selling organization, such as the physical appearance of the place of business. More generally, the selling organization tries to control expectations through its brand promise. A *brand promise* might be as simple as "one-stop shopping" or "be secure with us" or may be a more complex mix of implicit and explicit commitments. Either way, the idea of a brand promise is to offer an attractive proposition that creates expectations that the organization is able to meet and, ideally, exceed.

Meeting Expectations through Human Capital: The Continental Experience

Continental Airlines offers a fine example of a business that created a new brand promise and then aligned its human capital practices in support of that promise.[7] Just over a decade ago Continental was almost bankrupt after its unsuccessful attempt to serve price-sensitive leisure travelers. It also was performing poorly, landing at the bottom of industry rankings for on-time performance and customer complaints.

The company decided to change course and go after higher-margin business travelers who are more sensitive to service than are leisure travelers. A new brand promise was crafted from what Continental had learned from customers, employees, and travel agents. That promise was accompanied by many changes that were immediately visible to customers. The company got a new logo. Its aircraft got a new look both inside and out. New uniforms were issued.

More important, the company made extensive changes in its human capital practices to support the new business strategy. One marker of those changes was the public burning of the company's 800-page workplace policy manual and its replacement with a slimmed-down version of 80 pages. That was a clear sign that energy-sapping top-down control was out and that employees were being empowered to better serve customers, especially those in special circumstances.

The workforce also changed. Its high rate of turnover gave the company the opportunity to "repopulate" itself with people who bought into the new brand promise and the importance of fulfilling it. Internal communication practices were revved up and reoriented to get all employees to focus on the new brand promise. Cash bonuses were paid for each month in which the airline achieved its goal of being in the top three in the industry for on-time performance.

Continental's change initiative was successful and, importantly, sustainable. Although the entire airline industry has suffered financially, Continental has maintained high levels of customer performance and has not endured the unkind fate that several of its competitors encountered in the tough economic times after the year 2000.

What accounts for Continental's success? In an industry dominated by tangible assets, its leaders recognized the importance of managing their valued intangibles: brand and human capital. Although the new brand promise was not exactly original, Continental's strategy for delivering on that promise was uniquely its own. The company's enduring success testifies to the value of aligning human capital strategy with business strategy from the start.

Moments of Truth

Just as there is great variety in goods and services, there is great variety in customers' experiences when purchasing them. Attempts have been made in the service sector to identify the universal dimensions of the experiences that drive customers' evaluations of service quality. Most notable in this regard is the work of A. Parasuraman, V. A. Zeithaml, and L. L. Berry.[8] Their dimensions are as follows:

- *Dependability:* whether the service provider delivered what was promised. This is perhaps the dimension most closely aligned to the concept of fulfilling a brand promise.
- *Responsiveness:* timeliness.
- *Authority:* Was confidence inspired in the consumer that the provider was capable?
- *Empathy:* the extent to which the service provider could see things from the customer's perspective.
- *Tangible evidence:* indications that the service was actually performed (e.g., a replacement part left wrapped on the floor of the car after the car was serviced).

Note how prominently employees figure in these dimensions of experience. Empathy and authority are distinctly human qualities. Dependability and responsiveness can be qualities characteristic of machines providing services such as ATMs, but those qualities also can be the direct result of employee interaction with customers. Whether these are truly universal dimensions of customer experience is an open question. If they are or are close to being universals, the role of the service provider's human capital in influencing the service experience is clear.

Whether one embraces the idea that customer experience is driven by a few universal considerations or the idea that it is driven by the fulfillment of expectations that are particular to each brand or service, there is growing recognition that a few decisive moments determine customers' experiences. These are "moments of truth." Consider cable television service. Many possible moments of truth are experienced by the customers of a cable service provider, including the first phone to call to initiate the service, the work of the installer, the accuracy and timeliness of the monthly statements, service interruptions and outages, the quality of the programming, and the range of services offered. None of these "moments" determines the overall customer experience. The task for management is to identify the key moment and then orient human capital practices to its successful completion.

Measuring the Drivers of the Customer Experience

As we described at the beginning of this chapter, there has been no shortage of interest in establishing measurable links between human capital and customer behavior. Data is plentiful. Some of the data is subjective, dealing with the feelings, impressions, and private evaluations experienced at various moments of truth. Other data is more objective; it is the actual record of customer transactions, their frequency, and their value.

Many early attempts to link human capital data to customer data involved subjective reports from employees and customers. Benjamin Schneider and David E. Bowen reported a breakthrough study of this sort in 1985.[9] Those researchers found a significant correlation between employees' reports of their satisfaction and customers' reports of their satisfaction in bank branches. The next generation of research took this a step further, as illustrated by the work of Rucci and his colleagues at Sears. In that work employee attitudes measured through surveys were found to be related to customer satisfaction, also as indicated by survey responses. The next step was to relate customers' satisfaction to a measure of their behavior: spending. Here customer attitudes predicted store revenue. Thus, the employee-customer-profit "chain" was born. Although there was no direct link between employee attitudes and store revenue, the chain was put together by virtue of the data that linked customer satisfaction to both.

A third wave of linking human capital to customer behavior is in progress. It involves reading the objective record of workforce attributes and practices and assessing their impact on customer behavior. This, of course, involves the application of Business Impact Modeling (see Chapter 6) in the service of understanding the drivers of customer behavior and experience.

First Tennessee National Corporation engaged in this type of analysis, as we reported in Chapter 3. That case pointed out the substantial contribution of one workforce attribute—years of service—to both revenues from current customers and the acquisition of new customers. Among all bank employees, customers responded better to those who had more years of service with the bank. The way the bank managed its human capital also mattered to customers. For example, pay practices that emphasized individual performance, as evidenced by greater differences in base pay and base pay growth among employees in the same unit, were counterproductive. Those pay practices contributed to declines in revenue per employee by disrupting the delivery of effective customer service *in that environment*, which was team-based. Incentives that emphasized the individual over the team got in the way of effective team functioning. That effect could play out in many subtle ways, such as not sharing information with coworkers, not covering for them when they took breaks, intercepting customers, and not collaborating when necessary to meet a customer's needs.

Business Impact Modeling is well suited to understanding the drivers of customer experiences and behavior. A fact-based, data-hungry approach, it can take advantage of the wealth of employee and customer data maintained by organizations. It combines easily with data on both employee attitudes and customer satisfaction to create more complete assessments of the causes and consequences of the customer experience. Most important, Business Impact Modeling helps an organization identify the *most important* human capital attributes and practices in its system and set priorities for action.

Key Points

- Knowing your customers—who they are, where they live, what interests them—provides an important context for understanding the drivers of their experience and behavior.
- Thought about the linkages between employees and cus-

tomers has evolved substantially in recent years. There has been a movement from relatively simple and not very well supported notions that positive employee attitudes make for high-spending customers to more refined ideas about the importance of the system of human capital practices that drive both employee and customer outcomes.

- Customers' experience is an important stepping-stone on the path to understanding their behavior. Organizations can influence but not fully control that experience through implied brand promises and through their human capital management practices.
- Business Impact Modeling can be applied readily to the analysis of human capital drivers of customer behavior.

The Implications of Business Risk

WE HAVE ARGUED throughout in this book that the effectiveness of any human capital practice has less to do with the particulars of its design than with how well it is aligned with the business context into which it is introduced. Thus far we have had much to say about the internal business environment but have not said much about that *broader* business context: the external market in which an enterprise operates. That is the subject of this chapter, particularly as it is manifested in the very real issue of business risk.

Every organization is like a ship at sea. A ship has a destination, and the captain directs the ship's course to it. The officers and crew are responsible for the many tasks that maintain the vessel's safety and move it toward its destination. The sea, of course, does not care about the intentions of captains and crews. It has a life of its own, one that whips up adverse winds, squalls and gales, and other impediments to smooth sailing. Every ship on the sea—indeed, every shipowner, captain, and crew member—must deal with those hazards and the risks they entail.

For business organizations, the macroeconomy and the market

environment are like the mindless sea, buffeting financial performance and subjecting shareholders, managers, and employees to risks. Sensitivity to external business conditions varies across companies, depending on factors such as size, extent of diversification, financial structure, and management practices. Where a company falls along the spectrum of sensitivity has profound implications for the way it manages people and directly affects the likely costs and effectiveness of specific human capital practices such as recruitment, selection, training, staffing, and rewards.

Risk is a feature of every business and its environment. Risk lurks in the ups and downs of the economy, in the industry, and within the microeconomy of the enterprise. The important questions here are: How big are the risks? and Who will bear them? The second question is especially important because risk usually carries a cost. In free markets whose participants have alternative opportunities, few take on added risk without demanding greater compensation. What remains to be determined is who can manage that risk most efficiently and hence at the lowest cost.

This chapter deals with the role of risk and its implications for human capital management.[1] It presents a method for measuring the level of risk and its sources and for using that information to improve decisions about how risk should be shared among stakeholders, shareholders, and employees in particular.

How Risk Is Allocated

In principle, all the stakeholders in an organization can bear risk to a greater or lesser degree. Stockholders bear the risks of volatile share prices, which rise and fall in response to both company performance and external factors; they sometimes are subject to changes in dividend payments as well. Customers bear risk through changes in prices or service and/or product quality, which vary in their predictability. For this reason, branded companies can extract a premium for maintaining high levels of predictability in both of these dimensions of exchange. Vendors and suppliers bear risk through variability in the security of their relationships with customers. Demand may fluctuate. Contracts may be canceled. Customers in adverse circumstances may pressure them for price concessions as a condition for maintaining the business relationship. All these are forms of risk that manifest themselves in day-to-day transactions.

Employees feel the sharp edge of risk through their paychecks and their jobs, as is shown in Figure 10-1. Many companies manage fluctuations in company performance by adjusting employment—the *quantity* of the workforce—and its related expenses. When revenues fall, some workers are furloughed, partially buffering the effects of declining revenues on the bottom line and on the company's share price. This practice has been widespread mostly among unionized companies, which traditionally use "last in, first out" policies to determine whose jobs will be eliminated even though the people with the greatest seniority may *not* represent the greatest value to the enterprise. More modern forms of quantity adjustment include contingent staffing, such as part-time and temporary employment, and the use of contract employees. Those employees are like a reserve army, that adjusts quickly to changing business conditions and requires less of an investment to maintain. Like the low-seniority workers of yesteryear, they serve as a kind of release valve, absorbing the vacillating pressures of business risk.

Many companies, particularly nonunionized firms that rely on so-called knowledge workers, increasingly are opting for variable pay as a mechanism for buffering bottom line performance from business downturns. Variable-pay programs help companies protect the bottom line by automatically adjusting labor costs to changing market condi-

Figure 10-1

Risk And Its Allocation

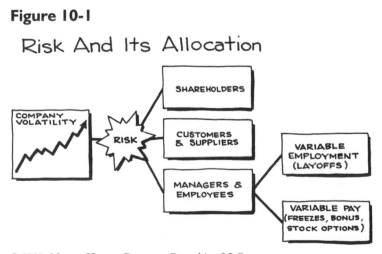

tions. By adjusting the price of labor, they remove some pressure to reduce employment, at least in the short term. This can help a company retain the human assets on which smooth-running operations depend, something that is more important for some organizations than for others. It also preserves investments in training that otherwise would be lost through layoffs.

Many employees now are compensated through plans that guarantee a certain level of base pay supplemented with a variable component that is linked to one or more measures of performance. Thus, a middle manager may be given a base salary of $60,000 with a stated opportunity to earn upward of another $15,000 if company, department, and/or individual goals are met. In this case one-fifth of the middle manager's annual compensation is at risk. Senior managers in the same company usually have a larger percentage of their potential compensation—half or more—at risk. That arrangement appears to make sense since senior managers presumably have greater control over corporate outcomes.

Interestingly, variable-pay programs seldom are introduced explicitly as instruments of risk sharing even though they inevitably have that result. Instead, they are instituted as incentive mechanisms that are designed to improve performance by tying rewards to business results. Such programs have exploded in recent years under the banner of "pay for performance." Particularly in the United States and among many companies in Europe and Asia, more and more employees, regardless of level or occupation, find that a portion of their pay is tied to some measure of group or organizational performance. Those incentives come in the form of annual bonus compensation, productivity gain-sharing, or profit-sharing programs.

For many companies during the 1990s the preferred vehicle for delivering incentives was stock or stock options. That certainly was the case for American executives. Spurred in part by new restrictions on the tax deductibility of base compensation over $1 million, compensation committees began to rely heavily on stock options as the basis of executive pay. Stock options confer the right to purchase company stock at a set price—the exercise price—during a specific period of time, usually 10 years. The purported benefits of stock options are twofold: The fortunes of shareholders and employees are linked directly, and the value of compensation is adjusted automatically to meet market conditions. Everyone has a piece of the action, and why not? Isn't this a logical way to motivate executives to increase value for shareholders? Isn't this form of pay for performance a perfect counterpart to a management creed that exhorts employees to be "results-oriented"?

Although the logic behind incentive compensation seems compelling, the record suggests that incentive programs are among the most problematic of all human capital practices. In the meta-analysis reported in Chapter 1 it was shown that financial incentives had by far the greatest variance in impact on performance outcomes. In some cases performance improved dramatically after the introduction of an incentive program, far more than was the case with any other intervention. In other cases the effects were negative. No other intervention tracked in the companies studied posed the risk of actually diminishing performance.

There are also serious questions about the efficacy of stock-based rewards. The collapse of the Internet bubble and retrenchment in the stock market overall have decimated the stock-based programs of many companies. Stock options for executives in those companies are deeply "under water," and the wealth accumulated during the 1990s generally has evaporated. Many executives have gotten the sudden, sobering news that their rewards have less to do with their own performance than with Alan Greenspan's.

In our view these problems reflect a failure by compensation committees or others in charge of incentive design to account for the role and costs of risk. Whatever their intent, incentive compensation and variable pay always involve *two* transactions:

- They price and allocate labor services.
- They price and allocate the risks associated with performance fluctuations.

Effectively addressing these two transactions with a single instrument is a major challenge. For those who view the world strictly through the motivational lens, it is easy to focus on the first transaction and neglect the second. Those people forget that if the second transaction is not managed appropriately, the results can be costly. Worse, the results can even undermine the motivational value of the supposed incentives. Indeed, when the efforts of employees are neutralized by environmental factors outside their control, those employees often cut back on their efforts. How well an incentive program balances both objectives ultimately determines its effectiveness.

Incentive schemes such as variable pay and stock options are based on the assumption that alignment between employee and shareholder interests is best accomplished through a *symmetry* of risk, that is, by putting both parties into the same boat. When one wins, according to this reasoning, so does the other. When one loses, others do as well. Basic economics indicates, however, that effective alignment sometimes requires an *asymmetric* allocation of risk for two reasons:

1. Under incentive compensation, performance volatility produces reward volatility even though performance volatility may be the result of random, external factors.
2. Shareholders and employees are not positioned equally to deal with risk.

To understand these positions more fully, it is necessary to dig deeper into the concept of risk.

Risk: A Definition

What do we mean by risk? In the financial world *risk* is defined as the uncertainty, or volatility, of returns. Thus, a company whose earnings fluctuate wildly is considered riskier for investors than is a company whose earnings fluctuate very little even if the two companies produce the same average annual earnings over a period of years. Figure 10-2 demonstrates this situation. Both companies produce the same average annual earnings of 10 percent over a 10-year period, but Company A's earnings are much more volatile than are Company B's. That volatility translates into higher risk in the minds of investors even though the outcome is the same in the long run. All else being equal, risk-averse investors would not value the two companies identically.

Investors do not like uncertainty and always respond to higher risk by demanding a higher expected return to offset the higher real or subjective cost. For example, corporate bondholders expect a higher return than do holders of bank certificates of deposit (CDs). Holders of B-rated bonds demand a higher rate of interest than do holders of A-rated bonds, all other factors being equal. Investors expect greater

Figure 10-2

Volatility Of Earnings:
Companies A & B

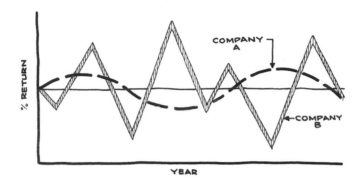

long-term rewards from their stakes in start-up companies than from their stakes in blue chip corporations. Thus, even though Company A and Company B produce the same average annual returns, investors will favor the steady ride of B by paying a higher price-to-earnings ratio for its shares than for shares of the riskier A.

By translating risk-return logic to the human capital market one can understand why employees demand more when company plans put their compensation at greater risk. Like shareholders, employees are investors—of their human capital—and expect a *risk-adjusted* rate of return on their investments. In effect, they say, "If you want to push the risk from shareholders' shoulders onto our shoulders, you'll have to increase the stakes." In a free and efficient labor market talented people can make that demand stick. All else being equal, expected or long-run average compensation will be higher the less certain their annual compensation is.

On the surface it may appear that the cost of risk is fixed regardless of who bears it. If management pushes risk off to shareholders, it will have to reward them with higher returns: Investors will not buy a company's stock at current prices. So share prices will fall to generate a more suitable risk-adjusted return. If management allocates more risk to employees, those employees will demand higher compensation. Thus, no matter how it allocates risk, a company seems to be stuck with the same net cost. This in fact is *not* the case because risk is not a zero-sum game. To understand why it is not, it is necessary to consider the component parts of risk.

The Components of Risk

In the business world risk has various components. For the purposes of this discussion we'll focus on shareholder return, although the discussion is pertinent to any measure of performance, particularly financial measures. Variations in share price may arise from three distinct sources:

1. *Market risk.* These are fluctuations driven by movements in the overall market or economy.
2. *Industry risk.* These risks originate in changes in the performance of the specific industry or sector in which the company operates.
3. *Firm-specific risk.* This type of risk is associated with performance fluctuations unique to the firm.

Volatility resulting from the first two sources of risk can be called *systematic risk*.[2] Volatility arising from the firm is called *unsystematic risk*.

Systematic risk is the uncertainty of return associated with the larger system in which an activity takes place. For example, a share of eBay stock is part of the larger market for corporate stock. The ups and downs of that market or system—result from factors over which eBay executives, employees, and company shareholders have no real control. Some of those factors are industry-related. For example, eBay stock is affected by investor sentiment about the Internet-based industry. When investors are disenchanted with that industry, even industry participants that are doing well often take a hit in the value of their shares. Broad, economywide factors that affect share price are also out of management's control, including consumer confidence, actions of the central bank, changes in tax policy, international conflict, and even terrorism. These factors create a level of volatility in the return of eBay shares as well as that of all other shares in the same "system." Thus the familiar expression "A rising tide lifts all boats."

Unsystematic risk, in contrast, is firm-specific. This is the part of a company's shareholder return that most directly reflects how investors perceive and value the company. It is independent of broader industry and market developments. Some of this volatility, to be sure, is associated directly with factors over which management and employees have control or substantial influence. For example, the success of eBay in implementing its unique strategy, managing costs, and confronting competitors has an impact on the ups and downs of that company's annual return, as do activities that directly influence investors' perceptions.[3]

Why do distinctions between systematic and unsystematic risk matter? Because investors can reduce or eliminate firm-specific risk through diversification: by putting their eggs in many different baskets. By diversifying into different companies and different industries, they can effectively reduce firm-specific risk and industry-specific risk and the costs associated with them. Doing this allows them to reduce their overall risk exposure and the associated cost.[4] They can balance their portfolios to calibrate risks and expected rewards to meet their objectives and match their individual risk tolerances.

Systematic (market) risk is another story. As long as their capital is in the market, investors are stuck with that component of risk. The only way to reduce market risk is to diversify *across different markets*, or systems, for example, by putting some capital into stocks, other capital into real estate, and still other capital into collectibles or precious metals.

Employees face a more daunting situation. They do not have real opportunities to diversify their human capital investments. They are stuck with the volatility caused by the market economy, the ups and downs within their industries, *and* the unique fortunes of their companies. A corporate employee whose monthly pay is linked to company performance (through variable pay) and whose net worth is tied up in company stock options or restricted securities could be dangerously undiversified. If the company has a bad year, variable-pay formulas make that employee's income shrivel. The employee even may be laid off. If the company collapses, employees like this lose their source of income *and* watch the value of their stock options and restricted shares melt away. If either the industry or the stock market is in a funk, the value of the employee's options and shares plummets. This situation imposes a cost on employees that must be compensated. Table 10-1 summarizes the three sources of risk and their impacts on investors and employees.

Table 10-1
How Investors and Employees Differ in
Their Ability to Diversify Risk

	INVESTORS	EMPLOYEES
Market Risk	Not diversifiable within market. Must be compensated.	Not diversifiable (via human capital investments). Executive *strategic* decisions.—e.g., regarding financial structure—may affect organization's susceptibility to market fluctuations.
Industry Risk	Diversifiable via portfolio investments in other industries.	Not diversifiable (via human capital investments). Executive *strategic* decisions—e.g., regarding M&A activity—may affect organization's susceptibility to industry fluctuations.
Firm-Specific Risk	Diversifiable via portfolio investments in other firms.	Not diversifiable (via human capital investments). But most directly influenced by employee decisions and actions.

Thus, there is a fundamental asymmetry in the positions of investors and employees with respect to the ability to bear risk. Investors can reduce risk through diversification in capital markets; that's the very reason capital markets exist. Employees are stuck with their risks. Labor markets afford no such opportunity for effective diversification. Investors therefore are positioned better to bear such risk, and at a lower cost compared with employees. This is generally true, but with two essential caveats. First, not all forms of risk can be diversified effectively through capital markets, as was indicated above. Second, the requirements for optimal risk management are often at odds with the requirements for delivering effective performance incentives, especially when it is difficult to observe the actual contributions of employees directly.

From a risk-sharing point of view, this situation seems to argue for firm-specific risk to be shifted entirely to investors, but that would not be a great idea. Since part of firm-specific volatility originates in the decisions and actions of executives and other employees, allocating risk completely to investors would give employees no incentives to perform well. This is the age-old insurance problem of moral hazard.[5] Insure the individual completely against losses, and the likelihood that losses will occur rises as diligence falls. That is why there are deductibles in insurance policies. Part of the risk must remain with the insured. This explains the need to have employees bear part of the risk associated with firm-specific performance. Indeed, incentives are strongest when they are linked to the firm-specific component of volatility.

Unfortunately, there is no optimal solution to the risk-sharing problem, only a difficult trade-off. Risk sharers are in what economists call a "second-best" world in which efficient risk sharing and optimal performance incentives cannot be achieved simultaneously. Doing better with one usually means compromising on the other. What is the solution? As usual in this book, measurement is the key. There may be no perfect solution, but the better able a company is to determine the sources of risk and weigh their relative impacts on performance variations, the better able it will be to mediate the tension between balancing risk and providing incentives. Before decisions can be made on how to allocate risk, it is essential to assess and measure its sources.

A Practical Tool

Performance Sensitive Analysis[SM] (PSA) is a proprietary statistical method that identifies and measures the different sources of volatility in a company's total shareholder return.[6] It can identify the portions of month-to-month volatility in shareholder return that are attributable to industry-driven, market-based, and firm-specific factors. (Sometimes one can measure volatility on a weekly or quarterly basis as well, depending on the circumstances.) With PSA output in hand, decision makers can better differentiate the true performance of a firm's human capital from the external factors that move its share price around. That makes it possible to establish clear, cost-effective incentives that lessen the exposure of employees to systematic risk.

How It Works

PSA measures the correlation of a company's shareholder return with indexes of both industry and general market performance over a designated period (usually three to five years). More specifically, it statistically decomposes the overall volatility of shareholder return into three components:

- General market volatility as measured by an index of stock market performance (e.g., Standard & Poor's 500, Datastream World Equity)
- Industry volatility as measured by an index of peer group performance
- Company-specific volatility: the part that is not statistically explained by industry and market movements

The third component is a "residual," the part of volatility that is not explained by movements in the two performance indexes. The analysis produces both market and customized industry "betas," which indicate the sensitivity of a company's performance to these external influences.

Two requirements must be met to decompose stock price volatility into its three component parts effectively. First, a peer group must be created to represent the industry or market segment or segments in which the company operates. Second, the likely correlation of industry and market movements must be accounted for; that is, the movements in industry performance that are driven by movements in the overall market must be filtered out of the industry index to avoid confounding the measures. Once two truly independent performance indexes are created, it is possible to statistically model the way changes in those indexes drive changes in a company's shareholder return.

The uniqueness and practical value of PSA stem from the methodology used to measure industry performance. Since industry-specific risk is in fact the great dividing line between investors and employees, imposing different costs on those stakeholders, the measure used to capture movements in industry performance is critically important.

The goal is to maximize the ability to draw statistical inferences about the effects of environmental factors on the performance of firms in the same sector. The degree of comovement between stock prices is a measure of the extent to which companies are affected by common environmental factors, both market-driven and industry-driven. Since the stock prices of firms exposed to the same environmental factors tend to move more in tandem than do others, more weight is assigned in the industry performance index to firms whose stock prices move more closely with that of the company of interest.[7]

PSA in Three Steps

1. *Identify the appropriate industry sector.* This is more difficult than it appears to be. What constitutes the industry, all industry segments in which the company operates significantly or only the industry segment from which it generates the highest percentage of revenues? This is a tough question for highly diversified companies.

2. *Construct a "filtered" industry return index.* This index is composed of peer group companies, with overall group performance weighted by the degree of comovement in stock prices. Statistical methods then are used to remove the effects of general movements in the stock market on the index.

3. *Use the industry and general market indexes to estimate the impact of general market and industry movements on the firm's shareholder return statistically.*

Applying PSA

Figure 10-3 describes how PSA methodology was used in one case to decompose total shareholder return (TRS) volatility (as measured by the variance of monthly TSR in the three-year period 1999–2001) into market, industry, and firm-specific factors. The companies involved were in the FTSE100 media and photography sector. It is clear that aside from differences in the overall volatility of those companies, the breakdown of risk varied dramatically as well. For instance, Reuters and WPP shares were found to be extremely sensitive to combined market and industry dynamics, whereas those of Reed International and EMI Group had the highest levels of firm-specific volatility. Like WPP, Granada has high volatility that is driven substantially by market dynamics, whereas Sky appears to be virtually immune to the influence of market movements. To draw conclusions about the risk profile of any one of these companies solely on the basis of knowledge of their sector clearly would be misleading.

Figure 10-3

Volatility Decomposition In FTSE
100 Media & Photography
Companies

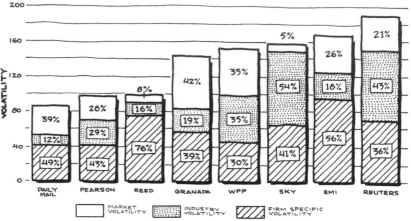

The observed differences in the risk characteristics of these companies bear directly on the impact and cost of transferring risk from investors to employees through the use of stock-based rewards. The market risks shown in the figure *cannot* be reduced by either investors or employees. However, industry risk, like firm-specific risk, can be reduced or eliminated by investors through diversification: Those investors can adjust their portfolios to achieve the risk-return relationship they desire. However, as we have noted, employees cannot diversify the human capital investments they make in their companies. Industry risk thus imposes a differential cost on them that ultimately must be compensated, often in the form of larger stock grants or other variable pay opportunities.

Returning to Figure 10-3, one can see that Sky and Reuters exhibit high levels of industry risk, which may mitigate against heavy reliance on stock-based rewards. Those companies need a mechanism for filtering out the effects of industry risk on their employees' rewards. In contrast, companies with high levels of firm-specific variation, such as Reed, may be able to use stock or stock options to deliver stronger incentives to their employees at a lower cost to shareholders than can others in the industry. Employees would see a stronger link between the rewards they received and what they actually did.

How to Use PSA Solutions

The examples given above underscore the practical value of PSA as a guide for dealing with risk in decisions about human capital policy and apportioning risk between shareholders and employees, especially through the vehicle of variable pay. At the very least, knowing the risk profile of a company's total shareholder return can help that company determine whether stock-based pay and other forms of incentive compensation are likely to be cost-effective as employee performance incentives. High levels of systematic risk, particularly fluctuations emanating from industry movements, raise a red flag about the likely effectiveness of such rewards. In these instances stock and even stock options are likely to prove costly to shareholders—say through dilution—even as they fail to deliver strong and consistent incentives for employees.

Does this mean that a company should forgo stock-based incentives completely? In some instances this may be the best solution. But of course stock-based pay has purposes beyond incentive considerations. It can be used to create a culture of cooperation, ownership, and responsibility for business outcomes. It is hard to imagine a true "ownership culture" without employees having a direct stake in shareholder value. Thus, finding ways to mitigate the adverse consequences of misallocated risk would be beneficial to all.

PSA provides a method to accomplish this goal. By measuring the components of risk, it provides a basis for developing risk-adjusted measures of performance, measures that to some degree filter out the effects of random environmental factors. Companies then can determine precisely how much systematic risk they want their employees to bear. They also can strengthen performance incentives by tying rewards more closely to the unsystematic component of performance. In this way, the "line of sight" becomes clearer.

This is not the place to undertake an exhaustive review of alternative ways to create risk adjusted performance measures, but let's be clear about the essential principle: Performance should be assessed relative to the risks that accompany it. One of the simplest ways to accomplish this is by measuring relative performance. This means basing incentive pay on a comparison to the company's performance relative to a weighted average of the same measure for peer group companies. Hence, if the focus is on total shareholder return, the company's TSR should be compared with the weighted average TSR for peer companies or for the market as a whole, depending on which measures most influence company performance. Financial gains should be realized if management demonstrates through this means that it is outperforming competitors or exceeding investors' expectations. Since competitors in the sector face similar environmental conditions, the use of relative performance filters out those influences and provides a better read on how the company's management and employees *actually* have performed.

For stock options, the use of relative performance could mean formally indexing the exercise or strike price of an option to changes in peer group and/or market performance. Alternatively, the company could adjust the size of grants offered to employees on the basis of how well the company performed compared with an established peer group. In this way executives and other employees in companies that outperform the

---

Myth Buster: Pay for Results? Not Always

It seems that every company these days exhorts employees to be "results-oriented," and why not? Shareholders are concerned with outcomes, not effort or intentions. Why should they reward anything but successful outcomes? For good reason, it turns out. Sometimes rewarding results makes it more difficult to achieve good results.

Take the case of stock. Since the primary duty of management is to increase the market value of their companies, it would seem sensible to link rewards directly to changes in shareholder value: the ultimate "result." But *whose* performance is being rewarded when rewards are linked to stock price? Although share price appreciation is the ultimate measure of *firm* performance, it is a very imperfect indicator of *management* or *employee* performance, especially in companies whose share prices are highly volatile and are driven by market and industry fluctuations. In those companies the presence of external factors over which executives and employees have no control transforms stock-based incentives into a kind of lottery in which bull markets generate large rewards and bearish ones wipe out gains.

What does running a lottery have to do with delivering performance incentives? Distinctions between competence and luck, between the results of business acumen and the effects of random market and industry factors, are blurred. As a consequence, those rewards end up providing little in the way of motivation even as they increase compensation costs. They also can lead to defections among valued personnel who find that their stocks or stock options are worthless even though they have performed well beyond market expectations. This is a sure way to undermine commitment and make those employees prime targets for recruiters representing rival firms who are cherry-picking talent in a down market. Net result: Company performance is hurt, not helped.

peer group are given larger grants in the following year. There would be no rewards for performance that increased simply because of systematic market and industry forces. Instead, employees would share only in value associated with firm-specific performance, value they have created through their diligence and effort.

These are just a few potential solutions for improving the effectiveness of incentive compensation systems. They add some complexity to incentive design, but that is far less onerous than the problems that often arise with more traditional pay for performance plans. Companies that fail to allocate risk efficiently through their incentive programs invariably end up with higher compensation costs (including dilution), higher turnover, skewed decision making, or a combination of all three.[8] The quality of decision making becomes compromised as executives are influenced more by their personal tolerances of risk than by a prudent evaluation of prospective shareholder returns. This could be the most costly outcome of all.

Layoffs

Our discussion of risk has focused mostly on pay, but we noted earlier that performance risk also can be allocated through changes in levels of employment. In a fragile economic environment no discussion of risk would be complete without considering the role of layoffs and reductions in force. Even when companies try to use forms of reduced pay to soften the blow and hold on to their employees, as Schwab and Agilent did, the pressure to cut costs often forces them to resort to workforce reductions. In these situations the systematic risks of the macroeconomy filter down to employees in the most severe form of all.

Are there any lessons to guide companies as they make decisions about the number of people they will employ? Businesspeople are inculcated with the notion that labor is a variable cost. The economics textbooks they read in school made that very clear, and in a limited sense it is true: Labor costs vary most directly with short-term changes in the volume of production. However, this is a superficial view of cost that fails to account for the investment component of human capital. To the extent that the capability of an organization's workforce resides in firm-specific human capital, labor may be the least variable cost of all.

Idle a plant or sell off machinery and a company can always buy them back. But shed firm-specific human capital through layoffs and those assets are basically gone forever. Reacquiring that asset is generally a costly and lengthy process. What's more, by using layoffs to buffer the bottom line a company may have destroyed the foundation of trust on which rebuilding must rest. Rock-solid firm-specific human capital requires an implicit contract between employer and employee that recognizes the value of employee commitment and uses rewards to induce employees to invest in specialized capabilities that are worth more inside the company than outside it. Because firm-specific know-how increases employee vulnerability even as it benefits the company, employees rely on the company to shelter them from volatility. Companies that are too quick to lay off employees break the implicit contract and damage their ability to reconstitute the workforce when they need it.

Some companies understand this and manage accordingly. Nucor Corporation, a highly productive and profitable steelmaker, resisted using layoffs even though it operates in a highly volatile industry. One of its four management principles is "Employees should be able to feel confident that if they do their jobs properly today, they will have a job tomorrow."[9] Instead of laying off employees during business downturns, Nucor uses that slack time for training, cleaning, and maintenance. This keeps everyone employed and keeps Nucor's highly productive work teams together.

The bottom line: Before making decisions about how to balance pay and employment adjustments for employees in the face of a recession, executives need a clear picture of the human capital on which their organizations rely. They need to know the relative worth of general versus firm-specific human capital for different parts of their businesses and for different occupational groups. People with general skills may be replaceable, but people with strong firm-specific skills are not. This is at least as important a consideration as current compensation expenses. For example, the firm-specific human capital of Sears's sales associates is probably limited and easy to rebuild with new hires. For that company the advantages of shedding and then rehiring sales associates as consumer demand fluctuates probably would outweigh the benefits of maintaining those employees through thick and thin. The opposite would hold for a private investment firm. The relationships between that firm's professional employees and its clients are worth millions. An investment consultant must have intimate knowledge of the client's needs and preferences, and the client must have full confidence in the consultant's ability and integrity. These are characteristics that only build over time. They cannot be bought, and when lost they are not easily replaced. Clients who use private investment services will not tolerate churn among the individuals who advise them. Therefore, the investment firm must be extremely careful in how it adjusts to market fluctuations.

These two examples focused on the extreme ends of the human capital spectrum. Most organizations lie somewhere in between. Moreover, the nature of human capital often depends on the function or the occupational group involved. When it does, negotiating the trade-off between layoffs and variable pay or, for that matter, deciding whether shareholders or employees will bear more risk is unquestionably more complex.

In the end it boils down to understanding a company's human capital, knowing the sources of its value to the company. Do you know where your company stands on the human capital spectrum? Do you know where the greatest value resides in your workforce? Do you know which segment of your workforce is the most productive? These are complex questions, but, thanks to the new science of human capital management, you can answer them.

Key Points

- Risk usually carries a cost. In free markets where participants have alternative opportunities, few will take on added risk without demanding greater compensation. The core question is *who* among an organization's stakeholders can bear the risks associated with performance more efficiently and thus at the lowest cost.
- Many companies use variable pay as a mechanism for buffering bottom-line performance during business downturns. When revenues shrivel, they automatically reduce employee compensation. Alternatively, companies may rely on layoffs. Which solution is better depends in part on the relative importance of general versus firm-specific human capital to company performance.

- Investors and employees are not positioned identically to bear risk. Investors can diversify away much of the performance risk, certainly the industry- and firm-specific components, but employees cannot diversify the risks to their labor investments. This suggests that *asymmetry* in the way risk is distributed between shareholders and employees is often better. They should not always be placed "in the same boat."
- One of the challenges in motivating and rewarding executives and employees is to determine which part of total shareholder return is due to their decisions and efforts and which part is due to market and industry volatility.
- Performance Sensitivity Analysis is a proprietary statistical method that identifies and measures the different sources of volatility in a company's total shareholder return. It can identify the portions of volatility in shareholder return that are attributable to industry-driven, market-based, and firm-specific factors. It can be used to develop better risk-adjusted measures of performance for use in incentive compensation programs. The result is stronger performance incentives for employees at a lower cost to shareholders.

PART IV

Implications

11

The Investor's Perspective

INVESTORS' CONFIDENCE HAS been shaken, and calls for transparent and complete corporate accounting are growing louder. In this atmosphere is it not borderline irresponsible for a corporation to fail to disclose information about the performance of what is usually its largest annual investment, its expenditures on human capital? That is exactly what most corporations do today.

The performance of a firm's investments in human capital must surely affect that firm's value. Investments in tangible assets such as equipment, land, buildings, inventory, and cash have always played a role in firm valuations. Rules and standards guide the calculation of tangible asset values at any point in time. As Accounting 101 teaches, calculating the value of tangible assets begins with historical cost: the price at which each asset was acquired. That value then is adjusted through depreciation to reflect loss of value through use or obsolescence. The firm's balance sheet rolls up the value of all its assets and, after reducing it by liabilities, provides us a proxy of its worth: its book value. Information on the firm's income statement provides a basis for assessing how well the company has used its tangible assets to produce revenues and profits.

However, something remains unexplained by this accounting. What an acquirer pays for a corporation almost always exceeds that corporation's book value, as does the market value of its shares. What explains this disparity?

The gap between book value and marketplace price is substantial and has grown over the years. Is this value expansion simply a function of "irrational exuberance" on the part of investors? One way to check is to determine whether the market-to-book gap closed in the wake of the American stock market collapse. Our assessment, based on valuations at year-end 2002, indicated that S&P500 companies still command a market-to-book premium of over three times book value. Although this is below the four to six times book value seen at the end of the 1990s, the gap between tangible asset value and market value remains appreciable.

What is the source of this discrepancy? Why do accounting measures fail to reflect the ways investors appraise corporate value? What is missing? The answer is intangible assets. Although their values are not reflected in corporate balance sheets, investors recognize and are willing to pay for those assets.

Intangible Assets and Measurement

Intangible assets take many forms. A recognized brand is one of the easiest to understand: the name Coca-Cola, the McDonald's golden arches, the Nike "swoosh." Each represents enormous value. The "relationship value" within a network of trusted suppliers and customers is another intangible asset that is not found on the balance sheet.

In many cases a company's greatest intangible asset relates to human capital. Human capital is the wellspring of many of the other intangibles valued by investors. Increasingly, investors see human capital as the engine of innovation in knowledge-economy companies, the source of winning strategies and business models.

Although the importance of human capital is undeniable, the calculation of its value is often a puzzle. Unlike a piece of equipment, the system of human capital practices deployed to create and manage human assets in an organization has no "purchase price" from which value can be determined. This lack of a transactional starting point led Martin Fridson and Fernando Alvarez to conclude, "Everybody acknowledges the value of a company's 'human capital' . . . but no one has devised a means of valuing it precisely."[1]

Human capital is different from tangible assets and other intangible assets in that companies can never wholly control people's motivation and productivity in the way they control physical capital. In addition, there is little unique value to a business in its employees' knowledge, skills, and experience since in principle they are available to all companies at prevailing market rates. It is only when they are combined with a company's management system and/or transformed into firm-specific capability that unique and lasting advantage is created.

That management system is a major determinant of economic productivity, yet it generally is overlooked in corporate valuations. The reasons for that omission include the difficulty of measuring the

Origins of the Human Capital Concept

To economists, the term *human capital* has a very specific meaning that appeared initially in the works of Jacob Mincer, Theodore Schultz and Gary Becker in the late 1950s and early 1960s and was developed further by Sherwin Rosen and Richard Freeman, among others.[2] Both Becker and Schultz won Nobel Prizes largely for their work in this area and made human capital a core concept in labor economics.

The original work in this area attempted to achieve a better understanding of decisions made by individuals and firms to increase the quality of labor through expenditures on education, training, and on-the-job learning. Individuals and organizations incur costs in improving labor quality in the hope of generating future returns through enhanced productivity and earnings. Therefore, their decisions are *investment* decisions. The analogy to capital investment has stuck despite recognized differences between human capital and physical and financial capital. Organizations invest current resources on training in the hope of generating higher productivity over time.

In 1985 Leif Edvinsson, the chief knowledge officer of Skandia Corporation, offered perhaps the first comprehensive report of human capital as a component of his firm's annual report. To Edvinsson, human capital embodied the sum of the knowledge, skills, and practical experiences possessed by an organization's employees and contractors.

management system and the fact that human capital is not a fungible asset. It cannot be traded or exchanged easily; more specifically, it is essentially indivisible and cannot be collateralized to secure other assets. Moreover, there are no markets for exchanging claims on future labor

Figure 11-1

The Intangible Asset Family

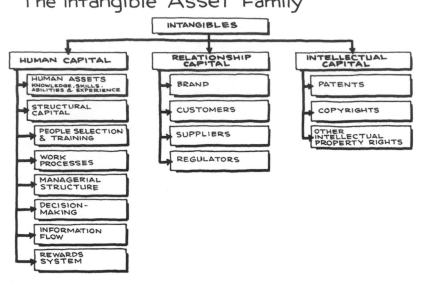

services. Also, human capital is only one of several types of intangible assets held by firms, as Figure 11-1 indicates. Despite the difficulties of measuring intangibles, many companies are making the effort.

Let us say at the outset that whereas estimating an asset value for human capital is useful for investors, it is clearly less useful for managers. The dollar value of an asset, although interesting, does not tell managers much. A manager's primary focus should be on putting in place and running the systems that create value from intangibles. Managers should know what creates value for investors and how to best manage it.

For the last 30 years attempts have been made to link human capital to shareholder value. Many approaches have been tried to proxy for a linkage or a way of measuring human capital, but all have failed to make the linkage explicit. Still, for investors (and some managers) who do not yet have access to the facts, those approaches represent a step in the right direction. Let's consider several of the most notable approaches.

The Lev Approach

Baruch Lev, an accounting professor at New York University's Stern School of Business, has for the last 30 years been pursuing measures for the value of intangibles. He stated to an interviewer that "one of the major problems with today's accounting systems is that they are still based on transactions, such as sales." As he explained:

> In the current, knowledge-based economy much of the value creation or destruction precedes, sometimes by years, the occurrence of transactions. The successful development of a drug creates considerable value, but actual transactions, such as sales, may take years to materialize. Until then, the accounting system does not register any value created in contrast to the investments made into R&D, which are fully expensed. This difference, between how the accounting system is handling value created and is handling investments into value creation, is the major reason for the growing disconnect between market values and financial information.[3]

Lev's proposed solution is to capitalize residual earnings: What is left over after the expected return from a business's financial and physical assets has been removed. These residual earnings are then attributed to intangibles. Lev's approach makes it possible for outside investors who are not privy to accounting and management system details to determine the relative differences in intangibles across competing firms. Lev's approach has the advantage of being less subjective than many of the following alternatives. Also, it can be implemented by using publicly available data, and the resulting valuations are not subject to the daily volatility of the stock market.

Further decomposing residual earnings to determine what proportion is attributable to different types of intangibles—people, brands, patents—would provide an additional degree of precision that would help isolate the earnings contribution of human capital per se. This would enable an investor to assess how well or poorly a company does at growing its human capital value.

Workonomics™

The Boston Consulting Group's Workonomics™ attempts to identify workforce (intangible asset) measures that are in effect the counterparts of traditional (tangible asset) accounting measures.[4] For example, workforce utilization is seen as the counterpart to asset utilization;

a workforce development plan is the counterpart of a capital investment plan. This approach is logical and appealing. However, it does not provide a means of pointing to which of the many possible measures are the few, most important indicators for a company to track. Ideally, a measure's importance should be determined by the extent to which that measure reflects a human capital attribute or management practice that is known to drive a firm's performance.

The Spencer Stuart Human Capital Market Index

The Spencer Stuart Human Capital Market Index (HCMI) is unique in its melding of financial market and labor market considerations. Its goal is to establish the rel-

---

Shareholder Value

Shareholder value analysis (SVA), which first was developed by Professor William Fruhan of Harvard Business School, is often a useful starting point when one is asking, What creates value? SVA rests on the assumption that a predictable relationship exists between market premiums and return on equity. Other value-based management models have followed, such as Economic Value Added (EVA), trademarked by Stern Stewart, which builds on Fruhan's model by subtracting the cost of capital from operating profit.

These approaches are used in an attempt to identify the value drivers that influence profitability. For example, a value driver for a maker of computer chips might be error rates in chip manufacturing. The chip maker does not simply want to know that error rates and profits are linked; it wants to know what will drive down error rates most efficiently.

Human capital valuation should pick up where SVA and other value-based management approaches leave off. It must determine the specific workforce and human capital practices and policies that account for economic profit and shareholder return and then report measures that are specific to those drivers.

---

ative value of executive talent—one part of overall human capital—at any point in time and then track changes in that value.

The index has four components:

- The number of executive jobs open relative to the number of unemployed executives; this is an indicator of the competitiveness of the labor market for executive talent.
- The ratio of gross domestic product to the number of people in the workforce between the ages of 35 and 55; executive talent is located primarily in that age bracket.
- The difference between the high and low stock prices divided by the average stock price as an indicator of company-specific

volatility; the value of management is said to increase with volatility.

- The ratio of market value to book value; this is an expression of the value of intangible human capital.

Changes in any of these components will change the overall index. For example, if there is a decline in the number of people in the workforce between the ages of 35 and 55, the value of executive talent will rise, all else being equal. The usefulness of the index would seem to lie in making statements about the changing value of a portion of a country's human capital. Its application to individual companies, however, is unclear.

The Watson Wyatt Human Capital Index®

This approach to intangibles converts the many human capital practices in an organization into a single number.[5] The resulting index does not address human capital attributes such as the number of employees in a certain age range; instead, its focus is on consolidating information about activities and programs. The data supporting the index come from a checklist-like survey that typically is completed by an individual in the human resources (HR) function.[6]

Bruce Pfau and Ira Kay have reported success in correlating responses to this survey with various financial measures of a company's performance, including shareholder return.[7] According to those researchers, some practices, such as the use of broad-based stock options, are positive contributors to business performance. Others are destroyers of value, with developmental training (for future jobs) and 360-degree feedback being two examples. The index thus becomes a basis for making universal assertions about the right and wrong human capital practices for all companies, all workforces, and all times—a seductive approach because of its simplicity but one that all too often fails when applied to individual companies.

The Balanced Scorecard

The Balanced Scorecard developed by David Norton and Robert Kaplan has been an especially popular approach for discerning the leading activities, along with their respective measures, responsible for financial and customer outcomes. There have been many views of strategy over the years. Remember SWOT (strengths, weaknesses, opportunities, threats) in the 1960s, portfolio approaches in the 1970s, Porter's model in the 1980s, and core competencies and strategic intent in the 1990s? The Balanced Scorecard does not contest those approaches but tries to focus on a few of their shortcomings and implementation practicalities.

Based on research conducted in the 1980s with a small group of companies, the Balanced Scorecard proposes that accounting measures are too narrow, too backward-looking, and too inclined to measure aggregated results. Norton and Kaplan suggest that other factors, ones that speak to the effectiveness and sustainability of systems, processes, and activities, should be included in any measurement system.[8]

Despite the popularity of this approach to measuring and managing, many attempts to implement the Balanced Scorecard have been unsuccessful. A key reason for those failures is the inability to determine which processes and innovation activities truly are linked to customer and financial outcomes. In the absence of clear linkages, Balanced Scorecard implementations often default to applying templates of "best practices," a "bad practice" if there ever was one.

Information for Investors

None of these approaches has gained broad acceptance in the investment community. Nevertheless, the importance of human capital, as difficult to measure as it may be, is apparent to the professionals who are most familiar with asset valuation, according to a 2003 survey by CFO Research Services. That survey asked financial professionals in 180 large organizations to assess the impact of their companies' human capital on business objectives such as profitability, customer satisfaction, and innovation. Those financial professionals overwhelmingly identified human capital as a main driver of almost every key metric of business performance, including profits.

In light of the acknowledged impact of human capital on the measures that matter to investors—customer satisfaction, profitability, and so forth—one has to wonder what investors are doing to obtain information about this critical but intangible asset. To what extent is the professional investment community inquiring about human capital issues? What issues are being considered? Which human capital measures, if any, are these people obtaining from companies?

The CFO Research Services survey provides some of the answers. According to its findings, financial executives in 49 percent of the publicly traded companies surveyed reported that the investment community was probing human capital issues to at least a moderate extent. Only 15 percent indicated that no one was asking.[9]

The level of interest in human capital issues appears to vary by industry. For example, financial services and computer-related firms reported greater attention to human capital issues by the investment community than did manufacturers. Even then, the focus of attention on human capital was limited. According to the survey, financial analysts who asked about human capital issues focused primarily on the leadership team and the existence of succession plans. A survey conducted in 2002 by the Conference Board involving 102 mostly large North American (63 percent) and European (37 percent) companies reported that investors were interested in information about human capital.[10] Just over a third of the respondents saw investors requesting measures such as employee retention, compensation, and workforce profiles.

Some of those requests have come from institutional investors with an intense interest in human capital. Consider Calvert Asset Management Company, which manages more than $8 billion of investment capital by using "socially responsible investment" criteria. To be an investment target for Calvert, a company must measure up to various social and environmental criteria, including workforce diversity, labor-management relations, workplace safety, and working conditions. CalPERS (the California Public Employees Retirement System) is an even larger investor and has been a pioneer in the movement to obtain and evaluate information about human capital from the companies in which it invests. CalPERS focuses on things such as employee turnover and opportunities for education in judging its investment candidates. Several European-based money managers also seek human capital data, SAM (Sustainable Asset Management) and Friends, Ivory & Sime among them. Those institutional investors seek out companies that meet two tests:

1. Demonstrated social responsibility
2. Acceptable risk-adjusted returns to shareholders

The companies that pass the first test are subjected to more conventional financial analysis that determines whether they pass the second test.

The use of human capital information to screen out socially unacceptable investments has been practiced for a long time. Calvert, for example, has been in existence for over a quarter of a century. In contrast, discerning which companies are best at creating value from human capital assets is a more recent, almost nascent pursuit. However, the importance of this information in investment decision making is apparent. Over 60 percent of the respondents to a 1999 survey conducted by Ernst & Young said that nonfinancial data drove 20 to 50 percent of their investment decisions.[11]

Interest in alternative investment metrics, some of which capture human capital information, is not limited to large institutional investors. Popular magazines have joined the action. Allison Kopicki and Tom Contiliano explained in *Bloomberg Personal Finance* how investors can use "key performance indicators" (KPIs) to supplement traditional measures of company performance.[12] Some KPIs can be calculated from figures reported in different parts of corporate financial statements; others require the disclosure of new information. KPIs linked to human capital include revenue per employee, changes in the attributes of corporate officers (e.g., cumulative experience in and out of the industry, diversity of background, global representation), and the ratio of R&D expenditures to sales.

To make matters more difficult for investors, some key performance indicators can be misleading, such as employee turnover. Many people regard employee turnover as a key indicator of how well a company is doing with its human capital asset. "People turnover is important in every industry" Kopicki and Contiliano report. The Conference Board agrees: "High turnover produces more mistakes, lower customer satisfaction, increased workload, and lower morale."[13]

Blanket proclamations such as these are intuitively appealing but often misleading because the link between turnover and organizational performance can vary widely across industries and firms. Further, who is turning over in an organization generally matters much more than the percentage of turnover. For example, 20 percent voluntary turnover among personnel who are either easy to recruit, never interact with customers, or need little training may have little impact on business performance. The same percentage of voluntary turnover in the R&D department of a high-tech company, however, could be crippling over time; those highly trained defectors would be difficult and costly to replace and would take significant intellectual capital with them, and their departures surely would set back important projects.

In some cases, such as turnover of poor performers, low turnover may do considerable harm to a business, such as the company Digitt that was described in Chapter 7. Those changes surely would have passed muster according to this narrowly defined turnover standard, yet low turnover was the single most powerful indicator that Digitt was depreciating its human capital assets. Investors clearly need more discriminating measures than these.

The test of whether turnover is a useful KPI is that it have an impact on business performance. This test must be performed separately for each business. Using a Business Impact Modeling approach, we have assessed the impact of employee turnover in many companies in several industries. In one company, a business-to-business services firm, turnover was running in excess of 20 percent annually and dramatically affected profitability. Thus turnover was a key performance indicator for that company. In a company in the food service industry substantially higher turnover was the norm, exceeding 100 percent in some years. However, turnover in that company had only a minor impact on a key business performance measure, earnings. Tracking turnover in that company and attacking it with expensive programs would be a fool's errand. In a third company, a financial services firm, employee turnover substantially reduced business performance, but only in certain employee segments. Here the *overall* employee turnover rate mattered little; it was the turnover rate in one segment of the workforce that affected the company's financial performance. Thus a segment-specific turnover number would be a useful KPI; a blanket number would reveal little of value.

From Platitudes to Useful Information

Although investors search for useful human capital metrics, few companies provide them. In their place companies offer platitudes such as "people are our most important asset." Fortunately, there are exceptions, and they may be harbingers of a new era of human capital reporting. National City Corporation is one of them. National City is among the largest banks in the United States, with assets in excess of $100 billion. Its chairman and CEO, David Daberko, went far beyond platitudes in his letter to stockholders in the company's 2001 annual report, in which he detailed National City's programmatic effort to change its value proposition to customers and cited the human capital practices that were being changed to support that proposition. Those investments, he acknowledged, would hurt short-term earnings but were essential to the longer-term success of the enterprise. Daberko reminded shareholders of those ongoing investments in his 2003 annual report letter, citing their importance to the company's operating strategy.

Another highly regarded bank, First Tennessee National Corporation, briefs financial analysts about human capital issues. Believing that its people practices are a source of competitive advantage, First Tennessee shares detailed human capital data with analysts, including the linkage between the retention of high-performing employees and business results.[14]

Third-party information vendors have begun to supplement the trickle of human capital data released by corporations. That information is narrowly focused, however, on corporate governance and the management of high-level employees. Interest in that information has risen dramatically in the wake of the heavily publicized scandals at

Human Capital, Productivity, and Shareholder Value

As part of our R&D effort, Douglas D. Dwyer conducted powerful research on productivity and shareholder value. That research revealed that there are substantial and often persistent differences in the productivity of manufacturing plants in the United States. Further, it was found that investors place a premium on firms with highly productive plants. In fact, on average a 10 percent gain in plant productivity that persists over time translates into roughly a 5 percent gain in market value. This suggests that persistent productivity advantages are in themselves a form of intangible assets.

This relationship between plant productivity and market value holds even after one accounts for other known drivers of a firm's market value, such as its physical and financial assets and its investments in R&D and advertising. This indicates that there are other reasons for differences in plant productivity, one of them being human capital management. That is, systematic differences between plants in their human capital and the way they manage it contribute to productivity and shareholder value.[15]

Enron and WorldCom. These vendors, such as Standard & Poor's, GovernanceMetrics International, and The Corporate Library, rate companies in terms of executive compensation, information disclosure, board structure and process, acquisition strategy, and related factors. The idea behind these rating systems is that nontraditional performance data, including information on how companies manage, organize, reward, and offer the right incentives to management, are important factors in investment analysis. At a minimum, the ratings indicate the likelihood that a company will experience a governance-based meltdown that could cost investors their entire stakes.

Although substantive reporting of human capital practices remains more the exception than the rule in U.S. companies, in Europe the reporting of human capital indicators is becoming required, often as part of a broader obligation to report social, ethical, and environmental indicators. France currently requires such reporting, Denmark will implement similar requirements in 2005, and the United Kingdom has the matter under consideration.

Although no similar legislation is on the horizon for U.S. companies, it is worth noting that some U.S. regulatory and governing bodies already require certain types of human capital reporting. The Joint Commission on Accreditation of Healthcare Organizations, for example, is implementing a requirement that hospitals report a minimum of two HR utilization indicators that have been judged to be relevant to the quality of patient care. The short list of potential indicators includes turnover, overtime, sick time, nursing care hours per patient day, and staff satisfaction. Other health-care providers soon may face similar reporting requirements.

What Information Should Investors Look For?

If you are an investor, you're probably asking yourself, "What type of human capital information should I be looking for?" Our suggestion is that investors look for three types of human capital information. The first concerns knowledge, skills, experience, and educational credentials. Companies that can provide detailed data about their workforces are attending to this intangible asset. The second type of information concerns investments being made in the workforce and the return on those investments. Finally, investors should seek information about how a company is making use of its human assets through practices of supervision, talent development, rewards, and the like. Those practices often are out of everyday view but can be glimpsed from stories in the business press and from internal corporate publications and communications.

Fuller Disclosure Is on the Way

Although the state of reporting on intangibles is generally poor at this time, the future looks promising. This *must* be the case because of the growing impact of knowledge, relationships, intellectual capital, and other intangibles on the fortunes of enterprises. Academics, the U.S. Securities and Exchange Commission, and investor groups are pressing to make intangibles more tangible for the investing public.

Myth Buster: Find the One Best Way to Manage Human Capital

Don't fall into the trap of looking for the one best way to manage human capital. What works well for one company may be the kiss of death for another. Indeed, if companies come off as mere imitators of the people practices of others, look elsewhere. Instead, assess a company on the basis of the amount of information it can provide about its internal labor market and how well that market serves business objectives. Seek an indication that the company understands the impact of human capital on key measures of business performance. Companies that are truly in command of their human capital practices should be able to speak to such issues, including the financial return on specific investments such as training and variable pay.

From an investor's standpoint, then, the critical thing to look for is information on the sophistication and skill with which a company manages what is often its largest investment.

The term *full disclosure* will take on a broader meaning. Information about human assets, which once was the domain of socially conscious investors, has a growing constituency in the financial community. Although the information being sought today is superficial, this may be a function of the paucity of solid reported data about human capital and the ways corporations measure and manage it. However, with the growing pressure for greater disclosure, we expect this situation to change.

As human capital data become more readily available, count on financial analysts to develop methods for integrating them into investment decisions. The greatest challenge will be knowing which of many possible measures are truly indicative of a firm's ability optimize its human capital. Finding the right measures for each company's unique context will be the key to better investment decisions.

If you are a CEO or financial executive, you might do your share price a favor by getting ahead in the disclosure game. Here are two things you should do:

1. Remember that investors cannot act upon what they cannot see or understand. Thus, if you are building the value of your human capital assets progressively but are not disclosing them, don't expect investors to reflect that progress in your share price. If you're treating human capital as a key asset, share the news. Your competitors cannot easily use that information to imitate you (and do so at their peril), but investors can use it to value your organization appropriately.

2. Get the facts and report them to investors. Understand the strengths and weaknesses of your company's internal labor market and communicate how you are implementing the changes needed to overcome any weaknesses. Develop solid metrics, track them, and report them. In particular, get the facts on what attributes and practices contribute the most to important outcomes for your business. Communicating that information to investors can truly differentiate you and your firm from the crowd.

Key Points

- Intangible assets, including human capital and its management, contribute substantially to the value of a company. However, there are no widely accepted conventions for valuing intangible assets.
- Investors' interest in human capital is increasing. Only a few companies have distinguished themselves in the disclosure of information about their human capital, how it is managed, and the impact on business performance.
- At this time investors have no magic formulas or easy-to-calculate ratios to look at in assessing a company's ability to cre-

ate value from its intangible human assets. Until those things are available, they should look for evidence that a company's leadership is in command of the facts about its workforce and about how workforce attributes and people management practices relate to business performance.

- The trend is toward fuller disclosure of intangible assets.

12

New Roles for Chief Executive Officers and Other Leaders

E ARLIER CHAPTERS IN this book laid out the bedrock principles of human capital strategy and used a number of cases to illustrate their applications. Companies derive substantial benefits when those principles are implemented properly. When that happens, the drivers of employee productivity and barriers to human performance can be identified and addressed. Executives and managers have the facts they need to make good decisions about the people side of the business. In many cases the impact of decisions about human capital on both performance and financial results can be predicted with a high degree of certainty. Executives finally can make the most of a critical asset.

The approach described in this book—a new science of human capital management—has great potential for improving business results. That potential, however, may not be fully realized under old organizational arrangements. Traditional divisions of responsibility between functions may become impediments to managing human capital optimally. Human capital is a strategic issue that has no functional boundaries. The increased attention on the part of boards and investors to human capital issues should energize everyone. The data needed to find the human capital drivers of value, for example, are not the province of human resources (HR), finance, marketing, quality control, or any other single function. It is necessary to cut across functional boundaries to obtain, analyze, interpret, and act on those facts and relationships properly.

To realize the potential of this new approach to managing human capital it is necessary to obtain the participation and encouragement of leaders in all the major functions of an organization. Their involvement may require a change in roles for key people. This chapter examines those new roles, starting with the chief executive officer (CEO), and examines how leaders can make the most of a firm's human capital strategy.

The Role of the CEO

The breadth of a CEO's job is considerable. When reduced to its essentials, however, that job is about optimizing the long-term return from the assets placed at the company's disposal. Those assets include physical plant and equipment and financial capital from shareholders, creditors, and ongoing operations. Of course, they also include human capital and the systems that are in place to manage it.

As earlier chapters have made clear, these intangible assets are usually the least understood and least optimized. At the same time, the outside world of investors and securities analysts is beginning to ask questions about the quality of people assets and how well they are being developed, retained, and utilized. The net result is an opportunity for CEOs and other executives to improve business performance and communicate something new and valuable to investors. Doing that requires two things: looking inside and looking outside.

Looking Inside

Looking inside is concerned with resource allocation and the alignment of resources with strategy. Let's consider resource allocation first.

Allocation

If our argument that employees should be approached as capital assets is correct, financial executives should stop viewing employees as an expense and start treating them as an investment. Once they have done that, they should ask the following questions:

- *What is the actual size of our investment in human capital?* Major components of that investment can be calculated readily, such as wages and benefit costs. Other components of the total investment may not be well known to organizations, such as the cost of leadership development tactics. Determining the level of investment being made in human capital is the first step in optimizing its long-term return.
- *How is human capital managed as an asset in this company?* What are the facts about how we acquire, develop, motivate, retain, and deploy our people? How well are we serving the needs of our business strategy? Answers to these questions emerge from an analysis of the internal labor market dynamics unique to every enterprise.
- *Which attributes of our people and which of our people practices affect business results, and how much?* Answering these questions requires formal analysis. The facts that emerge from that analysis are the key to making strategic human capital decisions.
- *Are the returns from our people investments satisfactory?* How can we best redirect our investments to achieve better returns and thus enhance our business success?

There is no doubt that isolating the returns from human capital investments from those attributable to other investments (technology, for example) is difficult in some circumstances. Nonetheless, the returns from discrete people practices and programs can be measured. Examples include investments in leadership development, retention of key employees, and targeted training programs. Do those programs produce a positive return? How much of a return? CEOs should ask questions like these. This is not a rhetorical exercise. Answers that are based on facts should be demanded.

Alignment

Aligning people practices with business strategy should be a constant concern. Everyone in business understands in principle the purpose and power of alignment. Alignment assures that everyone from the executive suite to the mail room understands the organization's strategy and the way his or her job contributes to it.

Several cases in this book have demonstrated that people practices also must be aligned with higher organizational goals. Remember the global manufacturing company described in Chapter 1? That company's goals of profitability and product quality were undermined by a career development practice that deliberately moved managers around rapidly. Those managers were learning general business skills at the cost of technical depth. The case of Digitt was also instructive. Digitt liked to think of itself as a company that honored and rewarded performance, and performance was what it needed to make its strategy work. However, the facts revealed a different picture: Digitt rewarded years of service more than it rewarded performance. Worse, even the poorest-performing employees were rewarded if they had the good luck to be members of teams that did well. As often as not their bonuses matched those of top performers. Those cases underscored the negative effects of misalignment on strategy.

The lessons for a CEO from those cases are clear:

- As you develop a business strategy, make sure you have the people resources capable of supporting it.
- Align people practices with that strategy but never assume that practices are aligned. Get the facts.

Looking Outside

For CEOs, two key outward-looking activities that relate to growth are acquisitions and investor relations.

Acquisitions

Chapter 8 examined the problems that corporations face when they get new resources through acquisition. There is good reason to believe that the poor results of acquisitions often are caused by neglect of the human capital aspects of those deals and failure to integrate the new people into the various businesses properly. This is where a savvy CEO can make a huge difference in a deal's outcome. Here is some advice:

- Be very cognizant of the differences in human capital between the acquiring organization and the target enterprise. Uncover and evaluate the facts about the workforces that are coming together. Those facts should inform your decisions.
- Remember that predeal due diligence usually focuses on

quantifiable balance sheet factors. Human capital issues generally are overlooked during due diligence even though they are often the most important parts of the deal.

- Estimate the potential scope of integration. Should the target company be fully integrated with the acquirer, partially integrated, or operated as a separate portfolio company? Differences in human capital and people practices can help a CEO find the answer.
- Always approach the combined organizations as a system. A change in one is likely to affect the other.

Investor Relations

Many securities analysts and a number of key institutional investors are looking beyond tradition-bound financial statements and current growth rates when they size up companies. They are asking about the "intangibles," including human capital, that command market premiums over book value. As was explained in Chapter 11, investors' attention to the people side of the business is growing. As a result, CEOs with a powerful story to tell about their people can expect an attentive audience. Those CEOs can differentiate their companies—and potentially garner higher share prices—if they can make a case that the following things are true:

- They have metrics in place that track human capital performance.
- They have a strategy for making the most of human capital.
- Their human assets are strengthened continually through rewards, training, career development, and targeted recruiting.
- People practices are aligned with the business strategy.
- Human assets are being allocated to their most productive uses.

If you are the CEO and have a powerful story to tell about your people, make that part of your investor communications. Don't hide your light under a bushel. If you don't have a strong story to tell, build one from the principles and practices advocated in this book. Otherwise you may not be able to differentiate yourself from rivals in your industry.

New Applications for Financial Disciplines

The modern chief financial officer (CFO) is usually the key adviser to the CEO and the board of directors. It is the CFO, after all, who assures that an organization is capable of meeting its financial obligations. The CFO is also responsible for obtaining the financial capital required to execute the business strategy. That capital must be deployed to its highest uses. When other executives advocate new initiatives, the CFO often plays the critical role of a skeptic, challenging assumptions and projections and tempering wishful thinking with objective analysis.

The CFO is also the master of measuring and monitoring. Indeed, the finance function audits transactions and sniffs out the costs and profitability generated by almost every operation. Want to know the average return on assets for the last five years? Whether financial performance in the company is improving or flagging? Which products are most profitable? Ask the CFO.

Despite their propensity for measurement, however, few financial executives have taken the measure of human capital. Only 16 percent say that they have anything more than a moderate understanding of returns from what is often the company's largest single investment— human capital—according to a survey done by CFO Research Services. Fourteen percent profess to be clueless (see Figure 12-1).[1] This poor state of understanding about human capital returns among every corporation's most skilled number crunchers suggests two things:

1. Many, if not most, companies are unable to apply financial discipline to their largest single investment.
2. Many CFOs are not equipped to give advice about resource allocation for the people side of the business.

This also explains why so few financial executives explicitly consider the value of human capital when decisions about layoffs are made. Knowledge, experience, and informational "nodes" in organizations— all assets with long-term value—are lost whenever this year's books are balanced by cutting payroll. However, only 38 percent of the respondents admitted to weighing those losses against the benefits of cost savings in the CFO Research Services survey. In the same vein, 30 percent of financial executives confessed to paying little or no attention to the future value of the individuals they let go during downturns.[2]

Figure 12-1

To What Extent Do You Know The Return On Your Aggregate Investment In Human Capital?

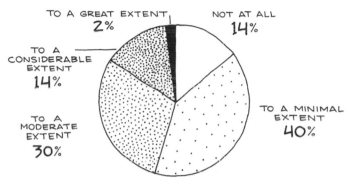

Source: *Human Capital Management: The CFO's Perspective* (Boston: CFO Publishing Corp., 2003), 3.

Fortunately, this situation is changing. More and more financial executives are recognizing human capital as a key driver of customer satisfaction, innovation, and profitability: the underpinnings of long-term value creation. Also, they are getting involved through greater partnering with HR managers and by factoring human capital into their valuations of acquisition targets. Many financial executives are seeking larger roles in decisions about human capital. Undoubtedly, some of this increased involvement is measurement-oriented, such as sponsoring the implementation of nonfinancial measures of performance to complement the financial measures. Although measures such as employee satisfaction should not be ignored, a financial executive should not be satisfied with nonfinancial measures that cannot be proved to be related to financial outcomes.

The measurement-based approach described in this book offers new tools for gauging the impact of human capital attributes and practices on business performance. Business Impact Modeling, for example, can enable finance executives for the first time to assess the likely returns of further human capital investments against the likely returns of alternative investments. The net effect of this new approach will redefine the role of CFOs, broadening their capabilities and responsibilities in the realm of human capital. Best of all, a CFO's expanded role will rest on a firm foundation of facts. A closer working relationship with the HR side of the organization will enhance the ability of the two to come together as informed strategic partners to drive business results.

If you are a financial executive, it is time to examine the issues raised in this section. The more informed you are about human capital returns and the investment aspects of people programs, the better an adviser you will be to the CEO and the board of directors. Becoming more informed calls for greater partnering with the head of HR. Working together, you can develop appropriate tracking metrics and find better ways to evaluate the economic returns of costly people programs.

A Different Future for HR

The HR function has come a long way. The business skills and acumen of HR leaders have increased, and their strategic importance continues to ascend with the increasing importance of human capital to business success. Organizations now look to HR to deliver the right human assets and to cultivate and manage those assets in ways that demonstrably return value to the enterprise. HR is no longer simply leading a war to acquire talent or handle back-office tasks.

Although HR is rising in the corporate pecking order, it still has a long way to go. It remains outside the strategic circle of many organizations, where it is perceived as a collection of programs or as a cost center absorbed with keeping payroll and personnel records, assuring compliance with hiring and firing rules, handling benefit programs, and doing other transactional activities. None of those very necessary activities, however, provide competitive differentiation for the organization. The result is that the head of HR is not at the table when new strategy is developed.

This situation is changing. We see a different future for HR as corporations start taking human capital strategy seriously. That future probably will coincide with structural changes within the HR function.

One significant change has been under way for some time, in fact. The transactional activities that currently dominate so much of HR management and are at the heart of the ubiquitous HR-as-cost-center perception are being moved out of the HR function in many cases.

Those transactions are being given over to outside vendors or, as a result of new technology, being given to the employees to manage. This already is happening with payroll and benefits administration at many firms, and why not? Those activities are not the ones that create shareholder value or competitive advantage. Delegating them to vendors or employees may free up the resources and attention required to advance the strategic agenda. When it is implemented properly, employee self-service reduces costs, and outside vendors can realize economies of scale better than the HR function can. Further, vendors serving many companies are likely to attain efficiencies that are not possible within the firm and pass them along as savings to their customers.

Work by the Society for Human Resource Management (SHRM) points to a possible bifurcation of the HR function as it evolves.[3] Administrative functions such as technology, call centers, and outside partner management will be run by core HR functional specialists, while thought leadership and strategic direction of human capital management will rest with a smaller group of professionals. The core HR departments are likely to be smaller in the future, and increasingly more decisions about human capital will move to line managers. This will be accomplished only by the smaller and more impactful strategic group providing the information directly to managers.

Whether or not the transactional parts of the job stays under the HR roof, the HR function almost certainly will take on greater strategic responsibility than has been the case historically. In some organizations a strong centralized HR function may emerge that oversees and coordinates human capital strategy across all parts of the enterprise. However, centralization is not a prerequisite for being strategic. The HR function in other organizations may be strategic yet decentralized. For example, each business unit in an enterprise may have a strong HR function that serves its strategic interests without reliance on a central HR office. That type of decentralized arrangement is most likely to appear in organizations with diverse business units that have distinctive strategies.

Whether decentralized or not, the HR function will take on more strategic responsibility. However, we also believe that with regard to human capital the "strategy pie" will expand. That is, human capital will take up an increasingly larger share of the strategic agenda of a firm. HR's slice of that pie will grow, but so will the slices claimed by the

CEO, the CFO, and business unit leaders. Simply put, human capital strategy will become a shared responsibility of organizational leaders as attention to it expands.

The changing agenda for the HR function that is elevating its strategic role is being signaled by a small number of U.S. corporations that have repositioned titles and renamed positions. This is analogous to what has happened with many information technology managers, who now find the title "chief information officer" on their business cards. On the HR side of the house, typical titles such as "vice president, human resources" are giving way to titles such as "chief human resources officer" (CHRO) and "chief human capital officer" (CHCO). Titles, of course, have to be backed up by substance, by capabilities and methods for delivering on the promise of the new titles and responsibilities. The capabilities to get the facts and focus needed to deliver as a strategic partner now exist, and there is likely to be more repositioning as those capabilities are extended. This trend will continue to the extent that HR managers do the following:

- Identify the true drivers of performance on the people side of the business
- Model the interactions between programs and employee behaviors, including unintended consequences
- Forecast the impacts of proposed people programs and investments
- Identify where cuts can be made without hurting performance
- Use analytic tools to identify optimal points of investment

Implications for Other Executives

So far we have considered the implications of the new science of human capital management for CEOs, CFOs, and senior HR executives. Those implications, of course, do not stop with these three managerial classes. In this section we briefly consider implications for leaders in two other functions: marketing and quality assurance.

Marketing

In many organizations the marketing function has a deep and detailed understanding of customer behavior. The attributes of the most profitable customers often are known: where they live, where they shop, how much they use the Internet, their ages, their estimated annual incomes, their expectations for the services or products they buy, and so on. These are very usable facts. Advertising uses them to make its messages better targeted, better crafted, and more effective.

Facts about the links between customer behavior and an organization's human capital practices and workforce attributes are less known despite general acknowledgment that the way human capital is managed is critical to meeting customers' needs. The head of marketing therefore should have a strong interest in the organization's human capital strategy and become a partner in the strategy-making process. The marketing function is, after all, the function most keenly in touch with the ways in which customers are changing. Customer changes generally have implications for human capital. New skills, for example, may be required by customer-facing employees. If this is the case, the organization will have to acquire those skills in the labor market or develop them from within. That choice should involve the marketing function.

Quality Assurance

Although quality is every employee's responsibility, oversight of quality often is delegated to a separate function or a specific set of employees. In health-care systems, for example, physicians typically occupy that role. In manufacturing companies, engineers often take on that responsibility.

Like the marketing function, the quality function maintains excellent data. Also like marketing, it has a clear interest in the human capital dynamics of the enterprise since some causes of poor quality can be traced to people and the way they are managed. Indeed, the root causes of quality problems often are found in rewards, training, employee selection, supervision, and other people practices. As a result, quality managers have an interest in setting human capital strategies, if only to ensure that the workforce embodies attributes that support quality and that employees are managed in ways that meet goals involving service quality.

In Chapter 6 it was explained how the head of HR at Quest Diagnostics obtained facts about employee turnover and its impact on critical measures of business performance. The quantification of that impact grabbed top management's attention. Once the magnitude of the business problem was known, the likely returns on investments to solve the problem were reasonably predictable. Operational leaders enthusiastically embraced the need for those investments. After all, those initiatives, if successful (which they ultimately were), would boost the very measures for which they were held personally accountable: measures of operating margin, quality, and customer service. Faced with the facts, the CEO, the board, and the company's operating managers all threw their support behind the programs. In effect, the HR chief had developed a fact-based business case for change that galvanized top management. Business Impact Modeling and Internal Labor Market analysis made it possible. Whatever the future holds, it seems clear that as those tools become more prevalent, decisions about human capital will become a larger part of every manager's job.

Key Points

- Investors and analysts are beginning to press CEOs on how they are using and optimizing their human capital, the asset that most CEOs understand the least. Those who have a good story to tell will find an attentive ear in those audiences. In turn, they should ask tough questions of their function leaders, especially HR and finance, regarding how human capital is being managed and with what effect.
- Finance is taking on a larger role in strategic human capital decisions. Although financial executives were not able to assess returns on human capital investments in the past, techniques for doing that with clarity and precision are now available.
- The HR role continues to evolve toward increased responsibility for strategic objectives. Carrying out that responsibility requires a fact-based understanding of the way those objectives are served by workforce attributes and people practices.

Managing Your Personal Human Capital

INVESTORS WANT TO make sure that their financial capital is invested in enterprises that are well managed. Specifically, they want returns commensurate with the risks they take. Whether you're the CEO or a line manager, you have comparable concerns when you invest your time, energy, and ideas in your company. Like a financial investor, you want to know how well you are leveraging those personal investments. For example, you probably know where your personal savings stand and know the value of your house and car. What about your worth as an employee? Is it increasing in value? Is the return on your investment commensurate with the risks you are taking as an employee?

Unlike the rest of this book, this chapter discusses *your* personal skills, knowledge, and experience: the choices you have made as you have invested in your education, experimented with different jobs, and made trade-offs over the course of your career. Even without access to information about your company's internal labor market, you can begin to manage your own human capital with the discipline of an investor by using some of the management principles explained in Part I. As the unwritten contracts that once bound employees and employers together dissolve in greater numbers, each person should be asking, "How am I managing my most valuable personal asset?"

Toward More Self-Reliance

U.S. corporations furloughed more than a million managers and staff professionals between 1979 and 1987. A smaller but still significant wave of layoffs began rolling through the corporate world in 1999. Those events neutralized whatever illusions people had about a long-term career with a single company, let alone lifetime employment. Many people nevertheless maintain long-term employment in the middle of this turmoil. Despite what people read in the news, they find that careers in organizations are alive and well. Job longevity in the United States actually has been growing, mostly as a function of the aging of the workforce. The average tenure in large companies hovers around eight years and is even higher for salaried employees.

Although careers remain alive and well for many people, others feel like free agents. What they do from day to day seldom has the feel of permanence. Change from job to job and from company to company is anticipated—with regret by some and with relish by others. Layoffs are not the only reason many employees have begun to feel like free agents. Corporate retirement policies also have played a role. A larger share of retirement planning and investment decisions has been pushed into the hands of employees, at least in the United States.

Not many years ago the great majority of pension plans offered by U.S. companies—large and small and across industries—provided "defined benefits" at retirement; that is, they promised a specific retirement income that was based on pay level and age. The organizations made annual contributions, made the investment decisions, and assumed all the investment risks. Today more and more employees—well over a third in the United States—find themselves covered by "defined contribution" plans. Like variable-pay and pay-for-performance arrangements, those plans shift the burden of risk and decision making onto employees. They make no promise about what people will get at retirement. Such plans range from glorified savings accounts in which employees provide all the savings to profit sharing–type plans. Employees in those plans are responsible for their financial futures even if many of them are less than fully prepared to assume that responsibility.

People who regret the loss of stability that characterized the workplace climate of the past can take some comfort from the fact that several developments have made managing one's own career less daunting. First, greater access to information about opportunities has made the search easier; second, the portability of retirement assets has made job transitioning easier. In the Great Stone Age before widespread Internet service, employers had a huge advantage over their employees and job applicants. Human resource departments with access to data on competitive wage levels could tell at a glance if their wage rates were high, low, or near the middle for every position. That gave them a substantial bargaining advantage. Information asymmetry always works to the advantage of the party with the most relevant information.

What Job? What Company?

Few stories have exploded the concept of the lifetime career and the notion of corporate permanency more humorously than one told by Charles Handy in *The Age of Unreason:*

> Thirty years ago I started work in a world-famous multinational company. By way of encouragement, my employers produced an outline of my future career. 'This will be your life,' they said, 'with titles of likely jobs.' The outline ended, I remember, with myself as chief executive of a particular company in a particular far-off country. I was, at the time, suitably flattered. I left them long before I reached the heights they planned for me, and by then I knew that not only did the job they had picked out no longer exist, neither did the company I would have directed nor even the country in which I was to have operated.
>
> Thirty years ago I thought that life would be one long continuous line, sloping upward with luck. Today I know better.[1]

Today, because of Internet access, there is a more level playing field. People can find where the jobs are and learn much more about opportunities, including compensation comparisons. For example, CareerJournal.com posts thousands of executive and professional jobs, and Monster.com nearly a million jobs in 22 countries. CareerJournal, Monster.com, Hotjobs, Careerbuilder, and other sites help job seekers and every person who is unhappy with his or her current situation. They also have helped companies reduce recruiting costs and announce job openings to a broader pool of potential candidates. Given the number of daily "hits" on those Web sites, one can imagine the number of hours spent by disgruntled employees searching for better jobs—often on company time! Employees who are not satisfied with the return they are getting on their skills and know-how can scan the corporate universe quickly for alternatives. The more people who use those job networks, the more valuable they become.

More information and more equal access to it are slowly creating a more efficient market for human capital, as they did earlier for financial capital. This development, if it continues, will have huge implications for individuals, companies, and the larger economy. Consider what is known about the impact of efficiency on free markets. Greater efficiency eliminates barriers between willing buyers and sellers. It reduces transaction costs and makes disparities between opportunities more visible. It narrows differences between what one party is asking and what another party is willing to pay. More important, greater efficiency directs resources away from moribund enterprises and to those with greater return opportunities. We have observed this in financial markets for a long time and now see something similar happening in labor markets.

Although the trajectory of efficiency appears promising, today's labor markets are fairly inefficient. Theoretically, greater access to job information should lead to better matches of people with employers. The fact that a high percentage of jobholders say that they would change jobs if they had the opportunity can be taken as evidence that many individuals and employers are not well matched. Part of this certainly is explained by the "transaction costs" of changing jobs, which often exceed the benefits. Alternatively, either companies are not providing individuals with sufficiently accurate information or individual workers are failing to obtain or use information properly. Whatever the cause, poor matching can be costly to both companies and individual employees. Next we'll explore in greater detail how these issues play out for you as an individual.

Toward a Self-Managed Career

The developments noted above all point in the direction of greater career self-management and apply to everyone: executives, managers, technical professionals, and rank-and-file employees. Companies are forcing people to take charge of their economic futures and shoulder greater responsibility for the risks and financial returns associated with them. Fortunately, greater geographic mobility, opportunities for training, and labor market information give people the means to do that. Goal definition and goal matching are the two building blocks of career self-management.

Goal Definition

What are your primary occupational goals right now: money, progressive promotions, a growing level of responsibility, intrinsic growth, personal gratification? You may want to broaden your range of experience and competencies or, conversely, become more and more skilled in your current specialty. Work-life choices often dictate goals, such as staying in the same community. Whatever goals you've chosen, make sure they are crystal clear.

Determining one's workplace goals is the first step toward the kind of thinking people should adopt with respect to the human capital they invest. An astute financial investor, for example, does not make a move until he or she has established an investment goal, and that goal should have a time component: short-term, intermediate, or long-term.

Although money is often not the prime motivator, the goals of human capital investment closely parallel those of financial investors. For example, financial investors cite goals that fall into any of the following four categories: safety of principal, current income, capital appreciation, and tax advantages. The first three apply directly to those who invest their human capital:

- *Safety of principal.* You don't want the value of your human capital to be diminished by obsolescence. This is a big concern for engineers and other technical professionals. You also may be concerned with the safety of social capital: protecting the relationships you have built up over time. This may incline you to remain within your current industry, geography, occupation, or employer.
- *Current income.* A high current return from your investment may override other considerations, particularly if you need a high income to put children through college, build a retirement nest egg, or meet other financial obligations. In this case you may be willing to forgo future opportunities for work that will maximize your net pay today.

- *Capital appreciation*. If you're in the early stages of your career, developing new skills and gaining experience may be a primary goal. These achievements may not pay off today, but they will build capital value and provide for higher earnings in the future. This is the basis of apprenticeships and internships that pay less than what an individual might earn in another position. Indeed, the path to capital appreciation is often one of delayed gratification. The higher lifetime incomes of college graduates are a good example of delayed gratification.

Goal Matching

Once you have defined your goals, identify a company or companies with which you can pursue them effectively. Start with the company for which you are working currently. Is there a match between your goals and the way that company deals with employees' careers? For example, if one of your goals is to become more expert at your craft, does your company encourage and reward specialization? Many do not.

Chapter 1 profiled a manufacturing company, ProductCo, whose pay and promotions agenda rewarded managers for doing the opposite of what the company needed to be successful; it put greater stock in generalists than in specialists. At TechCo we observed conflicting behaviors on the part of the company. While encouraging entrepreneurship and risk taking through its rewards, that company also enforced a regime of following rules and procedures and doing things by the book. At TechCo employees were bound to be whipsawed no matter what their goals were. No wonder the company was losing its best talent at ever-increasing rates.

The bottom line is that you always will be paddling against the current if your employer does not support or reward your goals. Thus, if you are comfortable doing things "by the numbers," find a company that rewards and encourages that type of work. If your goal is to advance progressively through the ranks, look for a company that has explicit career ladders that reward capable and ambitious individuals. *Career ladders* are formal programs for moving promising employees step by step up through the ranks, using training and various assignments to prepare them for each succeeding rung on the ladder. Those programs help employees build their personal human capital.

Risk and Return

In Chapter 10 we discussed how employees, unlike investors, cannot easily diversify their personal human capital investments. Therefore, no discussion of developing and investing human capital would be complete without dealing with risk. Every capital investment has a unique risk-return component, and human capital is no different.

In free and efficient markets an investment's level of risk is correlated positively with its expected return. Consider an investment in U.S. Treasury bills, debt securities with maturities of 90 days or less. Because the full faith and credit of the U.S. government stands behind T-bills, they are essentially riskless. Financial economists in fact use the T-bill rate as a proxy for the risk-free rate in calculating the expected returns from other types of investments.

Low-risk investments generally produce low returns. The only way to obtain a higher level of return is to take greater risks with one's capital. Financial scholars have described the relationship between risk and return by referring to the capital market line, a theoretical line that originates with the risk-free rate and intersects the expected returns of different classes of investments. Figure 13-1 indicates where familiar investment securities generally fall along the capital market line. Note the position of "Investment X." This "inefficient" investment provides its owner with the worst of both worlds: high risk and low return. A

Figure 13-1

The Risk-Reward Relationship

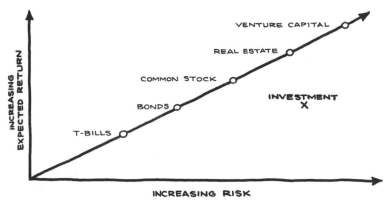

wise investor recognizes and avoids these situations, insisting that risk be commensurate with the level of return.

There is a clear relationship between the risks people take with their financial capital and the return that capital may generate. That relationship holds for human capital investments when labor markets are free and efficient. One obvious investment a person makes is in education, forgoing current earnings and investing in credentials and new skills in the hope of getting greater returns later. Many academic studies have quantified this with estimates of increases in annual earnings of 5 percent or more for each year of college. Our work, however, has shown that the returns to education vary considerably by job and employer.

Risk and return for human capital go far beyond education and training. Consider the situation faced by commission-based salespeople. Because returns on their labor are entirely subject to their individual sales production, they cannot forecast the size of their paychecks from month to month or year to year. Returns are highly uncertain, that is, highly risky. If they have more than a few bad quarters, they are likely to be dismissed. Being a commission-based salesperson is a risky proposition, but the potential returns are very high. In some companies commission salespeople are the top earners, earning more than the senior executives do.

In contrast, unionized employees manage risk differently. They work under a legal contract that guarantees a certain wage, specific hours, safety conditions, benefits, and in some instances protection from layoffs. The unions to which they pay dues also may provide unemployment subsidies and supplemental retirement income. Overall, the situation for unionized employees is much less risky than that for commission salespeople, but some union personnel pay for that security with lower returns on their labor.

What is the risk-return profile of your human capital investment? Is the return you're getting commensurate with the level of risk? In other words, is your investment "efficient?"

General Versus Firm-Specific Capital

Every working day presents opportunities for building a person's human capital—capital that will pay dividends in the future. Training seminars, negotiating sessions with third parties, challenging new assignments—each of these things and dozens of others add to one's storehouse of technical skills and know-how, at least in theory. Some, however, contribute to the riskiness of a person's capital while others reduce the risk. Consider these two examples:

- Helen is a control-room operator at a nuclear power plant. She is well paid and is viewed within the company as a member of a highly trained elite. The training required for her position was long and intensive, conducted in both formal and on-the-job settings. She is one of only 15 such employees in her company.
- Patrick manages a manufacturing plant with 180 employees. He too is well paid and highly regarded by corporate management. His plant operates production lines that produce three different types of automotive steering mechanisms. Patrick worked his way up to his current position through a string of progressive job moves within his current company and in two others. In addition, he is halfway through the MBA curriculum offered by a local university, which he attends two nights each week.

Helen has developed a very high degree of *firm-specific* capital. What she knows and what she does are very critical to her current job and to her company, and it pays her accordingly. Opportunities to employ that know-how elsewhere, however, are limited. By Helen's own estimate there are very few positions as a control-room operator in the entire country. Even if she took a position at another plant, Helen would have to receive additional training and be certified by a government agency on that reactor. Also, her know-how is not easily transferable to another industry.

Patrick, in contrast, has developed much more *general* human capital. He knows how to manage people and deal with budgeting, planning, and customer relations, skills that can be used in any business. He has spent a lot of time learning the specifics of manufacturing steering components, but much of that learning can be transferred to most other types of manufacturing.

Helen and Patrick have developed their human capital with major differences in risk. Helen's human capital appears to have a high inherent level of risk. If her job were eliminated tomorrow, there would be little or no demand elsewhere for her know-how. She might have to endure a long period of waiting and recertification before her capital would begin to provide a similar return. However, the uniqueness of her capital may be such that her company could not get along without her.

Patrick, in contrast to Helen, has developed substantial general skills for which many companies—even outside his current industry—will gladly pay. The many calls he receives from executive recruiters make this clear. Thus, if something adverse were to happen to his company or industry, he would be well prepared to shift his human capital elsewhere.

The downside risk of being a generalist like Patrick is twofold: Highly technical positions are closed off, and generalists are often replaceable by other generalists. However, the downside risk is offset to a large extent by the upside opportunities.

Where do you stand on the issue of specific versus general human capital? Everyone has some of both. Which is your stronger side, and which are you investing more in growing? Are your skills so specialized that mobility is difficult or impossible? Are specialized skills what your company rewards? (If you have a high proportion of firm-specific human capital, typically you should be demanding a greater return for investing in those skills, which have value only to your current employer.) If you are a generalist, does your employer perceive you as being easily replaceable? Does your company reward general human capital? Is the return you are earning on your human capital commensurate with the risk?

Use the Internal Labor Market Approach

During past job searches you may have observed career brochures being handed out that consisted of glossy pictures of a smiling diverse workforce. In the near future

Is This Where It's Heading?

More than half a century ago, Nicholas Butler (1862–1947), a former president of Columbia University, offered a wry view of generalists and specialists. The world, he told his listeners, had become one in which specialists spend their time learning more and more about less and less. Generalists, in contrast, are learning less and less about more and more. "Before long," Butler quipped, "half of the population will know almost everything about almost nothing, and the other half will know next to nothing about everything."

some companies will replace that kind of propaganda with clear facts about a firm's internal labor market and the investments made in developing employees who are aligned with the business's needs. Until that day comes, one of the tools described in this book—Internal Labor Market (ILM) analysis—can help you find a better match between your goal and potential employers. It can help you avoid the "say-do" trap described in Chapter 2. Your company may be saying things about its programs to help people like you build your capital and get ahead, but the reality—what it's doing through its system of training, advancement, and rewards—may be very different. It's your job to get to the truth, and ILM analysis can help you do that.

It is unlikely that you can produce an ILM map of your current or perspective employer or implement the model we use in doing a full-blown analysis. Doing either

---

Get the Facts

The case of Toyota Motor Manufacturing North America discussed in Chapter 2 revealed how a gap between employee perceptions and the workplace realities of pay and promotions almost caused the company to spend royally on revamping its policies in those two areas. By digging out the relevant facts, Toyota found that its policies were in fact working.

This case holds a lesson: Don't believe everything you hear about what is rewarded and how people get ahead. If your peers tell you that "those training programs are a waste of time; they won't help you advance" or that "staying put is the best way to protect your job; the people who make lateral moves usually get canned within five years," exercise scientific skepticism. Check the facts. Also check what the company tells you. It may also say one thing but do another. Ask the following questions:

- What are the potential career tracks from where I sit?
- What percentage of people who take additional training or accept new assignments actually are rewarded?

Ask the company to add a new chapter to "open book management." Encourage regular discussion of the movement of people within the organization.

---

thing requires access to HR data, access to senior executives, many hours of work, and a solid working knowledge of statistical methods. Still, you can capture some of the highlights of a company's internal labor market through observation and by asking the right questions. This is doubly true if you are a current employee of the company. Here are some things you can do to assess the opportunities provided by your employer:

- Determine the number of people employed at your job level and the next two higher levels. This will give you a starting point for further inquiry.

- Ask, "How many people moved from my job level to the next higher level during the last year and the year before?" This information will help you determine the probability of advancement.
- Estimate the value of an upward move in money, competency-building experience, and career progress.
- Find out how many jobs at the next higher level were filled through outside recruiting. That information will help you assess whether the company tends to buy or build its senior talent and the probability of your moving up.
- Identify career bottlenecks above your level. Are upward career movements blocked at certain levels? You can answer this question by comparing the number of people leaving the organization at particular levels with the number being promoted. Will those bottlenecks affect you?
- Learn what is rewarded at your level: years of service, individual performance, team performance, technical specialization, general capabilities, education, political savvy, and so on. How strong is the match between your strengths and the things that are rewarded?
- Does the organization have a formal or informal infrastructure for developing employee skills and experience and other forms of human capital? These might be training programs, formal career development, regular mentoring, or a policy of experience-building assignments.
- Learn as much as you can about why people stay and why they leave.

Gathering and analyzing this information will help you form a clearer picture of your current or potential employer. If that picture does not match your job-related goals, you may find a greener pasture elsewhere.

Help Others Manage Their Careers

Up to this point in the chapter we have looked at human capital investments through your eyes: how *you* can make the most of your most important asset. By doing what's best for yourself, you may be doing your company a favor. After all, the company will benefit if your long-term interests are aligned with its interests; if your skills, knowledge, and experience are utilized fully; and if your human capital is expanded through training, career development, or some other means.

What's good for you is also good for those you manage. As a manager, you should put yourself in the shoes of your direct reports and see human capital issues from their perspective. Are there mismatches between their individual goals and the company's interests? If there are, those mismatches eventually will produce frustration, lower productivity, and costly turnover, and you will fail to make the most of the human capital at your disposal. Thus, every executive and manager has a motive for supporting intelligent career self-management among employees.

Here's a short list of things you can do today:

- Encourage people to take more responsibility for their careers and to think like investors.
- Provide the facts. What is being rewarded? What is the likelihood of being promoted this year? Greater information creates a more efficient internal labor market and reduces the likelihood that either the company or the employee will have a misunderstanding.
- Challenge the "conventional wisdom" and anecdotes about hires, promotions, transfers, and turnover in the organization. Then take it further by testing deep-rooted beliefs about the way those internal labor dynamics affect business performance and your own success.
- Help employees understand the prospects for having successive careers in the same company, for example, moving progressively from technical professional to manager to executive.
- Provide all talented employees with a career ladder and the training and progressive assignments that will help them move from rung to rung.
- Help people understand the implications and risks of generalized versus firm-specific human capital both for themselves and for the company.

Doing these things will help your people make the most of their own capital, and in the long run this will pay dividends to you and the company.

Key Points

View your career and educational choices as investments. Awareness, not perfection, is what you should seek when examining the facts about your current employer's internal labor market. Working in a company that's billed as one of the best places to work is meaningful only if it's the best place for you. Keep in mind that you do not have to work in a company with a well-aligned human capital strategy to be able to reach your goals within that organization. Remember the following:

- Manage the risks and returns of your human capital with at least as much discipline as you apply to your investment portfolio.
- Ask the company leaders for more information on the internal labor dynamics at work, reminding them that this is in the best interests of the company and you.
- Just as everyone knows that work is not entirely about pay, people should understand that pay is not about what one is earning currently but about potential future earnings. Look at your probability of future pay growth, not just today's paycheck.
- Demand higher returns today for firm-specific skills than you would for more transferable skills.
- Although it is impossible to replace the value of trial and error in your career, you can accelerate the learning process through trained observation.

14

Into the Future: A Boardroom Conversation

The CEO stood to speak.

"Ladies and gentlemen," he said to the board, "I am pleased to report that in the past 12 months we successfully took control of our largest investment."

He said it for effect. Having seen the presentations the previous year on workforce costs and talent strategies, they knew perfectly well what he was talking about.

"And this year," he continued, "we will increase that investment to 40 percent of sales. Our results more than make the case for the increase. Indeed, our return on those investments grew last year at 15 percent while our actual labor costs dropped 3 percent."

There were some nods around the table.

He smiled.

They were obviously very pleased.

IN ONE YEAR the CEO had taken the company from making people decisions with wishes, guesses, and hopes to making them with substantiated hard facts. Human capital no longer would be a curiosity on the board's agenda; it would be a standing item.

He went on to report on the company's progress:

"As you know, last year at this time we admitted to ourselves that we didn't really know what we were getting for the $5 billion we spend each year on labor, recruiting, technical training, leadership development, performance management, information and knowledge sharing, and all the other things we do to build this huge asset.

"Let's face it, we didn't even know if employees' experience in the firm over time created value for us. We didn't know if giving employees more discretion in the way they work improves productivity or hurts it. We thought that pushing major operational decisions into the field made sense, but we weren't certain. We only hoped that our 43 different incentive plans did what we thought they did. We weren't sure whether we should expand our "university" or shut it down. The fact is, compared to what we knew about managing our financial assets, logistics, marketing—almost anything else—we were lost in the woods. Just admitting it was a major step forward."

It was strangely emancipating to throw out the myths and uncertainty. For the first time he was really comfortable with all the previously soft and squishy people issues. They were no longer ephemeral. They were measurable, and their patterns told him how to make large and strategic decisions.

"The next step was to change the whole dialogue about workforce decision making. I started asking new questions," he went on.

"My favorites are:

- Are we sure our human capital strategy is aligned with our business design? How do we know?
- What can we change—by cutting, reallocating, or increasing our investments—to manage people more effectively and to generate greater shareholder returns?

"And I always end by saying, 'Prove it.' Needless to say, some of those early conversations were awkward, but we began to think differently, and eventually we started acting differently. We moved from ad hoc hip-shooting to holistic decision making.

"We became convinced that getting serious answers to these questions would not only save money but actually create value for us—value in everything from customer service to net operating income. Perhaps just as important, we came to see that finding the right answers to these questions would provide us with a powerful competitive advantage because no one else was thinking this way. We would be the first mover, get a head start. Furthermore, we knew—unlike with marketing, technology, even products themselves—they couldn't copy the advantage we would be building because it was inherently ours. What would they do: Try to reproduce our history, culture, leaders, and all of our management practices?

"So we set out to manage these human capital practices with the same rigor with which we manage our tangible assets. Knowing that 'what gets measured gets managed,' we first specified for ourselves which factors needed to be tracked. In most cases we already had the information; we just didn't know it."

At that point the CEO turned on the projector. Pointing to the Internal Labor Market (ILM) maps for the five major business units, he flagged the differences for the board.

"Among other things, we learned that we operate very different internal labor markets in our different lines of business. You can see that the sharply pointed pyramid form in these units means there's ongoing and intense competition to capture one of the very few positions toward the top. The one with the bulge in the middle points to the reality of limited career growth beyond that point. In contrast, this rectangular map implies a less competitive structure in this group because there aren't a limited number of seats at the top. Our preliminary assessment suggests that the respective structures are appropriate to the different groups' business models. This means that one size fits all not only doesn't apply to companies; it doesn't even apply to all divisions. We really need to tailor our people management to these differences.

"I must say that when I was first introduced to these ILM maps, I thought they were interesting but wondered whether they were really that useful. What I came to realize was that in some ways they are merely symbols of a more complex system that can be analyzed in unprecedented ways.

"So, for instance, ILM modeling shows us the attributes of the managers who move through the organization most successfully. We discovered that all the MBAs we've been hiring from top schools don't perform any better than do MBAs from second-tier schools. And we're paying about 10 percent more to get the first-tier people.

"We also know if our managers are moving too slow or too fast. Or if they're gaming the system. What might be even more interesting going forward is determining what kinds of managers most predictably develop high-potential people."

He flipped off the projector. Not since last year's governance discussion had he seen them so engaged. He was on a roll.

"These kinds of findings are reshaping how we think about many management techniques we've taken for granted. For example, we used to think about all employee turnover the same way; that is, anything more than 15 percent a year was bad. I used to rail at Marty about that all the time. I really wanted us to make the '100 Best Places to Work' list, and I figured higher turnover would give us a black eye. Well, as they say, be careful what you wish for. Marty added turnover to his managers' MBOs, and they dutifully hammered it—dropping it by half. Next thing you know, they're doing a marvelous job at keeping their poor performers. Can you believe that? Needless to say, I've offered Marty a mea culpa, and we've put the teeth back in the performance management system.

"That experience emphasized that some turnover is good and necessary to run the business properly. More important, we now are positioned to have differentiated targets for turnover. We know if exits among our frontline customer-facing people—including our drivers—go above 10 percent, we will be hurt in both sales and customer turnover. Conversely, we know that our marketing people are rather easily replaced and that we shouldn't be alarmed unless we go over 30 percent. What's more, our turnover goals for managers now make sense. We can adjust our targets to reflect realities on the ground. Armed with our ILM models, we have a real handle on what it takes to retain top talent. We won't penalize the Cambridge leadership because they're still struggling with a tight labor market but we'll stop giving a free ride to the folks in Toledo, where there are no other opportunities that would make any employee want to leave us. Last year those guys in Ohio were paid over $2 million for having a good record on retention. Right—we unwittingly rewarded them simply for being in a weak labor market. No more of that, I assure you.

"In the same way, we've learned that certain things we did in the past to save money were simply wrongheaded. If we increase the number of part-timers above 20 percent, our savings in fixed pay and benefits costs are quickly wiped out by a rapid erosion of overall productivity. They cost less per head, but we needed a whole lot more heads to get the job done. So we're much less likely to be seduced by cost cutting than we were.

"Those kinds of discoveries have led us to rethink our staffing model and our propensity to lay off people in downturns. It's clear that experience on the job in most sectors of this company cannot be replaced by new hires, no matter how talented they are. To avoid that trap we probably will put more leverage in the variable-pay program so that pay automatically ratchets down with slow business performance. In any case, the goal is to preserve our long-term investment in people.

"I'd have to say one of the unexpected outcomes of this measurement-based management is our ability to predict various scenarios. Of course, we've long done that with macroeconomic projections and sales forecasts. Now we can do the same thing with human capital. We have, in effect, a set of levers we can pull. We know that if we raise overtime 5 percent, we net an 8 percent productivity gain. We now have all of these various factors loaded in a software program along with the ILM data, and so we can do what-if simulations.

"So now we use the $8 million HRIS system for something other than mailing enrollment materials," he said with a thin smile, knowing that his predecessor had been given a hard time for the delays and cost overruns in installing it.

He noticed the one or two predictable eye rolls and went on:

"All of this has been particularly helpful in planning our M&A activity. We better know what it takes to integrate an acquisition and what the implications will be for the careers of our existing employees as well as our labor costs. We take a keen interest nowadays in whether the target's internal labor market matches the division we'll be merging it with.

"Finally, I've found that Wall Street is really picking up on this line of thinking. In the most recent phone call, it was clear that our ability to specify the return on individual tactics such as larger spans of control and the management stock incentive plan really caught their attention. I could tell some of them thought it was smoke and mirrors, but the Goldman and Merrill guys got it. And Deborah What's-her-name from Morgan Stanley glommed on to the fact that we're going to shield our key people from layoffs. Those three in particular understood that something really different is going on here. It's dawning on them that we really are now managing our people like we would any other major asset. I am positive that this is going to change the way analysts think about our organization.

"It won't be long before somebody's going to figure out that we are creating a large and increasingly measurable intangible value for shareholders. When that becomes clear, our logo is going to be on the cover of *Business Week* and our stock is going to surge."

The meeting eventually moved to other topics.

During lunch the conversation turned back to the human capital strategy and the new metrics. Someone asked what the big "learnings" were from the last year. The CEO obviously had thought about it:

"There's so much. In some ways, it's shocking to think business has gone so long without cracking this measurement nut. But if I had to boil it down to several points, I'd say:

- We cannot make major strategic changes with the business model or the human capital strategy without considering all the essential factors in both the marketplace and within the organization itself.
- The way we choose to manage human capital strategy can be a source of unique and lasting competitive advantage.
- Determining how managers and employees actually behave is ultimately more important than simply listening to what they say (although having both perspectives is better).
- We must resist the temptation to manage primarily around cost. The focus needs to be on ROI.
- Specifically, we need to expect systems thinking, demand the right facts, and always—always—keep the focus on value creation. That's the message I want to see permeate all parts of our company.

"Indeed, those three considerations are going to shape all of our major decisions in the future."

After lunch they made their way back to the boardroom. Walking down the hall, someone overheard the CEO talking to the oldest board member:

"You know, Henry, a year or two from now I'll stand up in front of an employee meeting and say, 'People are our greatest asset,' and you know what? They'll believe it."

Gentle laughter filled the hallway.

"No, seriously. They will know it's true because they will have seen how we have changed how we run this business."

As they turned the corner, the CEO put his arm around the board member's shoulders.

"Shoot, I might even put that back in the employee handbook."

The Research Roots of the Six-Factor Framework

Overview

The six factors are the essential components of a firm's human capital strategy. Not coincidentally, they are the workforce drivers of an organization's productivity. The six factors:

1. provide a powerful, unified platform for addressing a wide range of "people" issues
2. differentiate an organization from its competitors
3. are deeply rooted in rigorous research linking human capital to business performance.

The bulk of this appendix summarizes research foundations for the framework. Toward the end, we address other assets and technology, and we recap the content and attributes of the six factors themselves.

Research Background

We reviewed and synthesized findings from hundreds of research studies in economics, psychology, communications, management, and related disciplines to identify factors that affect the productivity of people at work. The research foundation reflects more than 300 studies, over 1,000 organizations. Given the intense investment that research requires and the long-term nature of the studies reviewed, we estimate that the literature reflects at least 450 person-years of work.

Mercer looked for research that:

- was published, especially in professional research journals, between 1971 and 1996.
- took place in organizations engaged in producing goods and delivering services, thus excluding laboratory experiments, simulations, and research done in nonemployment settings.
- measured productivity objectively rather than impressionistically.
- emphasized tracking the effects of planned changes in human capital management practices.
- was rooted in economics, psychology, management, communications, or related disciplines.

The search focused on leading research journals. The highly selective process by which articles are chosen for these journals ensures that the findings were of the highest quality and provided significant insights. For example, in the *Journal of Applied Psychology*—a source of many of the studies that Mercer reviewed—the majority of research papers are rejected for publication. In many years, only 10% of the submitted papers are published and truly represent the "cream of the crop" of research efforts.

Each study had to have *objective* end measures. "Objective" simply means that productivity was assessed in a way that, no matter who did the measuring, the same result would be found. Objective measures include counts of the quantity of production and the frequency of errors, measures of the time required to perform a cycle of work activity, and calculations of revenue per employee. (Alternatives to "objective" measures include opinion, gut feel, and intuitive experience.)

We also focused on interventions with lasting productivity effects. Intervention studies represent "experiments" in which a change is made in the organization and the effects are observed over time, a form of research that provides strong evidence of cause-and-effect. The time between an intervention and the measurement of its productivity consequences ranged from weeks to over five years in the research reviewed. Studies that were not interventions tended to make use of statistical controls to rule out the possibility that some other factor was driving productivity.

We did not include laboratory experiments and simulations because such techniques tend to strip away the context. Our emphasis on the importance of understanding productivity drivers *in context* squarely fits with the choice to emphasize research done in ongoing enterprises.

The Six-Factor Framework—The Essence of a Human Capital Strategy

Mercer's six human capital factors driving organization results are:

1. *People.* Those who are in the organization (including its leaders), what skills and competencies they bring with them when hired, what skills and competencies they develop through training and experience, their qualifications (such as prior experience and education), and the extent to which they embody firm-specific and generalized human capital.
2. *Work processes.* How work gets done, indicated by such things as the extent to which work is team-based, flexibility in production and service delivery, the degree of interdependence among organizational units, and the role of technology in shaping how work is performed.
3. *Managerial structure.* What balance is struck between employee discretion and management direction and control? High managerial control is indicated by such things as a strong emphasis on performance review and management (e.g., frequent reviews), narrow spans of control, and widespread standardization of work procedures.
4. *Information and knowledge.* All aspects of how information and knowledge are communicated, including how much information/knowledge is exchanged among employees, how it is exchanged (vertically, laterally, through formal and informal means), and the extent to which information is exchanged between a company and its environment.

5. *Decision making.* How important business decisions get made and who makes them. Decentralization (i.e., pushing responsibility for decisions into lower levels), participation, and timeliness in decision making are ways in which organizations differ in how decisions are made.

6. *Rewards.* How monetary and non-monetary inducements are used in an organization. This driver has many relevant aspects – including the extent to which pay is at risk, whether the risk is controllable, whose performance (e.g., individual versus groups) is rewarded, the extent to which rewards are "backloaded" (paid later in one's career) versus paid here-and-now, and the extent to which the work itself is a source of motivation.

The implications of these six factors can only be weighed and acted upon in the context of each organization —its marketplace (competitors, vendors, regulators, etc.), its business model, and its management of physical assets (including technology).

Here is a sampling of research findings that illustrate the six factors:

- *People.* Firms that extensively trained employees experienced net sales per employee advantages of nearly 20 percent over firms that did not train, after statistically controlling for differences in company size, unionization, capital investments, employee occupations and education levels, and industry in a sample of several hundred firms.

- *Work processes.* Radical (quantum) reorganization was associated with higher ROA than incremental reorganization for three matched pairs of firms from three industries.

- *Managerial structure.* A metals company experienced significant increases in weekly tonnage in 10 mines following a program of increased managerial control through weekly production goals and review.

- *Information and knowledge.* The greater the employee participation and access to information, the greater the net sales per employee in 495 business units over two years.

- *Decision-making.* Health care planning groups produced higher quality and more innovative plans when planners fully communicated with each other and participated throughout the planning process, compared to planning groups following procedures intended to make their planning process more efficient.

- *Rewards.* A study of 52 engineering firms in the United Kingdom over five years showed that those firms with profit-sharing plans gained 3 to 8 percent in value added over those firms without such plans.

Overall Conclusions

While the overall pattern of research results points to the importance of the six factors, the impact of each factor on productivity varied considerably from study to study. This variation is evidence that *context matters*. That is, the impact of a human capital practice on productivity will depend on what other practices are in place as well as how well the practice fits the business strategy and environment. Interestingly, the productivity driver with the most variable effects on productivity is Rewards.

Complementarities

Complementarities exist when the two or more drivers *in combination* affect productivity more than would be anticipated by "adding up" the expected effects of each component driver. For example, research shows that the productivity gains from a combination of highly selective hiring and heavy investment in training is greater than the expected sum of the gains from either practice on its own.

The Intellectual Foundations of the New Science

THE NEW SCIENCE OF human capital management presented in this book has been made possible by three major developments: (1) advances in knowledge about human capital and its links to organizational performance derived from burgeoning academic research primarily in economics and organizational psychology as well as documented field experience, (2) the emergence of modern electronic information systems that make employee data and all forms of financial, operational, and customer data readily accessible for real-time analysis and tracking, and (3) advances in and technological applications of modern statistical methods that allow practitioners and researchers to tap those data far more quickly and effectively to inform decision making. When these factors come together, organizations have the capacity as never before to manage their human capital investments from a strong factual platform. This appendix provides an overview of the intellectual heritage on which our work is built and the core statistical methods behind the analytic tools we present.

Research in Economics

The approach and methods presented in this book draw extensively on research in the fields of labor and organizational economics. Traditional labor economics actually had little to say about human capital management in organizations. As a branch of microeconomics it was concerned primarily with market transactions, specifically with the way labor markets operate to generate and balance the supply of and demand for labor and determine wages and salaries. However, over time two critical insights led to a transformation of labor economics. The first was recognition that human capital is not just an input to production as is stipulated in standard production theory. It is also the output of a production process in which individuals and/or organizations invest time and resources to enhance the quality and capability of labor. Hence, it follows that economic analysis could be applied to understand that process better and determine the causes and consequences of investments in human capital. It was this idea that gave rise to human capital theory and a large body of empirical research to test its key propositions.

The second insight stemmed from the observation that many of the most critical transactions involving human capital actually take place inside organizations, not in external labor markets. The employment relationship is complex and varied. One observes in practice a wide variety of contractual arrangements governing the terms of employment—some explicit, some implicit—and sometimes nonmarket mechanisms such as administrative procedures and policies play the central role. However, those nonmarket institutions accomplish the same things that external labor markets achieve: They allocate people to tasks and jobs, price those jobs and the associated labor inputs, and deliver incentives for people to develop and supply the requisite quantity and quality of labor. This suggests that the same optimization framework used to explain market relationships might be applied productively to analyzing those transactions within the firm. These insights led to a new field of investigation focusing on the employment relationship and the internal workings of the firm. In its most modern incarnation this field is called the "new economics of personnel" (Lazear, 1995).[1]

Below, we briefly characterize each of those fields and its contributions to the new science.

Human Capital Theory

Broadly speaking, human capital theory is concerned with the causes and consequences of investments in human capital both for the individual employee and for employers. The original work on human capital, beginning with the seminal studies of Jacob Mincer (1958), Theodore Schultz (1963), and Gary Becker (1964),[2] examined the economics of decisions by individuals (and by extension firms) to increase the quality of labor through expenditures on education, training, and on-the-job learning. It was recognized that both individuals and organizations incur *current* costs to improve labor quality that generate *future* returns in the form of enhanced productivity and earnings (pay and pay growth). Thus, these decisions are in essence *investment* decisions and can be treated in much the same way in which capital investment is modeled by financial economists. That is, economic agents, acting rationally to optimize their own welfare, make investment decisions by comparing the costs of those investments to the present value of the income stream they produce. Investments are undertaken when the present value exceeds the associated cost and the return is greater than the returns from available alternatives. Applying that paradigm, labor economists have been able to explain much about observed patterns of labor supply, productivity, and earnings growth.

For the most part human capital theory has focused on the decisions made by individuals. The analysis has helped explain a variety of labor market phenomena, including income differences across individuals, the trajectory of earnings over an individual's work life, and investments in education and on-the-job training and their respective returns as well as patterns of occupational and job mobility and the duration of employment. It was from this work that the critical distinction between general human capital and firm-specific human capital arose. Since the development of firm-specific human capital makes separation more costly for both the employee and the employer, the balance of general and firm-specific human capital achieved by employees has direct implications for the expected relationships between employee tenure and both pay and turnover. Human capital theory provides a road map for understanding those relationships and the ways labor markets value the different types of human capital.[3]

Human capital theory also made it necessary for economists to deal formally with issues that involve the heterogeneity of labor. Traditional microeconomics had abstracted from this issue altogether, characterizing labor as a homogeneous input to production that was measured by headcount or labor hours alone. Since human capital develops differently, depending on the investment choices made, the quality of labor will vary considerably. Thus, labor markets have the additional burden of helping to match individuals to jobs and organizations in a way that finds the highest value for those resources. Theories of "matching," "job search," and job market "signaling" were developed, in part, to help explain how these objectives are fulfilled through labor market institutions and the conditions under which outcomes are optimized. These are important complements to—and, in some respects, extensions of—human capital theory.[4]

It is quite straightforward to extend the human capital paradigm in an attempt to understand the investments in human capital made by organizations. For economists, human capital in organizations represents the *stock* of human assets—consisting of the accumulated knowledge, skills, experience, creativity, and other relevant workforce attributes—that drive the *flow* of labor services to the firm. It is important to understand the distinction economists make between "stocks" and "flows." That distinction is equivalent to the difference between wealth and income. Wealth is a stock variable; it can be measured in financial terms at a given point in time. Income is a flow variable; it has no meaning without reference to time (it is measured as $X *per* year, month, etc.). Human capital is the equivalent of the accumulated human "wealth" of an organization: the productive *potential* of its workforce. Labor productivity is in effect the income generated from that wealth. Hence, an organization will invest current resources in training to improve the quality of its workforce and, it expects, generate higher productivity over time. Such enhancements in labor quality are viewed as increases in the organization's stock of human capital. Increased productivity, if it materializes, reflects an increased flow of labor services from that stock of human capital and can be used as a measure of the return on the organization's investment in human capital.

Contract Theory and the New Economics of Personnel

Optimizing the productive potential of an organization's workforce by itself cannot ensure that the workforce will generate the expected return in terms of actual productivity. Obviously, productivity also depends on how the workforce is deployed and motivated. To be efficient, labor markets and other labor market institutions, such as internal labor markets, must provide for optimal utilization of human capital as well. This is where incentives come into play.

Incentive problems arise because of imperfections and asymmetries in the information available to the employer and the employee. If employers could observe perfectly both the quality of labor they employ and the actual labor input (e.g., effort and diligence) employees provide to the firm, there would be no selection or incentive problems with which to deal. Screening would ensure that those hired had exactly the capabilities required by the business. Contracts would focus on labor inputs alone—not outputs—and pay only for actual services delivered.

However, reality is far different from this idealized picture. Indicators of labor quality such as education, prior job history, and even testing are incomplete and often erroneous. And usually only proxies for actual labor effort and diligence (e.g., hours worked) can be observed. For example, it is possible that "lower-ability" recruits will pass for "higher-ability" ones. An efficient employment contract should minimize this contingency. If, for example, the compensation arrangement provides incentives for the lower-ability people to join the firm when the need is for high-ability employees, there is an "adverse selection" problem that undermines performance. Similarly, if the compensation system provides incentives for employees to shirk or to free ride on the efforts of others, this incentive or "moral hazard" problem will lead to diminished productivity in the existing workforce.[5] Thus, the structure of the employment relationship matters a great deal.

Economists have focused considerable attention on understanding the employment relationship and the nature of labor contracting. Much of that research characterizes the optimal employment contract under different assumptions about the information available to the employer and the employee and differences in their attitudes toward risk.[6] Risk comes into play because of uncertainty about both the outcomes of productive activity and those of the employment relationship. Someone will bear the burden of those risks, but who? To what extent will it be shared between the employer and the employee? These are questions with which every employment contract must deal.

Using a classic optimization approach as well as applications of game theory, economists have examined conditions under which different types of employment contracts arise. Their research addresses multiple dimensions of the employment relationship, including pay, career progression, and employment security, among others. It addresses questions such as the following: What determines the relative efficiency of fixed wages and salaries compared with individual incentives such as piece rates? When are group incentives optimal, and what solutions exist for the free rider behaviors that often are associated with those rewards? Under what circumstances are relative performance measures more effective than absolute measures in incentive programs? When are competitive compensation schemes in which employees vie for promotion up the career hierarchy appropriate for optimizing workforce productivity? What determines the size of differences in pay across levels in the hierarchy? A series of theoretical models have been developed that shed light on the optimal design of employment contracts and rewards under different conditions. Those models are useful in assessing the likely effectiveness of contracts observed in practice.

That research has been extended to examine the implications of incentive problems for organization structure, addressing issues such as why and how hierarchies arise, the links between the intensity of supervision and compensation costs, and even the role and value of bureaucracy in organizations. It speaks to the systemic nature of human capital management, in which structure and practice interact to influence behavior.

The body of research cited above is invaluable for understanding internal labor markets and the productivity of human capital in organizations. It has guided us in developing our analytic tools, clarifying key relationships among variables, and providing a basis for interpreting empirical patterns uncovered through statistical analyses.

The theoretical and empirical models that have been developed tend to be more narrowly focused and less systems-oriented than are those in the psychological literature, but they are rigorously formulated and offer clear, testable predictions. When combined, they provide rich insights into and data on the ways internal labor markets function and the ways human capital affects performance. The theoretical work indicates what one should look for in evaluating data. The models specify efficiency conditions for various aspects of human capital management under different contingencies. They are context-sensitive. The empirical work provides a vast array of normative data concerning key relationships. Those relationships are best used not as benchmarks to be mimicked by an organization but as a way to understand the uniqueness of the organization and the reasons such differences may be appropriate.

No discussion of the research base of our work would be complete without reference to the growing body of empirical research on the links between human capital management and labor productivity. Much of the most significant empirical research consists of econometric studies of the relationship between specific types of interventions and productivity and/or a firm's financial performance.[7] Most of this research involves the statistical analysis of samples of firms in particular industries or across industries. The most common approach has been to estimate a production function that is "augmented" to include variables that represent the human resources interventions of choice. Control variables representing industry- or firm-specific characteristics and/or demographic attributes of employees often are used to take account of the contextual factors that may influence program performance. The performance variables that are used most commonly are value added, value added per employee, net sales per employee, and profitability.

Here too economic research has been focused more narrowly than has the work in organizational psychology. Empirical research in economics has been concerned primarily with financial incentives, employee participation, and a number of practices aimed at the selection and development of human capital, such as training and screening. A few studies have examined other aspects of human resources (HR) systems, such as job design, seniority-based promotion, supervision intensity, information-sharing arrangements, and managerial attitudes toward employees (i.e., "values").[8] However, such studies are quite exceptional. Nonetheless, they are a hopeful sign of the expansion of empirical research to complement the extensive theoretical work in personnel economics.

Research in Organizational Psychology

The perspectives and insights in this book also can be traced to the psychological sciences. In particular, psychology that has focused on the study of people in organizations—initially known as industrial psychology and called variously since that time personnel psychology, industrial-organizational psychology, organizational psychology, and work psychology—has been an essential influence. (For convenience we use the term *organizational psychology* and ignore any subtle differences implied by nomenclature.) Organizational psychology has always influenced and been influenced by related disciplines that also focus on the workplace, such as organizational behavior, labor relations, and human resources. However, it has not often been married with thinking originating in economics. That, we believe, is a strength of this book.

The emphasis on facts, a cornerstone of the new science of human capital management, is a familiar characteristic of organizational psychology. Various methods of inquiry are used to establish facts in the discipline. One method is the quasi-experimental assessment of the impact on productivity of a change in a workforce practice. Another is the sophisticated use of statistical methods of analysis to discern cause-and-effect relationships. These are prized activities for establishing facts. They shape the analysis of the business impact of human capital practices and the analysis of internal labor market dynamics.

Facts learned through the use of these methods are impermanent, as has been noted by Ghiselli (1974).[9] They change over circumstances and time, over people and places. Thus, facts that are demonstrably true for one time or one workforce may not be true for another.

A good deal of the impermanence of facts in organizations has to do with differences in context. The notion of generalizability—the transportability of facts from one setting to another—has been and remains a core concern of organizational psychology. For example, facts about the accuracy with which future performance in a job can be predicted from a test or interview done at the time of hiring usually are considered to be certain (or reasonably so) when they are rooted in a scientific assessment of accuracy in one work context. Begin changing the context, for example, such as by applying the test or interview to a different population or a different job, and serious uncertainty arises as to accuracy. On a more general level, as we have seen in this book, human capital practices that affect performance positively in one setting, such as incentive pay plans and employee development through internal mobility, may have no effects or negative effects in another. That facts are impermanent is not a catch-22. Our way out consists of the judicious application of measurement-based scientific approaches to testing the transportability of facts across contexts.

Although sensitivity to contexts has always been part of organizational psychology, the field has paid very little attention to all the dimensions of context, as Raymond A. Katzell (1994) notes in his overview of metatrends in the field.[10] For example, the field has long addressed individual behavior in the context of varying work groups and supervisory styles. However, it largely has ignored broad contextual influences such as differences in labor markets. Fortunately, economics has much to offer about labor markets and other broad contextual influences.

Systems thinking also has made its way into the core of organizational psychology. Early on relatively little explicit attention was given to principles of systems thinking, but like most of the social and behavioral sciences, the field began to embrace systems concepts in the 1960s. Concepts such as interacting parts, feedback, interchange with the environment, and equifinality have become part of the intellectual vocabulary of the field, according to Katzell. An especially important expression of systems thinking is the "sociotechnical" perspective that asserts the importance of optimally fitting human capital practices to the demands of technology and work processes vis-à-vis the environment. Thus, organizational psychology informs a second fundamental principle of this book: the importance of systems thinking.

Supplementing an insistence on systems thinking and the importance of facts, the third principle of this book is an emphasis on value. In organizational psychology that emphasis is evident in a perpetual interest in application. Indeed, the field defines itself as living at the intersection of science and practice. Discovering and interpreting facts is a critical part of any science. Doing that to deliver real value is a hallmark of organizational psychology.

Much of that value has been directed toward enhancing the individual consequences of working, that is, identifying practices that contribute to happiness, health, reduced stress, and a decrease in injuries. Such positive outcomes for the individual can have value for employers too. The field also has for a long time focused on drivers of individual performance at work. Higher levels of individual performance can benefit both the employer and the employee. More recently the field has focused on organizational-level outcomes such as profitability and customer retention.

This developing emphasis on organizational-level outcomes, and not coincidentally the adoption of systems thinking, is forcing those in the field to address relationships across different levels of analysis. As has been noted, individual behavior represents one level of analysis, and that of whole organizations represents another. In between are work groups, department, branches or facilities, divisions, and so on. Working across levels of analysis—such as by linking the volatility of the external environment to the power of equity as a reward for motivating individual behavior or identifying the attributes of a department that influence individual choices to stay with or leave the employer—opens organizational psychology to new theories and new methods of establishing facts. Working across levels also is an important practical matter, as Katzell points out. Identifying the levels at which the causes of workforce and business outcomes originate helps an organization design the right interventions.

Statistical Methods of the New Science

Various forms of multivariate regression analysis are deployed in the core diagnostic tools discussed in this book, including Internal Labor Market (ILM) Analysis and Business Impact Modeling. In this section we provide some illustrations of the actual statistical models used.

Internal Labor Market Analysis

ILM Analysis is used to measure and model the causes and consequences of an organization's workforce dynamics—attraction, development, and retention—as well as the rewards that motivate them. Statistical modeling is a critical tool for identifying the causes and consequences of internal labor market dynamics. Because in our view the internal labor market functions as a system, with the various workforce dynamics continuously interacting to create an organization's workforce, the models that characterize those dynamics are largely symmetrical, relying on a consistent set of explanatory or predictor variables. As was noted in Chapter 5, those variables include individual employee characteristics, organizational practices, and external market influences. Of course, each organization will have a different set of specific variables that reflect its unique business context. The following is an example of one such set that was used for an ILM Analysis of one of the companies mentioned in this book:

Figure B-1. Case Example of ILM Variable List

EXTERNAL INFLUENCES	ORGANIZATIONAL PRACTICES	EMPLOYEE ATTRIBUTES
Unemployment rates	Size of facility (location, growth)	Age
Location		Gender
Market share	Dispersion of incentive payouts	Education (level, specialization)
Competition (location, size, type, and number)	Supervision (structure, spans of control, stability)	Ethnic background
		Prior experience
Labor pool (demographics, income levels, education, occupations)	Turnover rate (location, team)	Recruiting source
		Termination reason
	Employee heterogeneity	Job family/occupation
		Salaried/ hourly
	Risk (variable pay, employment variability)	Union status
		Tenure (in position, with company)
	Workload	Pay level (current, prior)
	Performance (level and volatility)	Incentive earnings
	Line of business	Relative pay in grade
		Level (job grade, level)
		Promotion history
		Transfer history (business unit, job family, country)
		Location (work, home)
		Performance rating

The basic ILM analysis involves statistical estimation of models of the drivers of internal movements—promotion and lateral job changes—as well as the drivers of retention. It also involves statistical modeling of the drivers of compensation, including pay, total compensation, and annual pay growth.

Both linear and nonlinear regression techniques are used to estimate those models statistically. When the outcomes of interest (i.e., the dependent variables) are "categorical" or "dichotomous" in nature, as are events such as promotion, lateral movement, and turnover, we most often use "discrete choice" models, particularly in their binomial form. In these circumstances the outcome or event either occurs or it does not. That is how it appears in employee data. Hence, the dependent variable is restricted to those two alternatives, denoted 1 if the event occurs and 0 if it does not.

For binomial models, the objective of modeling is to determine the influence of specific explanatory variables on the probability that an event or outcome will occur. What is being estimated, then, is the probability that the event will occur given the values of the specified explanatory variables. Since the overall probability cannot be less than 0 or greater than 1, the mathematical expression or functional form relating those variables must restrict the outcome to the range between 0 and 1. A variety of probability distributions can be used for this purpose, the two most common being the cumulative normal distribution and the logistic distribution. We usually rely on the logistic distribution and employ logistic regression for estimation purposes.[11] Typically, the models are structured to estimate the probability of the particular event in a specific year based on the values of the explanatory and control variables at the end of the prior year.

A logit model generally is specified as follows:

$$P = \frac{\exp^{U}}{1+\exp^{U}} = \frac{1}{1+\exp^{-U}}$$

where P denotes probability and U is the vector product of parameter estimates, $\boldsymbol{\beta}$, and the values of the corresponding explanatory and control variables, $\mathbf{X}$. U is thought of usually as representing the level of "utility" that underlies an individual's decision, such as to turn over or not.

Variants of a logit model take the form of different specifications of U, the linear component in the equation above. An example of a turnover model estimated through logistic regression specifies the following linear structure (for U):

$U = \beta_0 + \beta_1{}^*$ local unemployment rate $+ \beta_2{}^*$ years of service $+$ $\beta_3{}^*$full-time status $+ \beta_4{}^*$degree_bach $+ \beta_5{}^*$degree_grad $+ \beta_6{}^*$supervisor's span of control $+ \beta_7$training taken $+ \beta_8{}^*$prior year pay growth $+ \beta_9{}^*$(promotion $= 1/0$) $+ \ldots + \beta_N{}^*$ business unit A $+ \varepsilon$

Therefore the model to estimate is:

$$P(turnover\ next\ year) = \frac{1}{1 + \exp^{-(\beta_0 + \beta_1{}^*\ local\ unemployment\ rate\ +\ \beta_2{}^*\ years\ of\ service\ +\ \beta_3{}^*full\text{-}time\ status\ +\ \ldots)}}$$

In this equation, the event of interest is on the left-hand side and the variables assumed to influence those events—the independent variables—are on the right-hand side. Statistical estimation produces estimates of these betas that reveal the significance and relative strength of each factor's influence on the probability of turnover. They can be converted readily into so-called elasticities that measure the expected impact of a change in a particular characteristic, such as an employee's performance rating or gender, on the probability that that employee will leave the organization in a particular year. Quite apart from its relevance to a retention strategy, just think how valuable such information could be to an organization that is evaluating its performance management system or its efforts in regard to diversity. Illustrations of such elasticities were presented in Figures 2-4 and 5-4.

For the models used to estimate drivers of continuous variables such as pay and pay growth we use ordinary and/or generalized least-squares regression. As was noted above, there is a vast literature in both economics and organizational psychology on the determinants and consequences of pay. The specific models we have developed as part of ILM analysis draw heavily on the established research but are more comprehensive in their coverage, especially in regard to organizational factors and individual characteristics that influence compensation.

Business Impact Modeling

Similar multivariate regression techniques are used for Business Impact Modeling. Once again a critical issue is to determine the functional form that will be utilized to characterize the relationships being studied. We noted in Chapter 6 that a family of methods is employed. Here we focus only on one—the production function—to illustrate what the actual statistical model might look like.

As was noted before, the production function is a mathematical expression of the relationship between inputs and outputs in the production process. The practical value of the production function is enhanced by augmenting the traditional specification of labor input on the right-hand side of the equation to reflect the broader array of workforce attributes and management practices that affect the productivity of human capital in an organization. In most instances it is possible to specify a form of production function that directly links critical business outcomes such as productivity and profitability to key characteristics of the workforce and the way human capital is managed. Here is an illustration:

Revenue per employee = β_0 + β_1*assets + β_2*average years of service + β_3*percent full-time status + β_4*urban location + β_5* office size + β_6*average supervisor span of control + β_7*average training expenditure per employee + β_8*percent bonus participation + ... + ε

In this adapted equation the business outcome on the left-hand side is revenue per employee, something that is tracked routinely. The purpose of the equation is to identify which among many possible human capital–related factors consistently drive revenue per employee after accounting for other influences, such as location and capitalization of the business units or facilities examined. Some of those factors seem intuitively plausible. For example, more experienced employees (measured as a count of years of service) and full-time employees (measured as 1 = full-time status and 0 = part-time) might be expected to produce greater revenue per employee in many organizations. Other factors are included as statistical controls in the model to allow for correct estimates of the key human capital parameters in the equation. For example, whether a sales location is in an urban area may have a substantial effect on revenue per employee. What if it turns out that most full-time employees work in urban areas and part-time employees work in suburban or rural areas and full-time employees on average produce more revenue per sale? Is the higher revenue per employee a result of the employee's full-time status—and all that implies about what hours the employee is on the job or his or her interest in the work—or is it a result of the fact that full-time employees happen to work mostly in urban offices? The action implications differ greatly depending on how this question is answered. Statistical models answer questions such as this one, helping to identify which of the many possible influences are indeed the most important and thus are priorities for action.

As in ILM Analysis, the betas (βs) for each element on the right-hand side of the equation are estimated through the modeling process. The overall equation, then, is a statement about which factors contribute to revenue per employee and how important each factor is in comparison to the others. Unimportant factors can be removed, and the remaining factors can be prioritized by their relative importance. These are key facts in setting human capital strategies.

In addition, the modeling can be used to test for productive interactions, or "complementarities," among different factors. For example, one might suppose, as research suggests, that training investments in employees have a bigger impact on labor productivity in environments where recruitment and selection criteria are more stringent or where the education level of the workforce is higher. Evidence of the latter relationship, for example, will be revealed if the overall weight of the variable "average training expenditure per employee" rises when that variable is statistically interacted with a measure of educational attainment (e.g., average years of education, percentage of the workforce with advanced degrees). Rigorous tests of interactions among these variables reveal whether and to what extent complementarities of these kinds materialize in the organization. You might recall from Chapter 3 that this kind of interaction was uncovered in the relationship between the utilization of part-timers and overtime. To everyone's surprise, overtime actually improved productivity at Healthco. However, that was the case because managers were using overtme to deploy their more productive full-timers more intensively. Certainly, understanding that relationship had important implications for the way overtime use should be regulated in that organization.

When is Business Impact Modeling of this kind feasible statistically? Two conditions must be met at a minimum. First, a sufficient number of measures of performance over time are required in order to fill in the left-hand side of the model. This means that one needs to find like units within an organization whose performance can be compared systematically. In a manufacturing organization those units might be factories. In a retail company they could be stores. For a financial services organization branches are the likely unit of observation. Within a single business unit departments and cost centers are likely candidates for comparison. All that matters is that there are common output measures that can be tracked and enough observations over time to make statistical analysis viable. Obviously, the measures must be tracked at a level that corresponds to a meaningful workforce unit as well.

In the example above, hundreds, if not thousands, of sales transactions would become the left-hand-side data. Our example addresses revenue per employee, but remember that any performance measure—profit, errors, customer attrition, speed, efficiency, and so on—can be subjected to this type of analysis. Data to fill in the right-hand side of the model, the human capital side, typically come from HR information systems, payroll records, and related sources. Often they are variables that are derived as outputs of an ILM Analysis.

The second requirement is that there be enough variation in the internal operations and/or external environment of the facilities for it to be possible to discriminate between alternative drivers of performance. Business Impact Modeling operates by simultaneously comparing performance across facilities in an organization and within any specific facility over time. If all the units within the organization were identical or remained completely unchanged in the way they were managed over time, there would be nothing to compare. Performance differences would be random and therefore uninformative. Fortunately, one seldom finds such uniformity in the operations of organizations. Even if organizations are run "by the book," the reality on the ground almost always differs across units. There are differences in business and labor market environments, differences in workforce demographics and ILM dynamics, and differences in operations. Those differences can be treated as a form of natural experiment that sheds light on the drivers of business performance, including those related to human capital.

By providing some simple illustrations of the models underlying ILM Analysis and Business Impact Modeling, we do not mean to suggest that there is a mechanical formulaic approach to addressing human capital management. First of all, there is nothing mechanical about the statistical analyses. In an actual assignment many statistical issues have to be addressed carefully, including determining the most appropriate model specification, determining the appropriate units of analysis, and deciding on the evaluation and treatment of the data (for instance, especially when perceptual data are introduced, one may need to perform a factor analysis to create valid summary measures of highly correlated responses that could cause multicollinearity problems otherwise). Testing the robustness of results to changes in model specifications and for estimation using different employee populations is usually important for building confidence in diagnostic results.

Most important, one must always keep in mind that the results of such analysis are only one source of information, albeit an important one. To determine their relevance to actual management practice, they should be filtered through the experience of those most familiar with the organization and combined with the results of more qualitative appraisals. As we noted in Chapter 2, good decisions require the right facts, and the right facts seldom are unearthed through the use of a single method.

Summing Up

This book presents principles of systems, facts, and value as well as methods for harnessing them to manage the human capital side of the enterprise. These principles and methods are deeply rooted in the disciplines of economics and organizational psychology. We acknowledge that great intellectual heritage and hope that our work advances the future collaborative efforts of those two disciplines.

Endnotes

Introduction

1. *Human Capital Management: The CFO's Perspective.* Boston: CFO Publishing Corp., 2003, 11.
2. "VW Plans 1 Billion Euros Investment in China," *Financial Times Information, Global News Wire–Asia Africa Intelligence Wire*, March 4, 2003.
3. "Chicken Out Rotisserie Announces $21.25 Million Equity Financing." *Business Wire*, October 14, 2002.

Chapter 1

1. Edward Lazear and S. Rosen, "Rank Order Tournaments as Optimum Labor Contracts." *Journal of Political Economy*, October 1981, no. 89, 41–64. See also J.R. Green and N.L. Stokey, "A Comparison of Tournaments and Contracts." *Journal of Political Economy*, June 1983, no. 91, 349–365.
2. Ann P. Bartel, "Formal Employee Training Programs and Their Impact on Labor Productivity: Evidence from a Human Resources Survey," National Bureau of Economic Research Working Paper, July 1989, no. 3026, 37.
3. Richard A. Guzzo, R. D. Jette, and R. A. Katzell, "The Effects of Psychologically Based Intervention Programs on Worker Productivity: A Meta-Analysis." *Personnel Psychology*, 1985, vol. 38, 275–291.

Chapter 2

1. David Matheson and Jim Matheson *The Smart Organization*. Boston: Harvard Business School Press, 1998, 6.

Chapter 3

1. Gordon Bethune and Scott Huler, *From Worst to First: Behind the Scenes of Continental's Remarkable Comeback*. New York: John Wiley & Sons, Inc., 1998.
2. Dwight L. Gertz and Joao Baptista, *Grow To Be Great*. New York: Free Press, 1995, 7–12.

Chapter 5

1. Peter B. Doeringer and M. J. Piore, *Internal Labor Markets and Manpower Analysis*. Lexington, MA: Heath, 1971.
2. This research has spawned a new field within labor economics called the new economics of personnel. The hallmark of this work is the application of classic optimization and modern game theory perspectives to the analysis of labor transactions inside a firm. This research has probed areas such as the determinants of pay; the provision of work incentives; human capital development; supervision; and organization structure. A landmark publication in this field is E. P. Lazear, *Personnel Economics*. Cambridge, MA: MIT Press, 1995. Other seminal works directly relevant for understanding internal labor markets include the following:

   - G. P. Baker, M. Gibbs, and B. Holmstrom, "The Internal Economics of the Firm: Evidence from Personnel Data," *Quarterly Journal of Economics*, 1994, no. 109, 881–919.
   - G. P. Baker, M. Gibbs, and B. Holmstrom, "The Wage Policy of the Firm," *Quarterly Journal of Economics*, 1994, no. 109, 881–919.
   - B. Holmstrom, "Moral Hazard in Teams," *Bell Journal of Economics*, 1982, no. 13, 324–341.
   - E. P. Lazear, "Agency, Earnings Profiles, Productivity and Hours Restrictions," *American Economic Review*, 1981, no. 71, 606–620.
   - E. P. Lazear and S. Rosen, "Rank Order Tournaments as Optimum Labor Contracts," *Journal of Political Economy*, 1981, no. 89, 841–864.
   - G. C. Calvo and S. Wellisz, "Supervision, Loss of Control and the Optimum Size of the Firm," *Journal of Political Economy*, 1978, no. 86, 943–952.

   Similar developments have taken place in other disciplines. Sociologists have studied differences between firms in employment systems and their implications for occupations and mobility (for example, see R. P. Althauser, "Internal Labor Markets," *Annual Review of Sociology*, 1989, vol. 15, 143–161). Others in the organizational sciences have looked at differences in the operation of internal labor markets within an organization (for example, see Jeffrey Pfeffer and Y. Cohen, "Determinants of Internal Labor Markets in Organizations," *Administrative Science Quarterly*, 1984, vol. 29, 550–572). Lawrence Pinfield's *The Operation of Internal Labor Markets* (New York: Plenum Press, 1995) describes the range of disciplines offering research-based insights into the concept of internal labor markets and notes the preeminent contributions from the disciplines of economics, organizational psychology, and human resource management.

Chapter 6

1. Cathy Cooper, "In for the Count," *People Management*, October 12, 2000, 28–34.1.
2. Atul Gawande, *Complications: A Surgeon's Notes on an Imperfect Science*. New York: Henry Holt and Company, 2002.
3. Robin M. Hogarth, *Educating Intuition*. Chicago: University of Chicago Press, 2001.

Chapter 7

1. Michael Beer and Nitin Nohria, "Cracking the Code of Change," *Harvard Business Review*, May–June 2000, 133–141.
2. Jeffrey Pfeffer, *The Human Equation*. Boston: Harvard Business School Press, 1998, xvi.
3. Ibid., 17.
4. See John Kotter, *Leading Change*. Boston: Harvard Business School Press, 1996.
5. For more details on Southwest versus United and Continental in the California Market, see case study by Charles O'Reilly and Jeffrey Pfeffer, "Southwest Airlines: Using Human Resources for Competitive Advantage (A)," Stanford, CA: Stanford University Graduate School of Business, March 6, 1995.
6. Richard Melcher, "Encyclopaedia Britannica's Trip to the Brink—And Back," *BusinessWeek Online*, October 15, 1997. Go to http://www.businessweek.com/bwdaily/dnflash/oct1997/nf71015c.htm.

Chapter 8

1. Michael E. Porter, "From Competitive Advantage to Corporate Strategy," in Cynthia A. Montgomery and Michael E. Porter, editors, *Strategy*. Boston, MA: Harvard Business School Press, 1991), 226.
2. M. L. Marks and P. H. Mirvis, "Managing mergers, acquisitions, alliances: Creating an effective transition structure," *Organizational Dynamics*, no. 28, 2000, 35–47.
3. J. S. Lublin and B. O'Brian, "When disparate firms merge, cultures often collide," *Wall Street Journal*, February 14, 1997, A9.

Chapter 9

1. Frederick Reichheld, *The Loyalty Effect*. Boston: Harvard Business School Press, 1996.

2. James L. Heskett, W. Earl Sasser, Jr., and Leonard A. Schlesinger, *The Service Profit Chain*. New York: The Free Press, 1977.
3. Anthony J. Rucci, Steven P. Kirn, and Richard T. Quinn, "The Employee-Customer-Profit Chain at Sears," *Harvard Business Review*, January–February 1998, 82–97.
4. A. H. Brayfield and W. H. Crockett, "Employee Attitudes and Employee Performance," *Psychological Bulletin*, 1955, 52: 396–424.
5. Anne Marie Ryan, Mark J. Schmit, and Raymond Johnson, "Attitudes and Effectiveness: Examining Relations at an Organizational Level," *Personnel Psychology*, 1996, 49: 853–888.
6. Benjamin Schneider and David E. Bowen, *Winning the Service Game*. Boston: Harvard Business School Press, 1995.
7. This account is adapted from Carla Heaton and Rick Guzzo, "Making Every Employee a Brand Manager," *Mercer Management Journal*, 2000, 12: 61–78.
8. A. Parasuraman, V. A. Zeithaml, and L. L. Berry, "SERVQUAL: A Multiple Item Scale for Measuring Customer Perceptions of Service Quality," *Journal of Retailing*, Spring 1988, 64: 12–40.
9. Benjamin Schneider and David E. Bowen, "New Services Design, Development, and Implementation and the Employee." In W. R. George and C. Marshall, eds., *New Services*. Chicago: The American Marketing Association, 1985, 82–101.

Chapter 10

1. This chapter draws on material from two previous articles by one of the authors of this book, Haig R. Nalbantian. "Performance Indexing in Stock Options and Other Incentive Compensation Programs," *Compensation and Benefits Review*, September–October 1993; and Haig R. Nalbantian and Wei Zheng, "Worth the Risk?: When and How to Use Stock in Executive Incentives," *World at Work*, Q3 2001, vol. 10, no. 3.
2. We recognize this definition is different from that commonly used in the traditional theory of finance. Financial economists adopt a purely investors' perspective, classifying as "systematic risk" only the part of stock price variation that is driven by the market. The remaining variation is classified as "unsystematic." In our discussion, we look at risk from the perspective of all stakeholders who "invest" in the company. We need a definition or taxonomy flexible enough to incorporate the perspectives of employees as well. Certainly, variations in stock price driven by movements in market and industry performance are "systematic" from the employee's vantage point. These movements together affect the employee's cost of bearing performance risk.
3. Some firm-specific risk is more random in nature. A takeover rumor, for example, can send the stock price gyrating even if it is completely unfounded. Yes, management can act to quell the rumor. But the effects will show up in the volatility we measure and certainly represent "risk" from both the investor and employee perspectives.
4. For risk reduction through diversification to work, the assets added to the portfolio must not be highly correlated. For example, adding the shares of a

particular regional bank to a portfolio composed entirely of regional banks would result in very little risk reduction, since the movement of shares of these firms is positively correlated to a high degree.

5. There is an extensive literature on the economics of incentives and risk sharing that characterizes the moral hazard problem, the conditions under which it arises, and alternative solutions. That literature is summarized in H. R. Nalbantian. "Incentive Compensation in Perspective." In H. R. Nalbantian, ed., *Incentives, Cooperation and Risk Sharing: Economic and Psychological Perspectives on Employment Contracts.* Totowa, NJ: Rowman & Littlefield, 1987, 3–43.
   Among the most important individual contributions are:

   - B. Holmstrom, "Moral Hazard and Observability," *The Bell Journal of Economics,* 1979, 10: 74–91.
   - S. A. Ross, "The Economic Theory of Agency: The Principal's Problem.," *American Economic Review,* 1973, 63: 134–139.
   - S. Shavell, "Risk Sharing and Incentives in the Principal and Agent Relationship," *The Bell Journal of Economics,* 1979, 10: 55–73.
   - J. E. Stiglitz, "Incentives and Risk Sharing in Sharecropping," *Review of Economic Studies,* 1974, 41: 219–256.
   - J. E. Stiglitz, "Incentives, Risk and Information: Notes Towards a Theory of Hierarchy," *The Bell Journal of Economics,* 1975, 6: 552–579.
   - J. E. Stiglitz, "Risk, Incentives and Insurance: The Pure Theory of Moral Hazard," *The Geneva Papers on Risk and Insurance,* 1983, 8. 1 33.

6. An early version of PSA was introduced in Nalbantian (1993). The article provides more detail on the methodology and its applications.
7. This approach to weighting industry peers is inspired by R. Antle and A. Smith, "An Empirical Investigation of the Relative Performance Evaluation of Corporate Executives," *Journal of Accounting Research* 24: 1–39.
8. There is evidence that executives heavily discount the value of stock options due to the risks they face. B. Hall and K.J. Murphy ("Stock Options for Undiversified Executives," NBER Working Paper No. W8052, November 2000) estimated that the value of stock options is granted at the money ranges from 21 percent to 64 percent of their Black-Scholes value, depending on executives' risk preferences and the diversification of their wealth. With such discounting, pressures to increase the size of grants is high. The cost to shareholders shows up in dilution of shares—a significant problem for many companies today.
9. See Nucor Corporation Web site, http://www.nucor.com/aboutus.htm, April 18, 2003.

Chapter 11

1. Martin Fridson and Fernando Alvarez, *Financial Statement Analysis,* 3rd ed. New York: John Wiley & Sons, Inc., 2002, 29.
2. The original thinking about human capital is captured in the following article and books:

- Jacob Mincer, "Investment in Human Capital and Personal Income Distribution," *Journal of Political Economy*, 1958, 66(4): 281–301.
- Theodore Shultz, *The Economic Value of Education*. New York: Columbia University Press, 1963.
- Gary Becker, *Human Capital: A Theoretical and Empirical Analysis with Special Reference to Education*. New York: National Bureau of Economic Research, 1964.

3. Interview with Baruch Lev by Juergen Daum. Posted at www.juergendaum. com/news/03_06_2002.htm. The full text of that interview can also be found in Juergen H. Daum, *Intangible Assets and Value Creations*. New York: John Wiley & Sons, 2002.
4. Felix Barber, Jeff Kotzen, Eric Olsen, and Rainer Strack, "Quantifying Employee Contribution," *Shareholder Value Magazine*, May–June 2002.
5. Bruce Pfau and Ira Kay, *The Human Capital Edge*. New York: McGraw-Hill, 2002.
6. The Watson Wyatt approach is consistent with a body of academic research in the 1990s that sought to link HR practices to various measures of economic productivity (e.g., sales per employee) and shareholder value. Some representative studies of this kind are:

   - Ann P. Bartel, "Productivity Gains from the Implementation of Employee Training Programs," *Industrial Relations*, 1994, 33: 411–425.
   - Mark A. Huselid, "The Impact of Human Resource Management Practices on Turnover, Productivity, and Corporate Financial Performance," *Academy of Management Journal*, 1995, 38: 635–672.
   - Casey Ichniowski, K. Shaw, and G. Prennushi, "The Effect of Human Resource Management Practices on Productivity," *American Economic Review*, 1997, 87: 291–313.

7. Bruce Pfau and Ira Kay, *The Human Capital Edge*. New York: McGraw-Hill, 2002, xvii.
8. Robert S. Kaplan and David P. Norton, "The Balanced Scorecard: Measures That Drive Performance," *Harvard Business Review*, January–February 1992.
9. *Human Capital Management: The CFO's Perspective*. Boston: CFO Publishing Corp., 2003, 12.
10. Stephen Gates, *Value at Work—The Risks and Opportunities of Human Capital Measurement and Reporting*. New York: The Conference Board, 2002, 13.
11. "Measures That Matter," Ernst & Young LLP, Paper, New York, 1999, 6–9.
12. Allison Kopicki and Tom Contiliano, "Reveal Your Stock's Secrets," *Bloomberg Personal Finance*, February 2003, 62–70.
13. Stephen Gates, The Conference Board, "Value at Work—The Risks and Opportunities of Human Capital Measurement and Reporting," 2002, 13.
14. *Human Capital Management: The CFO's Perspective*. Boston: CFO Publishing Corp., 2003, 13.
15. Douglas, Dwyer, "Plant-level Productivity and the Market Value of a Firm," Discussion Paper, CES 01-3, Center for Economic Studies, Bureau of the Census, U.S. Department of Commerce, June, 2001.

Chapter 12

1. *Human Capital Management: The CFO's Perspective*. Boston: CFO Publishing Corporation, 2003, 4.
2. Ibid., 30–31.
3. Based on comments by Helen Drinan, former president and CEO, Society for Human Resource Management, February 26, 2002.

Chapter 13

1. Charles Handy, *The Age of Unreason*. Boston: Harvard Business School Press, 1989, 6.

Appendix B

1. Edward P. Lazear, *Personnel Economics* (Cambridge, MA: MIT Press, 1995).
2. For actual references see Chapter 11, endnote 2.
3. A review of the literature can be found in Robert J. Willis, "Wage Determinants: A Survey and Reinterpretation of Human Capital Earnings Functions," in O. Ashenfelter and R. Layard (eds.), *Handbook of Labor Economics*, Vol. 1, Amsterdam: North Holland, (1986), 603–638.
4. See, for example, B. Jovanovic, "Job Matching and the Theory of Turnover," *Journal of Political Economy*, 1979, vol. LXXXVII, 972–990, and Dale T. Mortensen, "Job Search and Labor Market Analysis," in O. Ashenfelter and R. Layard (eds.), *Handbook of Labor Economics*, Vol. 2. (1986). Amsterdam: North Holland, 849-919 The seminal work on signaling is A.M. Spence, "Job Market Signaling," *Quarterly Journal of Economics*, 1973, vol. 87, 355–374.
5. For references concerning the issues of adverse selection and moral hazard and their relevance to employment contracts, see Chapter 10, endnote 5.
6. A more detailed survey of this research literature can be found in Donald O. Parsons. "The Employment Relationship: Job Attachment, Work Effort and the Nature of Contracts," in O. Ashenfelter and R. Layard (eds.), *Handbook of Labor Economics*, Vol. 2 (1986): Amsterdam: North Holland, 789–848.
7. Examples of this work include: A. Bartel, "Productivity Gains from the Implementation of Employee Training Programs," *Industrial Relations*, 1994, vol. 33, 411–425, J. Cable and N. Wilson, "Profit Sharing and Productivity: An Analysis of U.K. Engineering Firms," *Economic Journal*, 1989, vol. 99, 366–375, and F. R.Fitzroy and K. Kraft, "Cooperation, Productivity and Profit Sharing," *Quarterly Journal of Economics*, 1987, vol. 102, 22–35.
8. See, for instance, Casey Ichniowski, K. Shaw, and G. Prennushi, "The Effect of Human Resource Management Practices on Productivity," *American Economic Review*, 1997, vol. 87, 291–313, D. J. B. Mitchell, D. Lewin, and E. Lawler, "Alternative Pay Systems, Firm Performance and Productivity," in A. Blinder (ed.), *Paying for Productivity* (Washington, DC: Brookings Institution,

1990), 15–88, and Paul Osterman,"How Common Is Workplace Transformation and Who Adopts it?" *Industrial and Labor Relations Review*, 1994, vol. 47, no. 2, 173–188.

9. Edwin E. Ghiselli , "Some Perspectives for Industrial Psychology," *American Psychologist*, 1974, vol. 29, 80–87.

10. Raymond A. Katzell, "Contemporary Meta-Trends in Industrial and Organizational Psychology," in H. C. Triandis, M. D. Dunnette, and L. M. Hough (eds.), *Handbook of Industrial and Organizational Psychology*, 2d ed., Vol. 4 (Palo Alto, CA: Consulting Psychologists Press, 1994), 1–89.

11. A good reference source for the estimation of discrete choice models is William H. Greene, *Econometric Analysis*, 2nd ed., New York: Macmillan, (1993).

Index

About the Authors

Haig R. Nalbantian

A Worldwide partner at Mercer Human Resource Consulting, Haig Nalbantian is a founding member of the Strategy and Metrics group and is cochair of the company's global R&D Council. He is a labor/organizational economist, well recognized for his widely published work on incentives and organizational performance.

Richard A. Guzzo

Rick Guzzo is a Worldwide Partner with Mercer Human Resource Consulting and is cochair of the company's global R&D Council. He regularly consults with Fortune 500 companies and other large organizations regarding human capital. He is a Fellow of the Society for Industrial and Organizational Psychology.

Dave Kieffer

Dave Kieffer helps companies create competitive advantages for themselves by identifying their firm-specific workforce practices that most affect business results. He is also leader of the Strategy and Metrics group and a Worldwide Partner at Mercer Human Resource Consulting.

Jay Doherty

Jay Doherty has more than 20 years of management consulting experience with companies throughout North America, Europe, and Asia. As a partner with Mercer Human Resource Consulting, his expertise includes change management, organization design, and linking management practices to bottom-line results.

About Mercer Human Resource Consulting

Mercer Human Resource Consulting helps clients understand, develop, implement and quantify the effectiveness of their human resource programs and policies. Our goal is to help employers create measurable business results through their people.

We work with clients to address a broad array of their most important human resource issues, both domestically and globally. We have specialist expertise in all areas of human resource consulting, including compensation, employee benefits, communication, and human capital strategy. Of equal importance are our investment consulting expertise and the solutions we provide in program administration.

With more than 13,000 employees in some 140 cities and 40 countries, we have the local knowledge and worldwide presence to develop and implement global human resource solutions.

For more information, visit www.mercerhr.com. For specific information on the book, visit www.LastingAdvantage.com.